A Religion, Not a State

A Religion, Not a State

Ali 'Abd al-Raziq's Islamic Justification of Political Secularism

SOUAD T. ALI

THE UNIVERSITY OF UTAH PRESS
Salt Lake City

The Defiance House Man colophon is a registered trademark of the
University of Utah Press. It is based upon a four-foot-tall,
Ancient Puebloan pictograph (late PIII) near Glen Canyon, Utah.

13 12 11 10 09   1 2 3 4 5

LIBRARY OF CONGRESS CATALOGING-IN-PUBLICATION DATA

Ali, Souad Tagelsir.
    A religion, not a state : Ali 'Abd al-Raziq's Islamic justification of political secularism /
Souad Tagelsir Ali.
        p. cm.
    Includes bibliographical references and index.
    ISBN 978-0-87480-951-0 (pbk. : alk. paper)
        1. 'Abd al-Raziq, Ali, 1888–1966—Political and social views. 2. Islam and politics.
3. Islam and secularism. 4. Caliphate. I. Title.
    BP173.7.A4966 2009
    297.2'72--dc22
                            2009022891

To the memory of my beloved mother, Rayya

To my beloved father, Tagelsir

To my beloved families in the United States and the Sudan

CONTENTS

IN THE WAKE OF THE First World War—the year was 1924—the government of Turkey proclaimed the office of caliph to be abolished. About a year later, a little-known scholar at the Azhar University in Egypt published a book setting forth reasons why the office of caliphate was not essential to Islam and arguing that the Muslim community worldwide had no reason to think that without a caliphate Islam was deficient. His name was Ali 'Abd al-Raziq, and though not well known at the time, his book stirred up an enormous controversy which propelled him into the forefront of intellectual life in his day.

The book continues to command great interest throughout the Islamic world. Dr. Souad T. Ali's study is therefore very timely. Though not the first to write on Ali 'Abd al-Raziq, Dr. Ali provides the fullest and most accessible account of his political thought yet to appear in English. Scholars and educated laypersons in English-speaking parts of the Islamic world as well as in the West will benefit from Dr. Ali's readable and rich account. Though Shaykh 'Abd al-Raziq lived before the rise of what is currently called the "Islamist" movement, there is much in his arguments that a critic of the Islamist position might find useful.

Dr. Souad Ali's title says it all. Islam is, according to 'Abd al-Raziq, a religion, not a state. This statement implies both a certain view of religion and a certain view of Islam. By saying that Islam is not a state, 'Abd al-Raziq is saying in effect that it is not Islam's prerogative to do what a state does. By saying that Islam is a religion, he is implying that religions and states have their particular separate functions, which must not be confused with one another, and that the functions of a state are not intrinsic to the mission of the Prophet Muhammad, whereas the functions of religion are. The function of religion is solely to prepare people for the world to come—to prepare them in particular for facing God in judgment and for entrance into their eternal state. This message is an urgent one and it alone defines the prophetic mission. States, on the other hand, have the function of ordering this world in a manner that assures the stability of society in the here and now. The dichotomy of present world and world to come, of dunyā and ākhira, corresponds; it seems, with the dichotomy of religion and state, dīn and dawla.

Dr. Ali has produced a book that will raise many questions, as any good book should, in the minds of intellectually active—and not merely curious—readers. Was Ali 'Abd al-Raziq a seer of things to come? Is his notion of a non-state Islam—an Islam concerned with higher realities, with moral principles rather than with rules of law—bound to prevail ultimately? There are certainly plenty of people who hold a similar view of Islam's future, but there are many who do not. Perhaps the big question has to do with argument more than with vision. Historically, in the dialectical culture of Islam, a vision did not stand unless based on convincing argument. How will arguments be constructed in the future? The Shaykh is unusual in his belief that traditional argumentation utilizing methods like those propounded for centuries in the Azhar and elsewhere would still be persuasive in his time. What about our time? What about future time? Allahu a'lam.

BERNARD G. WEISS
Professor of Arabic and Islamic Studies
The University of Utah, Salt Lake City
2009

ACKNOWLEDGMENTS

I AM GRATEFUL TO A number of colleagues and friends whose support in different ways has been a great encouragement. My endeavor to think through the subject of this book has been significantly enhanced by invaluable intellectual and moral support provided by Professor Bernard Weiss who spared no time or energy to keep an insightful eye on the manuscript, reading through several drafts and providing vital feedback. Dr. Weiss's immense enthusiasm for the theme of this study, his important suggestions for the structure of the book, and his constructive criticism have been a crucial motivation that greatly helped me refine and develop my own argument. I am also indebted to a number of other colleagues, friends, and reviewers who read this work in part or in full in different stages and made useful suggestions for improvement: Dr. Mohamed Ahmed Mahmoud for valuable suggestions and for painstaking effort and meticulous review of the transliteration system; Dr. Ann Koblitz, Dr. Suzanne Lundquist, and Dr. Abdullahi Gallab for their valuable observations and moral support.

At Arizona State University, I would like to express my gratitude to a number of individuals and departments who provided unforgettable encouragement: Dr. Ann Koblitz and Dr. Cynthia Tompkins, whose invaluable mentoring, care, and support encouraged and helped me center my own ideas when I first joined ASU in 2004; Dr. Deborah Losse, dean of the Humanities, and Dr. Joe Cutter, director of my home School of International Letters and Cultures (SILC), for their constant encouragement and support; Dr. Linell Cady and the Center for the Study of Religion and Conflict (CSRC) for appreciated support in providing me with a research assistant for a semester. Dr. Joel Gereboff and Religious Studies; Dr. Mary Margaret-Fonow and the Women and Gender Studies Program; Dr. Stanlie James and the African and African-American Studies Program; Dr. Sally Kitch and the Institute for Humanities Research for their encouragement.

There of course remains the pleasant task of expressing my thanks and appreciation to Jeffry Halverson, initially my research assistant and later my colleague; and to Diana Coleman, my research assistant. I am immensely grateful to both of them for the many editorial hours they spent and for their insightful editorial work. My thanks go to Professor Hakan Yavuz, editor of the Turkish and Islamic Studies Series at the University of Utah Press, and to Peter DeLafosse, Glenda Cotter, and their staff at the Press. Thanks also to former Press director Joseph Herring.

I owe my warmest debt to my dear families in the United States and the Sudan: my husband, Abdullahi Gallab, who through his insight, untiring interest, love, and understanding has been a constant source of inspiration and encouragement; and to our lovely children, Ahmed, Azza, and Shiraz, for their patience and for tolerating too many hours of writing snatched from their own precious time. And to my dear family in Khartoum Sudan for their warmest love and support; especially my dearest father, Tagelsir Ali Elsheikh, whose encouragement, love, and support motivated me throughout the time of writing the book manuscript; and to the love and prayers of my dearest mother, Rayya Ahmed Elsheikh, bless her soul, who passed away a few months ago and did not live long enough to see this book in its final form.

NOTE ON TRANSLITERATION

GENERALLY ACCEPTED English forms of Arabic words and names, such as Islam, Muhammad, Ali, Shari'a/Shari'ah, Hadith, ulama/'ulama, etc., are used as they appear in their English format. For other Arabic terms I have used aspects of the Library of Congress transliteration system with some exceptions, such as when I use a capital D to emphasize the emphatic sound ض and when I use *Islamiyyah* instead of *Islamiyah*, given the fact that in the Library of Congress transliteration system, the *shadda* inflection is not emphasized when the same word is transliterated as Islamiyah; thus, the second (y) I use is meant to highlight the *shadda* pronunciation. In addition, the Arabic letter ح is transliterated as (ḥ) when it appears in the medial position or (Ḥ) when it appears in the initial position in Arabic terms that have not been added to the English dictionary. Also, while the Arabic letter ع is marked by the symbol (') as in 'Abd al-Raziq, the reversed symbol (') is used to indicate a *hamza*, as in *Hai'at*. Finally, to avoid confusion, I have not included the (h) to emphasize the *tā marbūta* at the end of a word except in very few cases such as in *khilāfah* (caliphate) and *Ḥukūmah* (government). The dropping of this silent final (h) has increasingly become the standard practice.

A Religion, Not a State

1

Introduction
Background and Overview

*T*HE PURPOSE OF this analysis is to elucidate to an extent not yet paralleled in any other study the arguments used by the Egyptian reformist scholar Ali 'Abd al-Raziq (1887–1966) to invalidate the notion of a universal Islamic polity headed up by a single individual qualified to bear the title of caliph. The study will evaluate 'Abd al-Raziq's conviction, that such a polity could be invalidated on Islamic grounds, as a modern development in Muslim thought. Through textual analysis, historical contextualization, and comparative approach, this study will endeavor to situate 'Abd al-Raziq's arguments within the context of previous thinking about the caliphate. Thus situated, 'Abd al-Raziq's position will show itself to be unique, in the sense that he uses an Islamic conceptual framework to declare the caliphate, considered as an Islamic institution based on a polity supposedly founded by the prophet himself, to be a human innovation, not a religious imperative. By bringing new insight to the issue of Islam and the state, this analysis critically challenges prevalent misinterpretations of Islam that have unfortunately endured for centuries.

The first chapter of this study historicizes the debate concerning the proper and desirable relationship between the state and religion within a Muslim context, then moves to examine the modern framing of the discussion. The chapter analyzes the strands of divided thought, "rootedness" (*asāla*) against the values of "modernity" (*ḥadātha*), as a healthy indication of the dialogue necessary to renew, revitalize, reform, and reconstruct religious thought. With the introduction of Ali 'Abd al-Raziq and his controversial publication in 1925 of a work pronouncing "Islam is a religion, not a state; a message, not a government," the foundation for the work is laid, namely, to reexamine the intellectual strength of 'Abd al-Raziq's work and his importance in the current Islamic political, philosophical, and religious thought. To my knowledge, 'Abd al-Raziq's work has not been published in English[1] in its entirety (although it has been translated into French and recently into Spanish), and therefore his chain of reasoning has remained largely unavailable to the English reader (apart from article and book references that I detail in the literature review section of this chapter). This text seeks to remedy this omission, by carefully tracing argument and counterargument through thoughtful analysis over the course of eight chapters. A brief synopsis of each chapter is included to aid the reader in previewing and reviewing the contents. Necessary historical background is provided at each juncture to maintain context for 'Abd al-Raziq's grounded argument that inserting state into religion was a human construct and not a religious imperative. Literatures responding to 'Abd al-Raziq's book are noted within a section at the end of chapter one, with an emphasis on modern references, and this discussion underscores the important contribution of this work to current academic, religious, and political scholarship.

Muslim debates over the relationship between the state and religion have their point of origin in the immediate aftermath of the death of the Prophet Muhammad in 632 A.D. During the prophet's lifetime, Islam had spread throughout Arabia and established itself as an organized system of communal life in Medina and beyond. However, because the prophet neither named a successor nor clearly delineated a specific form of government, Muslims have engaged in continuous discussion of, and experimentation with, various forms of governance throughout the last fourteen centuries. Jurists, philosophers, and theologians have set forth diverse theories of the state within an Islamic framework. Sunni jurists have for the most part focused on the *khilāfah* (caliphate), which originated with Abu Bakr and was ideally represented by him and the three who ruled after him, while their Shi'i counterparts have devoted attention to the more dynastic Alid *Imamah*.[2] However, a third voice among modern Muslims has advocated a theory of a secular state. Through the interaction of a diverse range of viewpoints, Muslim political thought has been shaped in both evolutionary and revolutionary ways, surviving conflict in one era and undergoing division and differentiation in another.

Beginning in the nineteenth century, Muslim discussions concerning the state, not only within the Middle East but also throughout the greater Islamic world, have been characterized by a conflict between two forces commonly described as "tradition" and "modernity." The main concern of these discussions has been with the question of the reconcilability of the relativistic values of "modernity" (ḥadātha) with the need for authenticity or "rootedness" (asāla). Advocates of rootedness argue that it is essential that the integrity of age-old principles be maintained in the face of changes[3] forced on Muslims from the time of colonialism—when indigenous Islamic cultures were threatened by the imposition of Western values. On the other hand, proponents of *tajdīd* (reform or renewal) and ḥadātha have been advocating the integration of Islam with modernity.[4] According to these Muslim intellectuals, Islam has always, in accordance with its primary texts, the Quran and Hadith, emphasized the inevitability and necessity of tajdīd. Furthermore, from its beginnings, Islam has had the capacity to revive itself in the "name of its high tradition, neither in the name of the West nor of its populist idealization of the folk culture."[5] Thus, renewal, revitalization, reform, and reconstruction of religious thought have extensive roots in the Islamic tradition. This sense of tajdīd, ingrained as it is in the Muslim tradition, is epitomized in the saying of the Prophet Muhammad: "God shall send to this *umma,* at the head of each hundred years, a person who shall renew its religion for it." This capacity for renewal has created and engendered a certain degree of vitality at the heart of Islam, evident in the practice of *ijtihād* (independent inquiry), through which equilibrium has been maintained. Simultaneously, it has fostered the institutionalization of the power, authority, and autonomy of the *ʿulama* (religious scholars) and the *mujtahidūn* (plural of *mujtahid*—independent inquirer) as the living conscience of the *umma* (Arabic for nation; can also refer to a community of Muslim nations; or, in general, the term is used to apply to the total community of Muslim believers), a development that militated against the manipulation of the religious establishment by the state. In effect, difference of opinion within the Islamic umma, as a famous Hadith remarks, has become "a sign of Allah's mercy." One example is the creation of Islamic jurisprudence, with its four schools of thought—the Hanafi, the Maliki, the Shafiʿi and the Hanbali—and the "elaboration of the law [as] the work of private scholars unaffiliated with officialdom, despite the aspirations of the caliphal regime to the contrary, and it was to remain so throughout subsequent centuries."[6] Both the Umayyad (661–750) and the Abbasid (750–1258) dynasties failed to manipulate the scholars and "the caliphate had to give up all claims to legislative power and to resign itself to being . . . the instrument of the implementation of the law of scholars, of books."[7] Nevertheless, later periods in Islamic history witnessed different forms of stagnation including the manipulation of the authority of such institutions and their ʿulama to serve the status quo and its political agenda. The latter period of the Ottoman Empire[8] could serve as an example of this.

The late Egyptian scholar Ali ʿAbd al-Raziq falls within the category of Muslim thinkers who advocated tajdīd—renewal—and who fell victim to the manipulation of religious authority by the state. In his case, it was al-Azhar

University that was manipulated by the Egyptian palace into condemning 'Abd al-Raziq's book.[9]

The publication in 1925 of *Al-Islām wa Usūl al-Ḥukm: Baḥth fī al-Khilāfah wa-al-Ḥukūmah fī al-Islam*[10] (*Islam and the Foundations of Rule: Research on the Caliphate and Government in Islam*) gave rise to a raging debate in Egypt whose dust has never quite settled in the years since. What made the debate so heated was the fact that Ali 'Abd al-Raziq was the first Azhar-educated scholar with the rank of *ʿālim* to declare that Islam is a religion, not a state; a message, not a government. The main thesis of 'Abd al-Raziq's explosive book was clearly at variance with the dominant Muslim view of that time, which perceived Muhammad to be the founder of a state as well as a religion. 'Abd al-Raziq's call for the separation of religion and state had the ring of a Western-inspired secularism that most Muslim scholars of the time felt they could only reject. So great was the upheaval that al-Azhar Supreme Council (*Haiʾat Kibār al-ʿUlamā*) condemned and denounced the book, expelled its author from the circle of ʿulamā, and terminated his membership in its council.

The debate continues more than eighty years after the publication of 'Abd al-Raziq's book, drawing even wider attention to his ideas and spreading his thought throughout ever-increasing intellectual and political circles. However, this ongoing debate is just one aspect of the many facets of the current Muslim condition, which includes debate on Islam and politics, Islam and modernity, and Islam and governance. This study examines 'Abd al-Raziq's book in light of these complex debates and attempts to evaluate the importance of the book as a modern and liberal development in Islamic thought. The urgency of such an investigation becomes particularly significant in the midst of the resurgence of Islamic "fundamentalism," or the Islamist ideology that advocates the idea of *al-Ḥākimiyyah li Allah*[11] ("sovereignty belongs to God"), a conviction that shapes the Islamists' ideological view of the state and governance. It was with this notion of *al-Ḥākimiyyah li Allah* with which Sayyid Qutb (1906–1966) influenced subsequent generations of Islamists, as reflected in recent years by such groups as the Egyptian Tandhīm al-Jihād and its leader Ayman al-Zawahri, who simultaneously occupies the second position in the hierarchy of the al-Qaʿida organization led by Usama bin Laden. Qutb held that Muslims had the responsibility to struggle against the forces of the *jāhiliyya* (ignorance) in the twentieth century—just as the prophet had fought the forces of the jāhiliyya of the seventh century—in order to reinstate the perfect Islamic community and, more importantly, to restore God to his place as the only rightful sovereign and to ensure that the *Shariʿa*, the divine law, was the only law governing the Muslim community.[12] The Islamist view, held by Qutb and others, stands in direct contrast to 'Abd al-Raziq's advocacy of the secular state and his separation of Islam and government. Unlike Qutb, 'Abd al-Raziq presented his arguments through traditional Islamic legal methods, utilizing the Quran, Sunna, *Ijmāʿ* (consensus) and *Qiyās* (reasoning by way of analogy), in order to prove that Islam is a religion, not a state.

This analysis is divided into eight chapters. Chapter 1, "Introduction: Background and Overview," sets forth the significance of this study as a critique of the caliphate as well as an investigation of the debate over Islam and politics, while also providing the synopsis of the chapters of the book. Chapter 1 ends with a review of scholarly literature on this subject.

Chapter 2, "Classical Juristic Theories of the Caliphate: From Idealism to Accommodationism," briefly reviews the development of Sunni theory of the caliphate from al-Baqillani through al-Mawardi, al-Ghazali, Ibn Jama'a, and ending with Ibn Taymiyya. The main point to be emphasized in this chapter is that as the contradiction between ideal and reality became more pronounced, the theory propounded by these jurists became more and more accommodating to reality. The ideal was a caliphate based on a contract with the community. Caliphs according to this ideal were to be elected to office by persons possessing the qualifications deemed necessary for this important function. Once elected, the caliph received an oath of allegiance from the community at large. The first accommodation was the acceptance of the notion of testamentary succession, whereby a caliph could, while still living, "elect" his successor and secure an oath of allegiance from him. Since the theory never stipulated how many electors were required, it was assumed that as few as a single elector could be sufficient and that this single elector could be the reigning caliph. As theory continued to develop, it reached the point of allowing seizure of office by force and finally (with Ibn Taymiyya) declared the caliphate to be a thing of the past and neither feasible nor necessary in the present. A ruler, no matter how tyrannical, held office legitimately as long as he provided an environment in which the law of Islam was respected and enforced. The Hanafi School adopted a similar view. The earlier caliphate had existed for thirty years only and ended with the Umayyad takeover in 661 A.D.

Chapter 3, "The Caliphate in the Colonial Era," explores caliphal developments that took place within the half-century prior to the publication of Ali 'Abd al-Raziq's provocative book *Al-Islām Wa Usūl al-Hukm*. The first of these developments is the use of the title of caliph by the Ottoman sultan Abd al-Hamid II (ruled from 1876 to 1909). Although the Ottoman sultans had always included "caliph" among their various titles, their use of this title had always been informal and honorific. Whenever Ottoman use of the title was challenged, the official response was to refer to a (probably fictitious) transfer of Abbasid caliphal authority to Salim I when he conquered Egypt in 1517. (A puppet Abbasid caliphate had been maintained by the Mamluk rulers of Egypt since the Mongol expulsion of the Abbasids from Baghdad in 1258). But the Ottoman sultans used the title with much caution, probably because the Hanafi School had declared the caliphate to be nonexistent since the death of Ali ibn Abi Talib (the fourth and last Guided Caliph) in 661. Abdul al-Hamid's proclamation of himself openly and assertively as caliph was quite unprecedented since it entailed taking on a role, in addition to the role of sultan of the Ottoman Empire, that no previous Ottoman ruler had thought of: the role of universal leader of all Muslims. The incentive for Abdul al-Hamid's bold undertaking was to bolster his own prestige at a time when the Ottoman Empire was collapsing rapidly. This action coincided with a perceived need on the part of many Muslims in India to have a Muslim world leader to look to at a time when the demise of the Mughal dynasty (a Muslim line of rulers) had created a power vacuum in India which had been filled by the British colonial authority there. This left, in Indian Muslim thinking, the Ottoman Empire as a remaining vestige of Muslim power in the world. The Young Turk regime (1908–1918)[13], anxious to promote the Ottoman Empire and enhance its influence, continued to maintain the fiction of an Ottoman caliph, knowing of the enthusiasm for such a caliph in the Indian Muslim community. Although among Indian Muslims there was an intense debate as to whether, in view of their not being descendants of the Quraysh, the Turkish sultans were qualified to be caliphs. Some said no, but many said yes. The latter became known as the Khilāfatists, who became an organized movement that was active from 1919 to 1924. In 1924 everything changed when the new Kemalist government of Turkey declared an end to the caliphate. It is interesting that they declared the end to the sultanate two years before declaring an end to the caliphate. Thus for two years, the new regime showed temporary deference to an ideal cherished by millions of Muslims. In the year or so after abolition of the caliphate, three important events occurred: (1) the British-supported Hashimite ruler of the Hijaz, Sharif Husayn, had himself proclaimed caliph, only to be soon after ousted by the Saudi occupying forces; (2) the ruler of Egypt, King Fuad I, made known his interest in the elevated post of caliph of all Muslims, seeing Egypt with its famed center of Muslim learning (al-Azhar) as even more worthy to be the seat of the caliphate than Istanbul (or Ankara); (3) Ali 'Abd al-Raziq published his book, affirming the nonvalidity of the very concept of caliph.

Chapter 4, "Ali 'Abd al-Raziq's Intellectual Formation and His Place among the Disciples of Muhammad 'Abduh," explores 'Abd al-Raziq's immediate Egyptian context and the complexity of the intellectual setting in which he lived, a setting marked by interaction between two tendencies: an Islamist tendency and a secular-nationalist tendency. The chapter deals with 'Abd al-Raziq's family background and his upbringing and education, and coordinates events occurring in his life with events in the larger world of Islam. For example, he was only seventeen when Muhammad 'Abduh died, and a young man of twenty-one, busy with his Azhar studies, when Abdul al-Hamid II was deposed by the Young Turk regime. At the time of the founding of the Khilāfatist Movement in India, he was thirty-two. Four years later, when the Turkish caliphate was abolished in 1924, he set out to write his famous treatise on the caliphate. The chapter also investigates his involvement in the circle of disciples of Muhammad 'Abduh. It explores especially the thought of 'Abduh, the two major tendencies among his disciples (following the famous dichotomizing of Albert Hourani further explored in chapter 4)—on the one hand, a conservative branch including the Manarist group represented by Rashid Rida and strongly connected with the Azhar, and a liberal branch represented by Ahmad Lutfi al-Sayyid and Ali 'Abd al-Raziq himself. At the same time, special attention will be given to 'Abd al-Raziq's uniqueness among 'Abduh's disciples. Unlike most liberals, whose arguments were couched in secular language, 'Abd al-Raziq phrased his in the language of traditional Islam, the language of al-Azhar. So in many ways, 'Abd al-Raziq stands alone in a third category. He is advancing secularization within Islamic idiom.

Chapter 5, "The Central Argument," reviews and analyzes the three main sections of 'Abd al-Raziq's book in great detail. The core of the book is his critique of the concept of the khilāfah (the caliphate) and his argument that Islam is concerned with spiritual matters unrelated to politics or government. He asserts that the Prophet Muhammad never established or headed a government and that he was merely a messenger assigned with the task of conveying and proclaiming a religious message. The main thrust of 'Abd al-Raziq's argument for the nonvalidity of the caliphate accords with the traditional methodology of *usūl al-fiqh* (the study of the sources of Islamic jurisprudence) on which 'Abd al-Raziq, as an Azharite who graduated with honors, would have been well read and well informed. The first question that systematic study poses is whether or not the appointment of a caliph is a duty of the Muslim community such that if the duty is not performed the community is in a state of sin. Most jurists take the position that it is a duty, but differ on the question

of whether its being a duty is known through reason or only through revelation. ʿAbd al-Raziq sets himself apart from historic Muslim thought on this
question, taking the position that it is *not* a duty. This requires that he refute
both the rational and the revelational proofs used by those who maintain it is
a duty. Refuting the rational argument poses no difficulty for him. In ʿAbd al-
Raziq's view, in order to establish that appointing a caliph is a communal duty,
incumbent upon the Muslim community, the reasons offered to support this
argument must prove that the Muslim community would benefit as a whole,
and that the appointment or election of a caliph is necessary to carry out those
governmental functions that are necessary for a society. He finds that the reasons are nonexistent, lacking, or unsubstantiated. As for revelational proofs,
these either come from the Quran or Sunna or entail methods grounded in
Quran or Sunna. It is not as though supporters of the caliphate do not quote
from Quran or Sunna. They certainly do. However, ʿAbd al-Raziq finds these
arguments to be ambiguous and inconclusive. As for attempts to find proof in
the consensus of scholars, these are for ʿAbd al-Raziq entirely unconvincing,
and he in fact makes the reader aware of the difficulties always entailed in ap-
peals to consensus. This chapter explores these revelational proofs in details
as well as proofs from consensus. The conclusion is that there are no certain
proofs that the appointment of a caliph is a duty; if it were, that would mean
that Islam without a caliphate is deficient.

Chapter 6, "The Ruling System in the Time of the Prophet," explores ʿAbd
al-Raziq's thinking about government as an institution distinct from religion.
He argues that all societies require government, including the earliest Muslim
society in Medina when disputes had to be settled and that Abu Bakr, Umar,
and others served as judges. Social harmony requires a judicial authority of
some sort. We know that the prophet himself exercised this judicial function
and that he appointed military leaders and regulated social interactions; however, we do not have details in these matters as they are all difficult to research.
And they were incidental to his role as prophet, whose mission it was to found
a religion, not a state. If it was a part of the prophet's mission to found a state,
we would expect more accessible guidelines.

Chapter 7, "Critiques of ʿAbd al-Raziq's Position," examines the attack on
the book that created quite a stir among the scholars of Egypt, compelling
them to grapple with the issue of whether the caliphate was a necessary part of
an Islamic order. Responses to and critiques of ʿAbd al-Raziq's book have been
written by both detractors and supporters of the author's argument. On the
one hand, the rage aroused by ʿAbd al-Raziq's book led to the immediate publi-

cation of several aggressively hostile responses that bitterly assailed the author and his ideas, while on the other hand, secular intellectuals, such as Taha Husayn, Muhammad Husayn Haykal, and Ahmed Amin, publicly defended the author's right to freedom of expression. In spite of such manifestations of support for 'Abd al-Raziq, it was the negative critiques of 'Abd al-Raziq's book that had the greatest impact on the Egyptian scene, creating an uproar against the book and the position it took on the relationship between religion and state. This chapter's main concern is to examine in detail the attack on Ali 'Abd al-Raziq's book by traditionalist 'Ulamā such as Muhammad al-Khidr Husayn, Mamdouh Haqqi, and Muhammad al-Bakhit al-Muti'i, who devoted serious studies to critiquing the book.

Chapter 8, "The Implications of 'Abd al-Raziq's Study for the Debate over Islam and Politics," shows that although this study was initially undertaken as an analysis of 'Abd al-Raziq's book, and to provide a new perspective on a work that has been at the center of debate for decades, it is also a case study of the relationship between Islam and the state and its complex representations, cultural discourses, and historical development. The continued debate over 'Abd al-Raziq's book is premised upon one of the most contentious issues of Islamic thought throughout the ages, namely, the relationship between religion and politics. Different historical periods have produced many political models and, with them, intellectual discourses. As such, it has become increasingly clear that an atmosphere of intellectual openness and tolerance is a major prerequisite for this debate to produce any fruitful results. This chapter also suggests that as long as 'Abd al-Raziq's argument continues to challenge existing ideas, his book will remain an important and pivotal addition to Muslim discourse in this field. As Charles Adams has argued, Ali 'Abd al-Raziq clearly belongs within the spiritual and intellectual succession of the influential Egyptian reformist Muhammad 'Abduh; and despite the fact that he exhibits characteristic differences in interpretation, he represents an important modern and liberal development in the movement which 'Abduh inaugurated.[14]

⇨   *Scholarship on 'Abd al-Raziq's Writings*

A GOOD BODY OF literature has been written in Arabic on 'Abd al-Raziq's book since its publication in 1925. As mentioned earlier, the immediate response to and critique of the book was formulated in the Arabic writings of Sheikh Muhammad al-Khidr Husayn, Sheikh Muhammad Bakhit al-Muti'i, and Mamdouh Haqqi, which have already been noted. A short response—of quite a different nature—to 'Abd al-Raziq's book by the Tunisian historian and intellectual Muhammad al-Talbi appeared in a long interview entitled, *'Iyāl Allāh: Afkār Jadīda fi 'Alāqat al-Muslim bi-Nafsihi wa bi- al-Ākharīn (Children of God: New Ideas on the Muslim's Relationship with Himself and Others)*.[15] In 1989 (also 1972) Muhammad 'Imarah wrote "Critical Observations" of 'Abd al-Raziq's book in which he pinpointed what he saw as weak points in the book that represent, in his opinion, negativity and a "flawed intellectual methodology." 'Imarah's critique is comprised of four instances of contradiction he claimed to have found in the book. Chapter 7 of this analysis elaborates on these critiques of 'Abd al-Raziq's book.

Other comments on 'Abd al-Raziq's book include the short commentaries written by Albert Hourani[16] and Charles C. Adams.[17] Both Hourani and Adams briefly discuss 'Abd al-Raziq within their analysis of Muhammad 'Abduh's disciples and students. Adams's book *Islam and Modernism in Egypt* was originally the first part of a doctoral dissertation submitted in August 1928 to the Graduate Faculty of the University of Chicago. The book format was first published in 1933. In the preface of the 1968 edition of the book, Adams mentions that the second part of the dissertation, which was not published for "various reasons," consists of a translation from Arabic into English of 'Abd al-Raziq's book *Al-Islām wa Usūl al-Ḥukm*. This translation was apparently lost and has never been published. Adams's book focuses mainly on the origin and development of the modern reform movement in Egypt, with special emphasis on Muhammad 'Abduh's biography and the principles, tendencies, reasons, and science of his doctrine. Hence, he briefly discusses Ali 'Abd al-Raziq as a young revolutionary writer influenced by 'Abduh, and tries to explore whether his liberal views bear any relation to the modern reform movement inaugurated by 'Abduh.[18] In 1962, Albert Hourani published his book *Arabic Thought in the Liberal Age: 1798–1939,* in which he was concerned about politics and society within the context created by the growth of European influence and power in the Middle East and North Africa. In his discussion, Hourani lays main emphasis on a number of individual writers and thinkers, including Jamal al-Din al-Afghani and Muhammad 'Abduh, as representatives of certain tendencies or generations. He basically traces the line of descent through four generations of thinkers. Within his discussion of the third generation (1900–1939) Hourani discusses 'Abduh and his disciples, including Ali 'Abd al-Raziq, as part of those "who continued to accept Islam as a body of principles, or at the very least of sentiments, but held that life in society should be regulated by secular norms, of individual welfare or collective strength."[19]

Recently, 'Abd al-Raziq's book has been referred to quite frequently, though briefly, in many articles and books written by a good number of scholars. Bassam Tibi (2002) made reference to the book in his article, "The Idea of an Islamic State and the Call for the Implementation of the Shari'a Law," from his book *The Challenge of Fundamentalism: Political Islam and the New World Disorder*.[20] In this chapter, Tibi discusses the diverse views regarding the notion of "the Islamic state," whether populist or totalitarian. He argues that two issues stand at the center of this debate: the implementation of the Shari'a law and the notion of the *Shūrā* (consultation), "whether as an Islamic substitute for democracy or, what some allege, as a specifically Islamic pattern of democracy."[21] Tibi's main discussion in this chapter focuses on Muhammad Salim al-'Awwa's book *Fi al-Nizām al-Siyasī lil-Dawla al-Islāmiyya (On the Political System of the Islamic State)*, which Tibi describes as an authoritative book—"the most comprehensive and most widely disseminated contribution of Islamic fundamentalism to the concept of an Islamic political system." In this book al-'Awwa repeatedly tries to refute 'Abd al-Raziq's secular theory of separation between religion and state, asserting that "Islam provided the first authentic political and legal system of state in the history of mankind."[22] While al-'Awwa refers to most of the early critique by al-Azhar concerning 'Abd al-Raziq's book, he focuses more on one critique by the Mufti of Tunis, Bin-Ashour, *Naqd 'Ilmī li Kitāb Al-Islām wa Usūl al-Ḥukm (A Scientific Critique of the Book Islam and the Basis of Rule)*." However, al-'Awwa's conclusion of 'Abd al-Raziq's book is that "the West has generated an 'imitative attitude' that has misled some Muslims, including renowned Muslim scholars, to plead for the separation of religion and politics."[23]

In chapter 26 of his book *The History of Islamic Political Thought: From the Prophet to the Present* (2001), Antony Black discusses Ali 'Abd al-Raziq as an Egyptian Muslim modernist who argued that the caliphate was merely a human institution, and that Muslims can organize their choice of government without necessarily adhering to it. In Black's analysis, this constitutes a break not only from traditional Islam, but also from the very enterprise of the Prophet Muhammad himself.[24] This is, of course, contrary to what 'Abd al-Raziq himself believed, as he argued that the prophet had never headed a state and was merely sent to profess a spiritual message. In his recent article, "Enlightenment in Islamic Thought," Nasr Hamid Abu Zayd discusses Ali 'Abd al-Raziq's book (and the dispute that emerged over its advocacy of separating religion from state) within the context of his discussion of Muhammad 'Abduh and Taha Husayn. Abu Zayd argues that 'Abduh is called the father of modern

Islamic thought because his response to the challenge of modern European Enlightenment accommodated the two extreme trends of modern Islamic thought: "the so-called enlightening trend and the traditionalist trend." On the other hand, Abu Zayd maintains, the dispute about Ali 'Abd al-Raziq's book nearly led to the destruction not only of the book, but also of the man himself. Abu Zayd also makes reference to another severe debate that appeared over Taha Husayn's book *Fī al-Shi'r al-Jāhilī* (*On Pre-Islamic Poetry*) (1927), when some critics did not accept Husayn's inclusion of critical remarks regarding some Quranic stories. It was no coincidence that Hasan al-Banna announced the formation of the Muslim Brotherhood Society just a year later, in 1928, as a reformist movement attempting to bring the whole Egyptian society "back to the track of Islam."[25]

    ❧   *Additional Studies on 'Abd al-Raziq*

THIS SECTION BRIEFLY reviews a number of relatively new studies that have been published associating, comparing, or contrasting Ali 'Abd al-Raziq with recent scholars. Ami Ayalon, in his article "Egypt's Quest for Cultural Orientation," discusses Ali 'Abd al-Raziq within his discussion of the recent case of Nasr Hamid Abu Zayd, the Egyptian philosophy professor who was pronounced an apostate by an Egyptian court in 1995. In this study, Ayalon explores the current developments of the war between culture and religion in Egypt, which has been going on for over a century with varying degrees of intensity, and attempts to place these reflections of cultural tensions in Egypt within their historical context. Hence, his reference back to 'Abd al-Raziq's book, the trial of 1925, and the severe punishment the author received by the al-Azhar Grand Council alluded to in the first part of this chapter. Comparing 'Abd al-Raziq's case with that of Hamid Nasr Abu Zayd, Ayalon argues that the resemblance between the two cases is striking, despite the major differences between them.[26] In the final analysis, he maintains, it is a valid comparison given the fact that both cases caused a political crisis in Egypt that led to removing 'Abd al-Raziq from the body of the 'ulama by the al-Azhar Grand Council on the one hand, and the pronouncement of Abu Zayd as an apostate by an Egyptian Shari'a court on the other.

    Leonard Binder, in his book *Islamic Liberalism: A Critique of Development Ideologies*,[27] provides a thorough discussion on 'Abd al-Raziq within his analysis of a number of scholars including and focusing on Albert Hourani and Muhammad 'Imara's treatment of 'Abd al-Raziq. Binder, however, dedicates the last part of the final chapter of his book to discussing 'Abd al-Raziq within the context of Muhammad Arkoun's account of "Islamic Structuralism." Arguing that the goal of Arkoun's epistemology is the removal of the distinction between "Islamic reason" and "philosophic reason," Binder concludes that Arkoun "shares in the rational and liberal tradition of Ali 'Abd al-Raziq and Taha Husain."[28] In Parvez Manzoor's analysis, the failure of 'Abd al-Raziq's work, according to Binder's liberalist rationale, is a statement on the need for an Islamic liberalism "which accommodates the traditional scripturalist conceptions of an Islamic government but which also supplies an interpretative framework capable of linking liberal political practices 'to an acceptably authentic hermeneutic of the Islamic tradition.' "[29]

Ted Thornton's article, "Sati al-Husri (1880–1968)," provides a discussion on a contemporary Syrian nationalist who advocated a similar "secularist" theory of separating religion from state. Sati al-Husri concurred with 'Abd al-Raziq that the entire caliphate system must be abolished, based on his similar belief that there was no historical or religious evidence to support it. An advocate of Arab unity, al-Husri did not believe in Islamic political unity—he believed that linguistic and cultural differences rendered such a dream unrealistic. In Ted Thornton's analysis, al-Husri carried Ibn Khaldun's famous concept of 'asabiyya (solidarity based on blood ties) a step further. He was attracted to the notions of *le lien social* and *esprit de corps*. Unity, for him, was more than mere blood; it also had a spiritual quality. However, al-Husri's thought differed from that of 'Abd al-Raziq's with respect to the form of government. In contemplating how to build Arab unity, he did not specify the form of government that would best suit Arabs. Furthermore, he did not rule out dictatorship as a political system for Arab nations, a point that reflects his awareness of the totalitarian tendency in his thinking.[30] While he can certainly be compared to 'Abd al-Raziq with regard to his advocacy of abolishing the caliphate and separating religion and state, al-Husri was an uncompromising secularist who believed that freedom did not mean democracy or constitutionalism, it merely meant national unity.[31] On the other hand, 'Abd al-Raziq, who was a scholar of Islamic law and simultaneously a product of the modern reform movement in Egypt, advocated a secular state, broadly speaking, within his concept of liberal Islam.

John Kelsay, in his essay "Civil Society and Government in Islam,"[32] discusses 'Abd al-Raziq within his discussion of the nineteenth-century transition of Muslim politics from the early caliphate to the modern systems. Although Kelsay sheds light on Ali 'Abd al-Raziq's defense of and reasons for abolishing the caliphate system, his main theme in this essay is to show that the existence of civil society is well established in the Islamic tradition. A clear association one can derive from Kelsay's argument with regard to ʿAbd al-Raziq is the parallel the author draws between Islamic discourses of moral society and notions of civil society present in Locke's ideas. ʿAbd al-Raziq has often been critiqued by his opponents as advocating a foreign concept of society and political systems derived from Western discourses; however, his (ʿAbd al-Raziq's) attempts to refute such accusations and, conversely, to show the similarities between the two with regard to civil society, were unsuccessful.

A brief reference to ʿAbd al-Raziq's ideas is also found in Kenneth Cragg's "Muslim Encounters with the West," in which he attempts to interpret Islam's experience with the West through examining Islam's own sense of how politics and religion can fit together. Cragg brings ʿAbd al-Raziq into the picture within his discussion of the Ottoman Empire after World War I, maintaining that

> [t]here was a lively disavowal by Egyptian writer and scholar Ali ʿAbd al-Raziq of caliphate's necessity to a right Islam on the grounds that its appropriateness in the aftermath of Muhammad's death and in the early centuries had been long superseded by developments in the self-perception of Islam and of law in and between nations. Islam could be happily rid of it and still fulfill itself in fully religious terms through a partial secularization of the state.[33]

ʿAbd al-Raziq's primary concern, then, has been to prove that Islam is a *dīn* (religion), not a *dawlah* (state). In his book *Political Islam: Religion and Politics in the Arab World* (1991), Nazih Ayoub provides a discussion on Ali ʿAbd al-Raziq in association with another al-Azhar Sheikh, Khalid Muhammad Khalid, who in the late 1940s had arrived at a similar conclusion (that Islam was a religion, not a state) without reading ʿAbd al-Raziq. He used the same argument that ʿAbd al-Raziq had used, that there is very little of a purely political nature stipulated in the Quran, that the political formulas adopted by the Muslims later on, such as the khilāfah, were human improvisations, and that the insistence on merging religion with politics would harm both.[34] However, Khalid did not maintain that position throughout. Apparently, the Islamist discourse of the 1970s had managed to persuade him away from his previous position. In 1981, Khalid published another book in which "he restated the *salafī* argument of the totality of Islam, including the concept of a specifically Islamic umma and a specifically Islamic State."[35] Yet, although

Khalid has reverted to the conventional Islamist terminology, he still advocates tajdīd (renewal) and still believes that Shūrā (consultation) is mandatory in Islam and is exactly equivalent to the concept of "democracy" in its current usage.[36]

In Armando Salvatore's analysis, 'Abd al-Raziq is eager to stress that the Quranic dīn is a religion not limited to reaching the principles of fraternity and equality, but one that aims at actively educating its followers to practice these precepts and, above all, that has forged norms inspired by them. Here, he clearly established that Islam constitutes, besides dīn (and as a consequence of its special character as dīn), a principle of civic life thereby affecting the *dunyā*, the worldly environment with its social obligations. This position comes quite close to the postulation of Islam as a "civil religion." Prominent in this argument is that it is precisely *because* of being this special sort of socially expanded dīn, grounded on values of equality and fraternity, that Islam cannot grant the necessary legitimation to any established power. As a result, Islam is *dīn lā dawlah*: religion, but not state.[37]

It is quite evident that Ali 'Abd al-Raziq's ideas have continued to be at the center of debate over Islam and politics since the first publication of his book in 1925. Such debate constitutes a serious intellectual event within contemporary Islam. 'Abd al-Raziq's message has resonated across eight decades, attracting both supporters and detractors. On the one hand, his book was met with opposition because it advocated a new perspective on matters which had been frozen into place through unquestioned religious doctrine, as Albert Hourani has noted. Such theory has been perceived by many as drawing "more from non-Muslim writers on Islam, who might be accused of trying to weaken its holds on its adherents, than from the fundamental Islamic sources, the sciences of Quranic interpretation and *hadith*."[38] This method, claimed to have been followed by 'Abd al-Raziq, was therefore construed by some critics of the book, such as Muhammad Rashid Rida, as "the latest attempt by the enemies of Islam to weaken it from within."[39]

On the other hand, the Islamic movement's radical reaffirmation of Islam as both state and religion remains challenged to this day by Ali 'Abd al-Raziq's counterargument that religion is religion and state is state with no necessary connection between them. As Muhammad al-Talbi has argued, despite the fact that 'Abd al-Raziq did not succeed entirely in his revolution, he has had many supporters spreading his ideas up to the present day.[40] In the words of Charles Adams, Ali 'Abd al-Raziq belongs in a spiritual and intellectual succession with Muhammad 'Abduh; and despite the fact that he exhibits characteristic differences in interpretation, he represents a modern and liberal development of a movement which 'Abduh inaugurated.[41] Clearly, 'Abd al-Raziq's book has provided a rich scholarly enterprise for researchers both in the East and in the West.

Throughout the course of writing *A Religion, Not a State*, I have used three separate editions of 'Abd al-Raziq's book: the original edition (Cairo 1925), which I could access at the Middle East Library (Marriott Library) of the University of Utah in 2002, when I first began working on my book; the Beirut 1966 edition because it includes Mamdouh Haqqi's critique of 'Abd al-Raziq, which I discuss in detail in chapter 7; and finally, the Sousa (Tunis 2001) edition, which was the only copy I was able to locate and order from Cairo after I moved to Arizona in 2004.

NOTES

1. 'Abd al-Raziq's book has been translated into French by Abdo Filali-Ansary as *L'Islam: est-il Hostile a la Laicite?* (Casablanca: Editions Le Fennec, 1997); and recently into Spanish as *El Islam Y Los Fundamentos Del Poder: Estudio sobre el califato y el gobierno en el Islam* (Granada: Editorial Universidad de Granada, 2007). Charles C. Adams's lost English translation (which was only referenced in the preface of his book, *Islam and Modernism in Egypt* [1933; New York: Russell and Russell, 1968]) is also noted in this chapter.

2. The Sunni and Shi'i concepts are discussed in greater detail in chapter 2 of this book.

3. John Cooper, Mohamed Mahmoud, and Ronald Nettler, eds. *Islam and Modernity: Muslim Intellectuals Respond* (London: I. B. Tauris, 1998), 3.

4. Ibid.

5. Ernest Gellner, *Nations and Nationalism* (Oxford: Blackwell, 1983), 12.

6 Bernard G. Weiss, *The Spirit of Islamic Law* (Athens: University of Georgia Press, 1998), 15–16.

7. Ibid., 16.

8. The dynastic empire (1299–1922) that was centered in what is currently Turkey. It controlled Asia Minor, the Middle East, and parts of the Balkans.

9. Muhammad 'Imarah criticized Muhammad al-Khidr Husayn for dedicating his book, *NaqD Al-Islam wa Usul al-Ḥukm* (1926), to King Fuad I of Egypt (1868–1936), an attempt that was largely perceived as appeasing the Palace at a time when it exerted relentless effort aimed primarily at controlling the al-Azhar as an academic institution of a unique religious status and depriving it of its independence ('Imarah 1989, 206–207). Original was in Arabic, English translation is mine. Muhammad 'Imarah's Arabic work on 'Abd al-Raziq is the most rigorous; it has documented most of the circumstances surrounding the publication of the book as I have discussed in chapter 4.

10. Ali 'Abd al-Raziq, *Al-Islam wa Usul al-Ḥukm: Baḥth fī al-Khilāfah wa-al-*

Ḥukūmāh fī al-Islam (Islam and the Foundations of Rule: Research on the Caliphate and Government in Islam), 1st edition (Cairo: Matba'at Misr, 1925).

11. It is useful to reflect on the earlier, contrasting meaning of the concept *lā ḥukma illā li Allah* (sovereignty is to God) advocated by the *Murji'a* (advocates of the doctrine of postponement) in their discussion on *imān* (faith) and *i'tiqād* (belief). The questions "who is the true believer?" and "does a Muslim remain a Muslim after committing a 'grave' sin?" seem to have been the first questions that were raised in Islam among the contending theological schools or political groups prior to 750, but the debate continued for a good number of years after that. The Kharijites reflected an extreme position and held that a "grave" sinner is not a believer and must, thus, be excluded from the Muslim community. In contrast, the Murji'a (those who preferred to postpone judgment on people until the Day of Judgment) argued that God alone, as reflected in their slogan, "la ḥukma illa li Allah," would decide the fate of a "grave" sinner. *Khawārij* (Kharijite)—those who seceded and broke away from the camp of Ali ibn abi Talib, the fourth Caliph, blaming him for not punishing the murders of 'Uthman, the third Caliph)—and Murji'a were, hence, diametrically opposed to each other in this regard. Whereas a "grave" sin from the former's perspective terminates one's status as a Muslim, the latter held that a sinner should not be excluded from the Muslim community because the decision on whether or not he/she is a sinner belongs to God alone and thus must be postponed. Both groups used their doctrines, primarily, for and against 'Uthman and Ali.

Montgomery Watt provides a useful insight into the doctrine of postponement when he writes arguing that though postponement meant in the first place postponing a decision about 'Uthman and Ali, the term was sometimes given other meanings in the course of the debate. Some opponents said that it implied asserting that the grave sinner is a believer, not merely that he is to be regarded as one; and in a sense this is indeed an implication of leaving the decision about him to God, and was accepted by the upholders of postponement. Again, there were later writers who said it meant postponing Ali to fourth place, a view which became the standard Sunnite. Another possible source is the Quranic phrase (9:106), "some are postponed for the command of God," and this verse was certainly used to justify the doctrine of postponement (Watt 1985, 121–126).

12. Charles Tripp, "Sayyid Qutb: the Political Vision," in *Pioneers of Islamic Revival*, ed. Ali Rahnema (London: Zed Books, 1994), 162.

13. See Stanford J. Shaw and Ezel Kural Shaw, *History of the Ottoman Empire and Modern Turkey*, vol. 2 (Cambridge: Cambridge University Press, 1988).

14. Charles C. Adams, *Islam and Modernism in Egypt: A Study of the Modern Reform Movement Inaugurated by Muhammad 'Abduh* (New York: Russell and Russell, 1968), 268.

15. Muhammad al-Talbi, *'Iyāl Allāh: Afkār Jadīda fī 'Alāqat al-Muslim bi-Nafsihi wa bi- al-Ākharīn (Children of God: New Ideas on the Muslim's Relationship with Himself and Others)* (Tunis: Sras Publisher, 1992).

16. Albert Hourani, *Arabic Thought in the Liberal Age 1798–1939* (Oxford: Oxford University Press, 1962).

17. Adams, *Islam and Modernism in Egypt.*

18. Adams's preface.

19. Hourani, *Arabic Thought in the Liberal Age*, vi.

20. Bassam Tibi, *The Challenge of Fundamentalism: Political Islam and the New World Disorder* (Berkeley: University of California Press, 2002).

21. Bassam Tibi, "The Idea of an Islamic State and the Call for the Implementation of the Shari'a/Divine Law," Middle East Information Center (2004), http://meddleeastinfo. org/article4480.html (accessed 2004): 17.

22. Muhammad Salim al-'Awwa, *Fi al-Nizhām al-Siyasī lil-Dawla al-Islāmiyya* (*On the Political System of the Islamic State*), 6th ed. (Cairo: al-Maktab al-Misri al-Hadith, 1983), 22.

23. 'Awwa quoted in Tibi, "The Idea of an Islamic State," 17.

24. Antony Black, *The History of Islamic Political Thought: From the Prophet to the Present* (Edinburgh: Edinburgh University Press, 2001), 318.

25. Nasr Hamid Abu Zayd, "Enlightenment in Islamic Thought" (2004), http://www. kath.de/akademie/rahner/vortag/enlight.html (accessed 2004): 7.

26. Ami Ayalon, "Egypt's Quest for Cultural Orientation," The Moshe Dayan Center for Middle Eastern and African Studies, Tel Aviv University, http://www.dayan.org/ D&A-Egypt-ami.html (accessed 2004).

27. Leonard Binder, *Islamic Liberalism: A Critique of Development Ideologies* (Chicago: University of Chicago Press, 1988), 128–169.

28. Ibid, 169.

29. Parvez Manzoor, "Islamic Liberalism and Beyond," in *American Journal of Islamic Social Sciences* 7, no. 1 (1990): 77–88.

30. Ted Thornton, "Sati al-Husri (1880–1968)," in *History of the Middle East Database*, online version (2004), 1, available at: http://www.nmhscool.org/tthornton/ mehistorydatabase/sati_alhusri.htm. See also William L. Cleveland's *The Making of an Arab Nationalist: Ottomanism and Arabism in the Life and Thought of Sati al-Husri* (Princeton: Princeton University Press, 1971).

31. Ibid.

32. John Kelsay, "Civil Society and Government in Islam," in *Islamic Political Ethics: Civil Society, Pluralism, and Conflict*, ed. Sohail H. Hashmi (Princeton: Princeton University Press, 2002), 3–37.

33. Kenneth Cragg, "Muslim Encounters with the West," in *The Encyclopedia of Politics and Religion*, ed. Robert Wuthnow, vol. 2 (Washington, D.C.: Congressional Quarterly, 1998), 538–543.

34. Nazih Ayoub, *Political Islam: Religion and Politics in the Arab World* (London: Routledge, 1991), 202.

35. Ibid.

36. Ibid.

37. Armando Salvatore, *Islam and the Political Discourse of Modernity* (Reading, U.K.: Ithaca Press, 1997), 89–90.

38. Hourani, *Arabic Thought in the Liberal Age*, 189.

39. Ibid. Rida trans. and paraphrased by Hourani.

40. Al-Talbi, *Children of God*, 94.

41. Adams, *Islam and Modernism in Egypt*, 268.

2

Classical Juristic Theories of the Caliphate
From Idealism to Accommodationism

*T*HIS CHAPTER TRACES the early theoretical underpinnings and brief trajectory of the Sunni caliphate, from the time of the Prophet Muhammad through the Umayyad takeover in 661, as addressed in the theories of Muslim jurists beginning with al-Baqillani and continuing through the writings of al-Mawardi, al-Ghazali, Ibn Jama'a, and finally Ibn Taymiyya and Ibn Khaldun. This background is crucial to understanding 'Abd al-Raziq's response to the Sunni doctrine of the caliphate. An examination of the theories proposed demonstrates a gradual accommodation to the profane or real world, as the divide between the conceptual ideal and human reality became apparent. This is first demonstrated in the successive accommodations conceded in the election process of the caliph, noting that a process which at its outset called for a qualified electorate (testamentary succession) in an ordered society devolved within a thirty-year period into a climate which accepted violent overthrow as legitimate, as long as Islamic law was claimed and upheld as the community standard. 'Abd al-Raziq's thought is grounded in Islamic sources and so this discussion necessarily begins with an examination of the early days of Islam.

Immediately following the Prophet Muhammad's death, the Muslim community was faced with many political challenges, including a problem of leadership. During his lifetime, the prophet of Islam had been the sole and uncontested religious and political guide and reference for Muslims through divine revelations, personal conduct, and communal guidance. Given the fact that the prophet did not name a successor, and that both the Quran and Hadith made only vague statements in regard to this matter, more than one faction claimed to have the right to the leadership of the Muslim community.

It was out of these circumstances that the caliphate arose in the year 632 when Abu Bakr, the prophet's close friend and father-in-law, was chosen by the Muslims of Medina to succeed the prophet as head of the Muslim community. The Shi'a secessionist movement also emerged out of the same circumstances.

In the Shi'a view, legitimate succession was restricted to a direct line of descent from Muhammad through Ali, his cousin and son-in-law. However, the majority position prevailed in choosing the successor from among the prophet's companions.

The caliph chosen had temporal and spiritual authority but was not permitted prophetic power, given the fact that such prophetic power was reserved for the Prophet Muhammad.[1] Therefore, the caliph could not exercise authority in matters of religious doctrine because the revelation of the Quran ended before the death of the prophet of Islam. Abu Bakr's caliphate lasted for only two years (632–634). He was succeeded by 'Umar ibn al-Khattab as the second caliph (634–644), who was followed by 'Uthman ibn 'Affan as the third caliph (644–656); then 'Uthman was succeeded by Ali ibn Abi Talib, the fourth caliph (656–661). Muslims recognize these first four caliphs as al-Khulafā al-Rāshidūn (the rightly guided caliphs).[2] The Shi'a, however, did not approve of this Sunni system of the caliphate and recognized Ali as the first caliph and ultimately the first imam of an Alid line of imams.

Within the Sunni caliphate system, Mu'awiya (661–680) became caliph after Ali's death, founded the Umayyad dynasty (661–750), chiefly by force of arms, and made Damascus his capital. In 750 the 'Abbasid family, descended from the prophet's uncle al-'Abbas, led a coalition that defeated the Umayyad family. The Abbasid dynasty (750–1258) transferred their center of power from Damascus to Baghdad. Another member of the Umayyad family, Abd al-Rahman I, escaped the general massacre of his family and fled to Spain; there the emirate of Cordoba was set up in 780. This later became the caliphate of Cordoba, or the Western caliphate, and persisted until 1031. A third competing caliphate was established by the Fatimids in North Africa, Syria, and Egypt (909–1171). After the fall of Baghdad to the Mongols under Hulagu Khan in 1258, the Abbasids fled to Egypt. The Ottomans captured Egypt in 1517 and Salim I assumed the title of caliph by asserting a questionable claim. The Ottoman sultans, however, kept the title until the last sultan, Muhammad VI, was deposed. A cousin succeeded him briefly, but in 1924 Mustafa Kemal Ataturk of Turkey abolished the caliphate. A year later Husayn ibn Ali, king of Arabia, proclaimed himself caliph, but was forced to abdicate by Ibn Sa'ud. Since then several pan-Islamic congresses have attempted to establish a rightful caliph.[3]

As was mentioned earlier, the Shi'a arose as a distinct movement in the context of the debate over how a rightful caliph should be chosen. They believed that Ali ibn Abi Talib, as the prophet's cousin and son-in-law, should have been the immediate successor. Ali eventually did become the fourth caliph, as noted, but he was immediately met with opposition from an already entrenched Muslim leadership.[4] Perhaps the most serious point of development regarding the dispute over leadership was marked by the murder of the third guided caliph, ʿUthman Ibn ʿAffan (d. 656). After the murder, a dissident group from among Ali's supporters—which later came to be known as al-Khawārij (the Kharijites)—revolted against Ali, blaming him for not being decisive in punishing the murderers of ʿUthman and perceiving his negligence as the ultimate betrayal. Both the Shiʿa and the Khawārij arose through dissent in determining the legitimate leadership of the Muslim community. Their respective positions regarding the question of the imamate has remained constitutive for both movements including the Shiʿa subdivisions.[5] The major threat to Ali, however, came from the Umayyad family in Syria. A civil war followed, Ali was eventually defeated and killed, and Muʿawiya assumed the throne and became caliph, thus establishing the Umayyad dynasty (661–750). As I have stated, the Shiʿa, on the other hand, continued their opposition and designated Ali as the first imam of their line of Alid legitimacy.

On the whole, although the theory of Alid legitimacy seems to be largely accepted by the different subgroups among the Shiʿa, this has hardly been the case in Sunni Islam with regard to the theory of the caliphate. Sunni acceptance of the four "Rightly-Guided Caliphs" (al-Khulafā al-Rashidūn), as well as their designation of a rank-based chronological order with Abu Bakr as first and Ali as last, implied that Sunni Islam aimed at being all-inclusive and comprehensive. On the other hand, the group that came to be termed as the Shiʿa resolved to reject the first three caliphs: Abu Bakr, ʿUmar, and ʿUthman, but accepted the fourth caliph, Ali, who became the first imam according to their doctrine. By taking this position, the Shiʿa parted company with the Muslim mainstream and resolved to be a sort of permanent opposition group to Sunni Islam, which ultimately enjoyed the support of the majority of Muslims. Further, "what marked them [the Shiʿa] off from Sunnites was also to a great extent their theological views."[6]

The Sunni Doctrine of the Caliphate

IN ORDER TO fully understand Ali ʿAbd al-Raziq's antithetical view on the Sunni doctrine of the caliphate, the following section provides an overview of accounts on the caliphate by Muslim thinkers beginning with al-Baqillani (d. 1013) through al-Mawardi (d. 1058), Ghazali (d. 1111), Ibn Jamaʿa (d. 1333), Ibn Taymiyya (d. 1328), and ending with Ibn Khaldun (d. 1406). The main emphasis will eventually be on al-Mawardi given the fact that his theory has been "generally regarded as the classic statement of the orthodox doctrine of the Caliphate/Imamate."[7]

In Sunni Islam, there was no one universally accepted doctrine of the caliphate—evidenced by the fact that such an assumption finds little support in the writing of Muslim jurists and scholars on the subject. Although al-Mawardi's[8] theory of the imamate was accepted by later generations of Muslim scholars as an exposition of an ideal form of government, such an acceptance was a different matter from accepting it as an exposition of the *only* recognized Sunni doctrine.[9]

ABU BAKR AL-BAQILLANI, D. 1013

Abu Bakr al-Baqillani's views on the imamate were first articulated in his *The Preface (al-Tamhīd): On the Refutation of Attribute Denying Apostates, Extremist Shafi'ites, Kharijites and Mu'tazilites.* He does not discuss whether the imamate is necessary by revelation or reason. In his opinion, the functions of the imam as leader of an Islamic state are to defend the umma from any enemies; to restrain oppression and redress grievances; to enforce and exact the punishment laid down by the law; to divide the revenues derived from conquest among the Muslims; and to make safe the pilgrimage. If the imam errs or transgresses in any of the above, the umma should set him right, correct him, and extract from him his duty. In selecting the imam, al-Baqillani argues, the umma should look for the most excellent (*al-Afdal*), but in case of disagreement over who is the most excellent, and to avoid the danger of civil strife, it is legal to select the less excellent. Further, al-Baqillani does not approve of the legality of the existence of two or more imams at the same time. It is quite important to emphasize that al-Baqillani insists that the imam must be of Qurayshi descent of any branch, implicitly refuting both the Khariji doctrine that any upright Muslim who can carry out the duties of the imam might become one, and the Shi'i doctrine of limiting the imamate to the descendents of Ali ibn Abi Talib.[10]

Although al-Baqillani does not discuss whether the caliphate is necessary by revelation or reason, he does not dispute that it is obligatory. Ali 'Abd al-Raziq takes note of the disagreement among Muslim scholars as to whether the obligatory character of the caliphate is based on revelation or reason. However, he indicates that such disagreement is not of as much interest to him as what the two sides in the debate had in common, namely the conviction that the caliphate is an obligatory institution. In other words, Muslim scholars have come close to reaching a consensus on this fundamental point, a consensus noted by Ibn Khaldun, as will be explained.

ABU AL-HASAN ALI IBN MUHAMMAD IBN HABĪB AL-MAWARDI, D. 1058

Abu al-Hasan Ali ibn Muhammad ibn Habīb (d. 1058) has been known in historical and juristic sources as al-Mawardi, given his family's work in producing and selling rose water (*mā' al-ward*).[11] He was born in Basra in 972 and lived there during the years of his early youth as he studied Islamic jurisprudence from the scholar and jurist Abi al-Qasim al-Saimary. Al-Mawardi then moved to Baghdad, the very center of the academic world of his time, to complete his education in the field of jurisprudence with the Shafi'i scholar al-Isfirā'īnī. While in Baghdad, he also studied the sciences of the Arabic language, Hadith, and *tafsīr* (exegetical works). He died in 1058 and was buried in the city of al-Mansur in Baghdad. Despite the wide fame he enjoyed during his life in Baghdad, historical sources do not provide us with many details of his family life as he lived it.[12]

In his book *al-Aḥkām al-Sultāniyya wal Wilāyāt al-Dīniyya* (*The Ordinances of Government and the States of Religion*), al-Mawardi argues that: "The Imamate is established as a successorship to prophethood (*li-khilāfat al-nubuwwa*) in respect to the protection of religion (dīn) and the governing of the world (dunya)." He maintains that the imamate is *wājib* that is necessary by revelation, not by reason. He claims that the Quran has made that clear in Surat al-Nisa 4:59: "Obey God, obey the Prophet and those in authority among you (*ulū al-amr*),"[13] among other scriptures. Like Ibn Khaldun, he does not specify the meaning of "authority." Interestingly enough, this is the same scripture cited by Muhammad Rashid Rida and all those who opposed 'Abd al-Raziq's argument. Yet, as has been and will be further seen within the course of this discussion, 'Abd al-Raziq refuted these scholars' employment of the above verse as evidence of their conviction of the necessity of the caliphate.

In his detailing of the system of the amirate[14] and its obligations, al-Mawardi does acknowledge that its arrangement is "contrary to the principles of Shari'a government," but justifies it on the grounds of necessity (*darura*). "Necessity dispenses with conditions that are impossible to fulfill, and fear of injury to public interest justifies a relaxation of conditions that would not be justified in private affairs."[15] Al-Mawardi's political thought is thus mainly found in *al-Aḥkām al-Sultāniyya wal Wilāyāt al-Dīniyya*, although only a small portion of the book is devoted to political theory while the rest of the book discusses details of public administration and rules of government.

Nonetheless, the portion on political theory is very important because it has largely been perceived as the first attempt in Islamic history at setting forth a comprehensive theory of the state, which has left an enduring influence on the course of Muslim political thought.[16] As the above and following discussion will show, excepting Ibn Khaldun, none of the Muslim jurists, theologians, and political philosophers who have followed al-Mawardi's line of political thought has made any improvement on his political theory.[17] In Qamar-ud-din Khan's analysis, it is evident that although the book *Usūl al-Dīn* (*The Sources of Religion*), written by 'Abd al-Qadir al-Baghdadi (d. 1037), a contemporary of al-Mawardi, provided a more comprehensive discussion on the caliphate compared to al-Mawardi, "the conclusion is that most of al-Mawardi's ideas are partly a heritage of the past and partly a clever manipulation of the opinions current in his own time."[18] However, al-Mawardi was hardly a mere recorder of facts, evidenced by what he wrote in the introduction of *al-Aḥkām al-Sulṭāniyya wa-al Wilāyāt al-Dīniyya* maintaining:

> Since these principles of royalty [the ordinances of governance] are mainly concerned with the conduct of rulers, since the direct application of these principles to the entire business of government prevents the rulers from an inquiry into their true nature, and since these rulers are too much engrossed in state affairs and diplomacy, I have brought out a separate book discussing all these principles in obedience to the behest of one whose allegiance is essential, in order that he may be informed of the different schools of law, may know what the people owe to him so that he may demand its fulfillment, and so he may know what he owes to them so that he may try to fulfill it. (And he has asked to be informed about these things) out of love for justice in his enactments and decisions, and for the sake of equity in his imposts and rewards. I ask God's help.[19]

The necessity of the imam or caliph as guaranteeing the survival, continuation, and very existence of the community is emphasized by al-Mawardi in the preface of *al-Aḥkām al-Sulṭāniyya*. He argues that God ordained a leader for the community through whom he provided the vicegerency of the prophet and through whom he perfected the religious community. He entrusted the leader with politics so that the management of affairs should proceed on grounds of the right religion so that there would be unanimity on an opinion which should be followed. The imamate became the principle upon which the basic foundations of the community were established—by which the interests of the community were regulated and the affairs of general interest were made stable, and from which particular public functions emanated. Because of this, it is necessary to deal with the ordinances of the imamate before any other matter, and it is important that the concerns of the imamate should precede any other religious considerations so that the ordinances regarding public functions may be arranged according to their proper classifications and similarity of their ordinances.[20] As Ann Lambton explains, al-Mawardi's conception of the imamate is not quite the same as that of al-Baqillani, who argued that the imam is a *wakil* (an agent) of the community that chose him and stood by him to set him right and to exact from him his duty. It is also different from al-Baghdadi's account of the imamate who considered it the duty of the community to correct the imam to the right path, if he erred, or to withdraw their support and elect another imam.[21]

As previously noted, the first point in al-Mawardi's political theory of the imamate is his assertion that the caliphate is necessary as a requirement of revelation, not as a requirement of reason, an argument largely disputed by Ali 'Abd al-Raziq. Thus, the appointment of the caliph or imam by the consensus of the Muslim community is wājib (obligatory) in al-Mawardi's opinion. It is *farD kifāya*, just like jihād, which should be undertaken by a few individuals, not the whole community, but in the case of farD kifāya, it is most likely that these representatives would be drawn from the 'ulumā.[22] This is the same conclusion reached by al-Baghdadi in his above-mentioned book, *Usūl al-Dīn*. The qualities that the imam must possess are seven in al-Mawardi's theory, and they are very similar to Ibn Khaldun's caliphate prerequisites mentioned earlier. First and foremost is the quality of justice/probity. The second quality is knowledge conducive to Ijtihād and independent judgment with regard to certain rules. The third quality is soundness of the senses and sensory faculties. Fourth is physical fitness that allows the imam to move quickly and appropriately. The fifth quality is insight (*ra'y*) conducive to good leadership and responsibility to members of the community. The sixth quality is bravery— courage helps protect the community from enemies. The seventh and last quality required in the imam is descent from Quraysh.[23] Al-Mawardi places great importance on this last quality, emphasizing that this is based on Hadith texts in addition to Ijmā'[24], a point that has been disputed by 'Abd al-Raziq, as explained in chapter 1. Al-Mawardi, on the other hand, argues that if anybody objects to such a quality on the basis that it excludes candidates from outside of the Quraysh tribe from being able to attain the caliphate, such an objection should not be considered. He justifies his defense of this point with reference to a Hadith as well as a point in Islamic history claiming that the Qurayshi descent quality was defended by the first caliph, Abu Bakr, as grounds for preference in the election on the *Saqīfa*[25] day when the Ansar paid allegiance to Sa'ad ibn 'Ubadah.[26]

Al-Mawardi further argues that the imam may either be elected by *ahl alḥal wal-'aqd* (literally, *people of authority* who loosen and bind communities, or those who bring issues to a solution), or be nominated by the ruling imam before his death by testamentary designation. Al-Mawardi emphasizes the debate among scholars regarding the first case of electing the imam, arguing that some of these scholars support the view that the imam must be elected by all members of the community. Other scholars disagree, arguing that only the people of Medina, not the whole land of the Hijaz, elected Abu Bakr. Another group of scholars proposed that only five people might elect the imam, supporting their argument with reference to the elections of Abu Bakr and 'Uthman, the third caliph. Other scholars said three, and some even argued that only one person might be sufficient to elect the imam. After presenting and discussing the different opinions by various scholars on the election of the imam, al-Mawardi concludes that a single elector suffices for electing an imam, citing the incident of al-'Abbas and Ali Ibn Abi Talib, the fourth caliph. The story claims that the prophet's uncle, al-'Abbas, asked his nephew Ali to stretch his hand and then paid him the *Bay'ah* (the oath of allegiance), arguing that when people came to know this fact nobody would dispute Ali's imamate.[27] Qamar-ud-din Khan argues that "the above extreme opinion has been advocated by al-Mawardi to advance another important opinion"[28] discussed in his book where he argues that in the case of two candidates equally qualified for position of imam, "the electoral college may nominate any one of the two without assigning any reason."[29]

With regard to the imam's title, al-Mawardi is wary of the title *khalīfat Allah* (caliph of God), explaining that the imam is called caliph because he succeeded the prophet of God in his community, thus it is most appropriate to call him *khalīfat Raasūl Allah*, or just *khalīfah*. He maintains that "the majority of scholars do not allow the title *Khalīfat Allah* and consider it as a sin to address the Imam as such."[30] They argue that it is permissible for the imam to be representative of someone absent or even dead; however, God is neither absent nor dead. To confirm his point further, al-Mawardi cites the incident when Abu Bakr rejected the title *khalīfat Allah* and told his companions: "I am not the Caliph of God but Caliph of the Prophet of God."[31] As noted above, al-Mawardi disapproves of the legality of appointing two imams simultaneously, arguing that "it is not permissible for a community to have two Imams at the same time even though some people went out of the norm and made it permissible."[32]

Once an imam has been named and approved, there are duties that he should undertake. These include safeguarding and protecting the origins of religion as established by the consensus of *salaf al-umma* (the ancient authorities). If anyone tries to be innovative or to deviate from this, it is the imam's duty to clarify the right way for him, using *hujja* (evidence) and proper argument of the Shari'a, and thus the religion is saved from any error and the community from heresies.[33] The second duty of the imam is to implement the *Aḥkām* between those fighting each other—within the context of dispensation of justice—preventing the strong from doing injustice to the weak and helping the weak to become strong. The third duty is to maintain security in the land so that people can lead a peaceful life and travel safely without fearing for their lives and money. The fourth duty is to implement and uphold the *ḥudūd* (punishments) as specified in the Quran to ensure God's *maḥārim* (prohibitions) are respected and that people's rights are protected. The fifth is to fortify the borders and defend them against foreign invasion in order to guarantee the security of both Muslims and those allying with them. The imam's sixth duty is to wage jihād against the obstinate who refuse to embrace the call to Islam until they either become Muslims or accept protection, as non-Muslims, within the territory of an Islamic state.[34] The seventh and eighth duties are to collect *fay* (taxes) in accordance with the Shari'a laws based on both the Quran and Ijtihād and to approximate stipends and allowances (*'atāyā*) from *Bayt al-Māl* (the state treasury) while avoiding both extravagance and parsimony. The ninth duty is to delegate authority to honest and reliable individuals, appointing people of integrity to the offices—including the treasury of the state—in order to secure efficient administration and protect the finances of the state. The tenth and last duty is for the imam to personally maintain supervision over all affairs of the state so that he oversees and directs the state policy, ensures people's safety, and protects their interests. The imam should not entrust such state affairs to others in order to engage himself in religious devotion or luxurious activities.[35]

Al-Mawardi then argues that if the imam performs his duties as detailed, observing the rights of the community, he has fulfilled God's trust in him as a leader to his community. In such a case community members' duties toward him include two obligations: obeying and supporting him—unless he changes. Such a change that prompts loss of the right to the title and authority of the imamate is of two kinds: first, if the imam loses his sense of justice/probity; and second, if he becomes physically disabled. Loss of sense of justice/probity is determined in two ways. First, if the imam becomes a slave of his inordinate desires and his sensual passions, openly flouting the prohibition of the Shariʿa, he is neither qualified to become an imam, nor can he continue as one—this behavior curtails the election and continuity of the imamate. Second, whoever commits such an act (after being elected an imam) and repents may retain his sense of justice but not the imamate, except through a new contract. The second change conducive to losing the imamate is a change occurring in the body of the imam. This is divided into three categories: loss of physical senses, loss of bodily organs, and loss of ability to behave in a sound manner with regard to managing state affairs. With regard to loss of physical senses, only loss of the mental faculties or loss of eyesight are considered conditions that would preclude an individual from election to the imamate or maintaining the position if already elected before the disability. With regard to loss of bodily organs, only loss of either both hands or both feet—making a person incapable of performing his duties normally—renders a person unfit for the imamate or forfeits the continuity of an existing imam.[36]

As will be detailed in chapter 5, in refutation of al-Mawardi's idea of the political system of the caliphate as a necessity by revelation, ʿAbd al-Raziq contends that the system of the caliphate is foreign to Islam and has no basis in its acknowledged sources, especially the Quran, Sunna, and Ijmaʿ (consensus).

ABUHAMID GHAZALI, D. 1111

In the imamate section of his book *al-Iqtisād fil Iʿtiqād* (*The Golden Mean in Belief*), Ghazali begins by stating clearly that researching the imamate is neither possible nor important, yet it opens doors for *taʿassobāt* (social cohesions within a tribal society). Thus, he maintains, the person who refuses to engage the subject is better than the one who attempts it even if the latter is ultimately correct. Problems arise if the one who opts to broach the topic is wrong. The potential for harming the community must be taken into account. Nonetheless, Ghazali decides to deal with the subject, briefly dividing it into three categories: first, the necessity of inaugurating an imam; second, requirements of the imamate and imam; and third, the belief of ahl al-Sunna in the prophet's companions and the guided caliphs. Concerning the first category, Ghazali declares that the imamate's necessity is based primarily on *sharʿ*, revelation, not on reason, which remains secondary. Consensus of the umma on the imamate follows. An ancillary basis for the imamate relates to the benefits it provides through ridding dunyā (life) of all harm.[37] On the requirement of the imamate, Ghazali elucidates further that the imam should first be qualified to lead, then must possess other characteristics such as knowledge and piety. Judges, on their part, should be male, mature, and should have sound reason, freedom, and impeccable oratorical skills, in addition to possessing perfect senses of hearing, sight, justice, and integrity. Most importantly, Ghazali endorses the belief that the imam should be from a Qurayshi descent (the prophet's tribe) based on the alleged Prophetic Hadith that, "Imams are from Quraysh."[38] Throughout the second section of his book, Ghazali continues detailing how authority should be bestowed on the imam and how *bay'ah* (the oath of allegiance) is sworn. In part three of the imamate section, Ghazali discusses the belief of ahl al-Sunna on the prophet's companions and the four guided caliphs, maintaining that people held their own opinions of them sometimes to the extent of extremism, engendering both positive and negative exaggerations. He further explains that those who engaged in positive hyperbole ascribed certain qualities to the prophet's companions and the four guided caliphs to such an extent that over time some followers assumed the infallibility of the imams. Conversely, there were those who attacked the Saḥāba (the prophet's companions), stabbing them in the back through the use of invectives and maligning their reputations through verbal backstabbing, as well as those who remained moderate in their remarks. Ghazali then explicitly emphasizes Muslims' need to follow the path of the golden mean in belief, *al-Iqtisād fil I'tiqād*,[39] a concept that he eventually chose to be the title of his entire book on this notion.

In summary, Ghazali holds an intermediary position between al-Mawardi (unity of the polity) and Ibn Taymiyya (political pluralism). Religion (dīn) and temporal power (dawlah) are twins: dawla is the guardian and preserver of dīn. Humans tend toward strife and need power (*sultan*) to keep order. However, the exercise of power requires a norm, and this can only come from *fiqh*. The appointment of an imam is a duty based on consensus, prophetic example, and utility. Ghazali was centrally concerned with the relationship between the imamate and the sultanate. For him, the only method of appointment of an imam that was realistic was the method of appointment by the one actually holding the reins of power; in other words, the sultan appointed the caliphate, and then the ruling aristocracy Seljuk and men of state, along with the ulama, gave their recognition (bay'ah).[40]

As Lambton has noted, according to Ghazali, the sultan naturally possesses circumstantial authority; he acquires legitimate authority through association with the imam. Since the imam lacked the necessary component of power, the sultanate was vital to the imamate. The ulama are also a crucial component, since only they can authoritatively declare the Shari'a. Ghazali thus regards the imamate as a complex institution consisting of three elements: imam, sultan, and ulama.[41]

BADR AL-DIN IBN JAMAʿA, D. 1333

In his book *Taḥrīr al-Aḥkām fī Tadbīr Ahl al-Islām*,[42] Ibn Jamaʿa goes further than his predecessors: he recognizes the de facto ruler as imam and regards seizure of power as itself according authority, a self-validating act. Whereas Ghazali had absorbed the sultanate into the imamate, Ibn Jamaʿa absorbs the imamate into the sultanate. He uses the terms imam and sultan interchangeably.[43] Ibn Jamaʿa's basic concern is with social order, and for this reason he holds that obedience should be rendered to a tyrannical ruler unless it entails sin. "The tyranny of a sultan for forty years is preferable to the flock being left without a master for a single hour."[44] "If a ruler acts with justice, the reward is his and it is for the people to give thanks; if the ruler is tyrannical, the crime is his, and it is for the people to be patient."[45] The ideal is, of course, that of the just sultan, and Ibn Jamaʿa has a lot to say about justice. But the ideal is not always, or even generally, realizable. Ibn Jamaʿa posits two kinds of imamate:

1. The elective imamate: follows the classical pattern, except that Ibn Jamaʿa includes umarāʾ (princes), ruʾasāʾ (leaders) and wujahāʾ al-nās (dignitaries) along with the ʿulama among the ahl alḥal wal-ʿaqd (leaders who loosen and bind communities basically to bring issues to a solution).
2. The imamate conferred by force: the only kind currently in existence. The bayʿah occurs after the fact. Both kinds of imamate are contractual in that both parties acquire rights and duties.

AHMED IBN ABD AL-HALIM IBN TAYMIYYA, D. 1328

In his book *al-Siyāsa al-sharʿiyya*,[46] Ibn Taymiyya does not equate the Islamic state with the imamate. Whereas all previous thinkers maintain the centrality of the idea of the imamate, Ibn Taymiyya uses the term *walī al-amr* (holder of authority; plural, ulū al-amr) instead of imam. He upholds the superiority of the first generations of Muslims (al-salaf al-sāliḥ). While the classical caliphate belonged to that period, it is not for all time, argues Ibn Taymiyya. In Ibn Taymiyya's opinion the Shari'a is the key concept: it requires the exercise of coercive power in its interests; this results in well-being in this world and the next. Both reason and revelation required Shari'a.[47]

He maintains that sovereignty devolves upon the entire community of in-terpreters of the Shari'a. His departure from previous political thought centers on his belief that a universal caliphate on the order of the original one is not obligatory. Furthermore, he maintains that there may be more than one imam or walī al-amr (guardian), thus advocating political pluralism. He even went further to claim that the concept of election is not valid; there never has been a bona fide election, in his opinion. What is of the essence is the contract (*mubāya'a*) between the ruler and the "influential" (including 'ulamā), with rights and duties on both sides. What Ibn Taymiyya envisions is a society in which there is harmony between ruler and the influential, with the 'ulamā playing a key role.[48]

After reviewing previous theories of the caliphate—and realizing the dete-rioration of Islamic thought, and in order to accommodate the existing reality (or to lend it some legitimacy), drifting away from the Shūrā (consultation) theory—Ibn Taymiyya criticized many of the negative phenomena in the Is-lamic society and looked at the political problem from the angle of the Shari'a and how it could be accommodated within the system of authority. He offered what has been perceived as a realistic perspective of authority, similar to Ibn Khaldun's socio-historical theory, which separated the different political sys-tems that the Islamic world witnessed from the prophetic message (*nubwwa*), which he believed lasted only for thirty years; then later on was confused with *mulk* (monarchical rule) or transformed to pure mulk. Ibn Taymiyya based his historical analysis of authority on a Hadith which referred to the Prophet Muhammad.[49] Accordingly, he maintained, mixing Khilāfah with ruling is permissible in the Shari'a. Most importantly, he argued that the caliphate is preferred, not obligatory, and that choosing a king is permissible in the Islamic Shari'a, as it was in other laws, provided that it is a right based also on the just authority.[50] However, Ibn Taymiyya did not mention in his book the issue of inaugurating the imam because he believed that the guided caliphate ended in the first thirty years after the prophet's death and would never come back given that it was based on texts and was not based on Shūrā.[51] In addition, he believed that the "Imamate of the Guided Ones" itself was based on strength and control. He maintained that "the Imam is the one who is obeyed, the one with authority whether just or unjust."[52] Based on this analysis, Ibn Taymiyya justified establishing political systems based on power, oppression, and con-trol, elucidating that the imamate is confirmed by the consent of *ahl alshawka* (those with power); and the person will not become imam until ahl alshawka agree, given that through their obedience to him the objective of the imamate is realized. This is based on Ibn Taymiyya's conviction that what is meant by the imamate is realized by capability and sultan.[53]

Ibn Taymiyya further believed that the imamate is established on two main bases: power and honesty based on Quranic texts in which power is mentioned before honesty such as, "You are with us powerful and safe"; or "the best you hire is the powerful and honest." In his opinion, accepting the philosophy of power required renouncing many ideals and conditions mentioned by previous Sunni 'ulama and confirmed by numerous prophetic Hadith narratives dealing with the characteristics of the Muslim ruler, such as belonging to Quraysh, piety, justice, knowledge, ability, consent of the community, and the oath of allegiance of ahl alhal wal-'aqd.[54] Thus, the principle that was established by his predecessors that Ibn Taymiyya abandoned was Shūrā in ruling, based on his conclusion that the Islamic umma deviated from its right path and deteriorated to the extent that Islam became estranged from its roots.[55]

Given that Ibn Taymiyya excluded most Muslim denominations and their branches, including Sunni Ash'arites, from the circle of ahl alḥaqq (people of truth), his concept of umma was a partial one (not the comprehensive concept that includes all those who take Islam as their religion based on its historical development). In his article, "Ibn Taymiyya supports the theory of oppression," Ahmed al-Katib[56] argues that Ibn Taymiyya's concept of the umma was exclusive of ahl al-Hadith, the Quran, and ahl al-sunna wa-al jamā'a. Thus, since ahl al-Hadith or ahl alḥaqq do not necessarily form a majority all the time, it was impossible for Ibn Taymiyya to consult Shūrā and the rule of the majority, or to make it a condition that the leader should receive the approval/consent of the umma. It was thus natural for Ibn Taymiyya, maintained al-Katib, to lean toward the theory of oppression and control and to lend legitimacy to ḥukūmāt al-amr alwāqi' (governments of reality), irrespective of the means through which it might come to power or assume authority.[57] In summary, ignoring the political struggle of the time, Ibn Taymiyya focused heavily on the Shari'a regime as the best for the Islamic umma. His main concern was a community guided by the prophet's sunna (exemplary behavior) regardless of how tyrannical the leaders of such a community might be.

IBN KHALDUN, D. 1406

The opinion of Ibn Khaldun (1332–1406) on the caliphate/imamate, articulated in his landmark al-Muqaddimah (An Introduction to History), was that royal authority implies a form of organization necessary to mankind. It requires superiority and force, which are expressions of the wrathfulness and animalistic tendencies of human nature. The decisions of the ruler, therefore, necessarily deviate from what is right. They will be ruinous to the worldly affairs of the people under his control. These choices will often conflict with, or impede, the worldly affairs of the people under his control. This situation will, of course, differ according to the intentions found in different succeeding generations. For this reason, it is difficult to be obedient to the ruler. The subsequent disobedience frequently manifests as turmoil and bloodshed. It is, therefore, necessary to have reference to ordained political norms which are accepted by the masses and to which they dutifully submit. The dynasty that does not have a policy based on such norms cannot fully succeed in establishing the supremacy of its rule. If these norms are ordained by the intelligent and leading personalities and minds of the dynasty, the result will be a political institution with an intellectual and rational basis. If they are ordained by God through a lawgiver who establishes them as religious laws, the result will be a political institution with a religious basis, which will be useful for life in both this and the other world.[58] Worldly interests, thus, have bearing upon the interests in the other world since, according to the Prophet Muhammad, all worldly conditions are to be considered in their relation to their value for the other world. Thus, Ibn Khaldun asserts, the caliphate is a substitute for the Prophet Muhammad inasmuch as it serves, like him, to preserve and protect the religion and to exercise political leadership of the world. This institution is called the caliphate or the imamate, and the person in charge of it is called the caliph or the imam.[59] In contrast to 'Abd al-Raziq's argument, Ibn Khaldun declares that the position of the imam is a necessary one. In his view, the consensus of the people around the Prophet Muhammad and the people of the second generation shows that the caliphate or imamate is necessary according to the religious law. After the death of the Prophet Muhammad, people proceeded to render the oath of allegiance to Abu Bakr and to entrust him with the supervision of their affairs; and so was the case in all subsequent periods of time. In no period was the Muslim community left in a state of anarchy or chaos. This was so by general consensus, which according to Ibn Khaldun proves that the position of the imam is a necessary one.[60]

Ibn Khaldun maintains that some people have expressed the opinion that the necessity of the imamate is apparent for rational reasons, and that the consensus which happens to exist merely confirms the authority of the intellect in this respect. In their view, what makes the caliph or imam rationally necessary is the need of human beings for social organization and the impossibility of their living and existing independently. One of the necessary consequences of social organization is disagreement, because of the pressure of cross-purposes. Yet, if there is no ruler who exercises a restraining influence, this leads to trouble that, in turn, may lead to the destruction and uprooting of mankind. Thus, the preservation of the species is one of necessary intentions of the religious law. Ibn Khaldun then draws quite an interesting association as he elucidates that this very idea of necessity is the one that the philosophers had in mind when they considered prophethood as something intellectually necessary for humankind. However, Ibn Khaldun emphasizes his critique of what he sees as essentially flawed reasoning. He maintains that one of the premises of such flawed reasoning is that the restraining influence comes into being only through a religious law from God, to which the masses submit as a matter of belief and religious creed. In Ibn Khaldun's opinion, this premise is not acceptable. Instead, the restraining influence comes into being as the result of the impetus of royal authority and the forcefulness of the mighty, even if there is no religious law. This was the case among heathens and other nations who had no scriptures and had not been reached by a prophetic mission.[61]

Having already stated that the caliphate institution is necessary by consensus, Ibn Khaldun emphasizes that this institution is a community duty and is left to the discretion of all competent Muslims. He maintains that it is Muslims' obligation to see to it that the caliphate is functional, and that the entire community has to obey the caliph after the Muslims have set up the caliphate.[62] Like most scholars critiqued by 'Abd al-Raziq, Ibn Khaldun underscores that such obedience is in accordance with the Quranic verse: "Obey God, and obey the Prophet and those of authority among you" (Quran 4:59). However, like most of them, he does not explain how "authority" can be determined or defined, though Ibn Khaldun is in agreement with al-Baqillani, stating that it is not possible to appoint two imams at the same time and emphasizing that religious scholars are generally of this opinion on the basis of certain traditions. 'Abd al-Raziq of course argues that none of the scholars who affirmed the obligatory character of the caliphate had been able to present evidence from the Quran to support this position. Whatever they presented, he maintains, does not constitute evidence and is open to many interpretations. With regard to the verse on "Obey God, Obey the Prophet and those of authority among you," 'Abd al-Raziq contends that the best meaning this verse could indicate is that Muslims have a group of people among them who can be consulted, and matters can be deferred to them. In his opinion, this is a much wider and general meaning than the caliphate in the context these scholars mention, and that such a meaning is quite contrary to the other and has almost no relation to it.[63]

The prerequisites governing the institution of the imamate are five in Ibn Khaldun's opinion. The first is knowledge, which he considers to be obvious because the imam can execute the divine laws only if he knows them. Further, the imam's knowledge is satisfactory only if he is able to make independent decisions. Blind acceptance of tradition is a shortcoming, and the imamate requires perfection in all qualities and conditions. The second prerequisite is probity, which is required because the imamate is a religious institution and supervises all the other institutions that require this quality. The third prerequisite governing the imamate is competence, which means that the imam is willing to carry out the punishments fixed by law and to go to war if necessary. He must therefore understand warfare and be able to assume responsibility for getting the people to fight. He also must be knowledgeable about group feeling and the fine points of diplomacy. He must be strong enough to take care of political duties. The fourth prerequisite that an imam must possess is freedom of the senses and limbs from any defect that might affect judgment and action. Such disabilities include insanity, blindness, muteness, deafness, or any loss of limbs—such as missing hands, legs, or feet—that might affect the imam's full ability to act and to fulfill his duties. The fifth and last prerequisite is descent from the Prophet Muhammad's tribe of Quraysh, a condition based upon the consensus obtained among the men around the prophet on the day of Abu Bakr's elevation to the caliphate.[64]

Abd al-Raziq's revolutionary conception of the state stands clearly as a modern antithesis of the classical Sunni theory of the caliphate discussed in the preceding pages. As noted, 'Abd al-Raziq's call for political secularism was an attempt by a scholar of al-Azhar to Islamize secularism.[65] This is quite an interesting argument and reverses the claim that 'Abd al-Raziq's ideas were borrowed from Western thought. 'Abd al-Raziq hardly perceives his ideas to be alien to Islam since his arguments always drew upon the classical sources: the Quran, Sunna, Ijmā' (consensus) and Qiyās (reasoning by way of analogy), and he is quite certain that these sources do not indicate that it is *dīn* and *dawlah* (religion *and* state) but only that it is *dīn lā dawlah* (religion *not* state). Thus, his ultimate perception is that, based on the teachings of the Quran itself, Islam is a religion and only a religion.

NOTES

1. "Caliphate," in *The Columbia Encyclopedia*, 6th Edition (New York: Columbia University Press, 2001), http://www.bartleby.com/65/ca/caliphat.html (accessed 2004).

2. Ibid.

3. Ibid.

4. Daniel Bates and Amal Rassam, *Peoples and Cultures of the Middle East* (Upper Saddle River, N.J.: Prentice-Hall, 1983), 60.

5. Wildred Madelung, "The Shiite and Kharijite Contribution to Pre-Ash'arite *Kalam*," in *Islamic Philosophical Theology*, ed. Parviz Morewedge (New York: SUNY Press, 1979); see 120–141 for Madelung's entire argument.

6. Montgomery Watt, *The Formative Period of Islamic Thought* (Oxford: Oneworld, 1998), 278.

7. Malcom H. Kerr, *Islamic Reform: The Political and Legal Theories of Muhammad 'Abduh and Rashid Rida* (Berkeley: University of California Press, 1966), 19.

8. Abu al-Hasan Ali al-Mawardi (972/364–1058/450).

9. Hamilton A. R. Gibb, *Studies on the Civilization of Islam*, ed. Stanford J. Shaw and William R. Polk (Boston: Beacon Press, 1962), 148.

10. Abu Bakr al-Baqillani, *Al-Tamhīd*, ed. Mahmoud Muhammad al-Khudayri and Muhammad 'Abd al-Hadi Abu Rida (Cairo: 1947), 185–186. See also Ann Lambton's *State and Government in Medieval Islam* (Oxford: Oxford University Press, 1981), 73–76.

11. The Arabic (ورد ورد) mā' ward is the noun, hence the nisba adjective, (ما ء) ورد) mā Wardī. The adjective وردي (wardī) in its independent form denotes the English adjective rosy (masculine), while (وردية) wardiyya is its feminine form, given the gender-specific nature of Arabic.

12. Abu al-Hasan Ali al-Mawardi, *Al-Ahkām al-Sultāniyya wa-al Wilāyāt al-Dīniyya* (*The Ordinances of Government and the States of Religion*), ed. Ahmed Mubarak al-Baghdadi (Kuwait City: Dar ibn Qutayba Publications, 1989.

13. Ibid., 3.

14. The terms amirate, imamate, and caliphate are sometimes used interchangeably. Amāra(h) or imāra(h) (transliteration is used differently by different authors) is often not a title but a function. It means authority, i.e., governmental authority. Imāmah and khilāfah are a bit different in that they do not have the versatility of amāra. They are offices with titles. The caliph himself was called Amīr al-Mu'minīn (Prince/Commander of Believers) as used in the early days of Islam. However, when amir is a title, it usually means governor of a province, the one who holds the amāra (or amirate) in the province either independently or under the authority of the caliph.

15. Ibid.

16. Qamar-ud-din Khan, *Al-Mawardi's Theory of the State* (Lahore: Bazm-i-Iqbal, [n.d.]), 20.

17. Ibid., foreword.

18. Ibid., 20.

19. Al-Mawardi, *Al-Ahkām al-Sultāniyya*, 1.

ولما كانت الأحكام السلطانية بولاة الأمور أحق، وكان امتزاجها بجمع الأحكام يقطعهم عن
تصفحها مع تشاغلهم بالسياسة والتدبير، أفردتُ لها كتاباً إمتثلت فيه أمرٍ من لزمت طاعته،
ليعلم مذاهب الفقهاء فيما له منها فيستوفيه، وما عليه منها فيوفيه، توخّياً للعدل في تنفيذه
وقضائه، وتحرّياً للنصفة في أخذه وعطائه، وأنا أسأل الله تعالى حُسن معونته، وأرغب إليه في
توفيقه وهدايته، وهو حسبي وكفى.

20. Ibid., 1–2.

إن اللّه جلّت قدرته ندب الأمة زعيماً خلف به النبوّة، وحاط به الملة، وفوّض إليه السياسة، ليصدر
التدبير عن دين مشروع فكانت الإمامة أصلاً عليه استفسرت قواعد الملة منه ما يصلح لسياسة
الدنيا، وانتظمت به مصالح الأمة حتى إستثبتت بها الأمور العامة، وصدرت عنها الولايات
الخاصة، فلزم تقديم حكمها على حكم سلطاني، ووجب ذكر ما اختص بنظرها على كل نظر ديني،
لترتيب أحكام الولايات على نسق متناسب الأقسام، متشاكل الأحكام.

21. Ann K. S. Lambton, *State and Government in Medieval Islam* (Oxford: Oxford University Press, 1981), 85.

22. Ibid., 4.

23. Ibid., 4–5.

24. It is important to emphasize at this point that Ijmāʿ is the third source of Islamic law. Ijmāʿ is defined as agreement or consensus of opinion of the jurists among the followers of the prophet in a particular age on a question of law. The Ijmāʿ authority as a source of law is founded in certain Quranic and Sunna texts such as, "Obey God, and obey the Prophet and those of authority among you." The four Sunni Schools of Law hold Ijmāʿ to be a valid source of law upon not only the authority of the above-mentioned texts, but also the unanimity of opinions to that effect among the community of jurists or scholars. The law laid down by consensus of opinion is authoritative and binding. Opinion is reached through ijtihād or independent inquiry. An opinion within Ijmāʿ is authoritative for the jurists and their followers. It is ijtihād that makes an opinion authoritative—not Ijmāʿ—but Ijmāʿ raises opinion to the level of certainty. Although an opinion is authoritative and does not need agreement to be so, Ijmāʿ places the ruling at a higher level of certainty that makes the entire community follow it. Hence the importance of the relationship between authority and certainty follows. There were minor disagreements between the schools of law regarding what constitutes Ijmāʿ. Bernard G. Weiss, *The Spirit of Islamic Law* (Athens: University of Georgia Press, 1998), 122–127. For critiques on Ijmāʿ see M. H. Kamali, *The Principles of Islamic Jurisprudence* (Islamic Texts Society, 2003), 175–179.

25. The day when the Ansar and the Muhajirīn met to elect a leader in the aftermath of the prophet's death.

26. Ibid., 5.

27. Ibid., 6–7.

28. Khan, *Al-Mawardi's Theory of the State*, 24.

29. Ibid.

30. al-Mawardi quoted in Khan, *Al-Mawardi's Theory of the State*, 24.

31. Ibid., 22. . لستُ خليفة الله ولكني خليفة رسول الله

32. al-Mawardi, *Al-Ahkām al-Sultāniyya*, 10.

33. Ibid., 22.

34. Ibid.

35. Ibid., 23.

36. Ibid., 24–27.

وإذا قام الإمام بما ذكرناه من حقوق الأُمَّة فقد أدَّى حق اللّه تعالى فيما لهم وعليهم، ووجب له
عليهم حقان: الطاعة والنصرة ما لم يتغير حاله. والذي يتغير به حاله ويخرج به عن الإمامة
شيئان: أحدهما جُرح في عدالته، والثاني نقص في بدنه. فأما الجرح في عدالته وهو الفُسق فهو
على ضربين: أحدهما ما تابع به الشهوة. والثاني ما تعلق فيه بشبهة للشهوة وانقيادا للهوى، فهذا
فسق يمنع من إنعقاد الإمامة ومن استدامتها. فإذا طرأ على من إنعقدت إمامته خرج منها، فلو
عاد إلى العدالة لم يعد إلى الإمامة إلاّ بعقد جديد... وأما ما طرأ على بدنه من نقص فينقسم
إلى ثلاثة أقسام: أحدها نقص الحواس، والثاني نقص الأعضاء، والثالث نقص التصرّف. فأما
نقص الحواس فينقسم إلى ثلاثة أقسام: قسم يمنع من الإمامة وقسم لا يمنع منها، وقسم مختلف
فيه. فأما القسم المانع منها فشيئان: أحدهما زوال العقل، والثاني ذهاب البصر. وأما فقد
الأعضاء ... ما يمنع من عقد الإمامة ومن إستدامتها ... هو ما يمنع من العمل كذهاب اليدين أو
من النهوض كذهاب الرجلين ....

37. Abu-Hamid al-Ghazali, *Al-Iqtisād fī al-I'tiqād*, with commentary by Dr. Insaf Ramadan (Damascus: Kotaiba Printing, Publishing and Distribution Press, 2003), 169. Original was in Arabic, English translation is mine.

38. Ibid, 169–170.

39. Ibid, 172–173.

40. Ibid., 171–174.

41. For the full analysis of this point, see Ann Lambton, *State and Government in Medieval Islam* (Oxford: Oxford University Press, 1981), 115–129.

42. *Tahrīr al-Ahkām fī Tadbīr Ahl al-Islām*, ed. Khair Eddin al-Tunisi (Beirut: Dar al-Kutub al-'Ilmiyya, 2003).

43. For a full account of Ibn Jama'a, refer to Erwin Rosenthal, *Political Thought in Medieval Islam: An Introductory Outline* (Cambridge: Cambridge University Press, 1958), 43–50. All subsequent references are from this source.

44. Ibid.

45. Ibid.

46. Ibn Taymiyya, *Al-Siyāsa al-Shar'iyya*. Online original Arabic text. http://arabic.islamicweb.com/Books/Taimiya.asp?book=8, accessed July 2007. All subsequent references to Ibn Taymiyya's book are attributed to this source.

47. Ibid, 5.

48. Ibid, 7.

49. Ibid.

50. Ibid, 9.

51. Ibid, 11.

52. Ibid, 12.

53. Ibid, 14, 15.

54. Ibid.

55. Ahmed al-Katib, "Ibn Tamiyya Supports the Theory of Tyranny and Oppression," http://www.iraqcenter.net/vb/archive/index.php/t-3276.html, accessed June 2007.

56. Ibid.

57. Ibid.

58. Ibn Khaldun, *The Muqaddimah: An Introduction to History*, trans. Franz Rosenthal, ed. and abridged by N. J. Dawood (Princeton: Princeton University Press, 1989), 154.

59. Ibid., 155.

60. Ibid., 156.

61. Ibid.

62. Ibid., 157–158.

63. 'Abd al-Raziq, *Al-Islām wa Usūl al-Ḥukm*, 15.

64. Ibn Khaldun, *The Muqaddimah*, 158–159.

65. Muhammad 'Imarah, *Al-Islām wa Usūl al-Ḥukm: Dirāsa wa Wathā'iq* (*Islam and the Foundations of Rule: A Study and Documentations*) (Beirut: Arabic Association of Printing and Publishing, 1972), 9.

3

The Caliphate in the Colonial Era

IN THE FIVE decades prior to the publication of Ali 'Abd al-Raziq's work *Al-Islām wa Usūl al-Ḥukm* in 1925, the Muslim world witnessed renewed interest in the caliphate. A number of efforts developed to revive the office of the caliphate, beginning with the Ottoman sultan, Abd al-Hamid II, in 1876. The title of caliph had long become simply honorary, but Abdul al-Hamid sought to reclaim the title as the leader of the entire Muslim world. With the collapse of the Ottoman Empire after World War I, his attempt to renew the caliphate was interrupted, though efforts were made to maintain the appearance of a functional system. The British colonial powers used this interest in the caliphate to their advantage. Aware of the void left behind after the collapse of the Mughal dynasty in India, they traded on the prestige and collective memory the title still held with India's Muslims. These developments were followed by three significant occurrences: (1) the short-lived claim by the Hashimite ruler Sharif Hussain bin Ali to the position of legitimate caliph in al-Hijaz in Arabia; (2) the King of Egypt, Fuad I, revealed his interest in becoming caliph of all Muslims, believing that Egypt, with its foremost seat of learning, al-Azhar, was worthy as the seat of the caliphate; (3) the publication of Ali 'Abd al-Raziq's book, which rejected the validity of the concept of the caliphate itself. The interplay between the power structures of the West and the Muslim world during the colonial period will now be examined to provide the necessary context and background in which to place the development of 'Abd al-Raziq's political thought and the reaction to his book *Al-Islām wa usūl al-Ḥukm*.

Abdul Hamid II, 1876–1909

THE FIRST KEY development, in the half-century prior to the publication of 'Abd al-Raziq's book, was the use of the title of caliph by the Ottoman sultan Abdul Hamid II. As alluded to previously, although the Ottoman sultans had always included "caliph" among their various titles, their use of this title had been informal and honorific. Whenever Ottoman use of the title was challenged, the official response was to refer to the (probably fictitious) transfer of Abbasid caliphal authority to Selim I (1512–1520) when he conquered Egypt in 1517. (A puppet Abbasid caliphate had been maintained by the Mamluk rulers of Egypt since the Mongol expulsion of the Abbasids from Baghdad in 1258.) But the Ottoman sultans used the title with much caution, probably because the Hanafi School had declared the caliphate to be nonexistent since the death of Ali ibn Abi Talib (the fourth and last guided caliph) in 661. Abdul Hamid's proclamation of himself openly and assertively as caliph was quite unprecedented since it entailed taking on a role, in addition to the role of sultan of the Ottoman Empire, that no previous Ottoman ruler had thought of: the role of universal leader of all Muslims. The incentive for Abdul Hamid's bold undertaking was to bolster his own prestige at a time when the Ottoman Empire was collapsing rapidly. In 1924, everything changed when the new Kemalist government of Turkey declared an end to the caliphate. It is interesting that they declared the end to the sultanate two years before declaring an end to the caliphate. Thus for two years, the new regime showed temporary deference to an ideal cherished by millions of Muslims.

Before Abdul Hamid II, the avoidance of using the titles of caliph, imam, and *Amir-ul-Mu'minin* (Prince/Commander of Believers) in official descriptions of the Ottoman sultan was thus possibly due to the fact that the Hanafi School of Law, which the Ottomans embraced, had come to adopt the view that the caliphate only existed for thirty years, up to the death of Ali, and that afterward there was only a government by kings. Such was the view of al-Nassafi (1068–1114).[1] This explains the fact that it was not until Abdul Hamid II that the title of caliph was officially used by an Ottoman sultan since the demise of the Abbasid dynasty in Baghdad in 1258. It is worth noting again that Abdul Hamid's assertive claim of himself as caliph was quite unparalleled in that all other Ottoman leaders had confined their duties to their position as sultans and no previous Ottoman sultan had thought of assuming the role of a universal leader of all Muslims. In addition to strengthening his own prestige at a time when the Ottoman Empire was deteriorating, Abdul Hamid was also motivated by another factor. As Stanford J. Shaw and Ezel Kural Shaw explained,

> The most widespread ideological force in the Ottoman Empire during Abdul Hamid's years was Islamism, calling for a return to the fundamental of values and traditions of the civilization of which the empire was the most

modern manifestations. Though encouraged and used by the sultan, this movement transcended him in both time and scope. It began in the late Tanzimat period, mostly in reaction to the manner in which millions of Muslims were being treated by the Russians as well as the newly independent Balkan states. Stories of persecution and savagery from the Crimea to Belgrade and Sarajevo were mingled with accounts of oppression from India to Algeria and contrasted with the toleration and good treatment provided for non-Muslims in the great Muslim empires, including that of the Ottomans.[2]

Although Abdul Hamid did not initiate the idea of what the Shaws call "Islamism," he realized how popular it was among his people and cunningly decided to use it to "strengthen his hand against enemies both at home and abroad."[3] During his reign, the empire focused more strongly on Islamic education, building schools and encouraging Islamic education to compete successfully with non-Islamic forms of education. Mosques and other Islamic venues were repaired, Islamic holidays were largely emphasized, and the use of the Arabic language was encouraged at the expense of other languages in the empire. Secular schools further added Arabic and Islamic studies to their curriculum. Given these efforts, Abdul Hamid was greatly successful in his endeavor, and despite all the negatives and complaints about his regime, his own image and the institution of the sultanate-caliphate were highly revered by the mass of the subjects.[4] Not only that, but, as Shaw and Shaw further elucidated, Islamism did intimidate foreign powers, despite their subsequent professions to the contrary. The fact that European aggression against the Ottomans greatly diminished after the British occupation of Egypt in 1882 and that the imperialist rivalries of the powers were diverted from military to economic competition during the rest of Abdul Hamid's era can also be attributed, at least partly, "to the success of his use of Islam as a weapon to ward off the aggressors."[5]

Realizing that an idea such as Ottomanism, even with its *Tanzimat*[6] system, would not bring national unity among the diverse peoples of the Ottoman Empire, Abdul Hamid began to focus on the idea of the Islamic caliphate to counter internal political unrest. Since 1907 many uprisings had been taking place throughout the Ottoman Empire. The main internal opposition that Abdul Hamid faced was the Committee of Union and Progress (CUP) that eventually led to the formation of the Young Turk Revolution, one of the strongest of its kind in Turkish history. Despite all of his efforts to suppress these uprisings, Abdul Hamid was eventually forced to give up most of his powers in the face of the Young Turk Movement. Although the crises that led to these uprisings were basically financial, not ideological,[7] Abdul Hamid was able to use the Islamic sentiment to delay the demise of his regime.

In the words of Jamal al-Din al-Afghani (1838–1897) as he reflected on the abilities of Sultan Abdul Hamid II, if weighed against the genius of four men combined, he would have *rajaḥahum* (outweighed them heavily) in cleverness, cunningness, and politics, especially in taming his companions.[8] However, al-Afghani held quite a negative view of Abdul Hamid with regard to the issue of the caliphate. His view was based on his firm belief that the dreams of the succession of incapable men who claimed the caliphate, save the first four "Guided Caliphs," fell short of the high status of the original caliphate with all its required qualifications and imperatives.[9] Referring to subsequent kingdoms and emirates of the time that were labeled "Islamic," al-Afghani questioned the very validity of those kingdoms' claim to the caliphate. "Where is the power that is to be used to avert the humiliation, colonization, or enslavement of Muslims in their own countries and homes?"[10] he asked. Al-Afghani also openly criticized Abdul Hamid asserting that, "the sultan plays with the fate of millions of his nation as he likes and none of them protested."[11] Not only that, but he renounced the oath of allegiance he paid to the caliph Abdul Hamid, elucidating that

> I came to request you to absolve me of the oath of allegiance that I paid you as caliph because I renounced that. Yes, I paid my oath of allegiance to you as caliph, but the caliph is incapable if he does not fulfill his promise. You have the choice not to promise, but if you promised you must be honest and fulfill your promise. I requested something of you and you promised to do it but you did not comply.[12]

Yet, the epitome of al-Afghani's criticism of Abdul Hamid, and other Muslim leaders of his time, is succinctly expressed when he said, "How can someone who is incapable of reforming himself become able to reform others."[13]

⇨   Caliphate in India under the Mughal Dynasty and British Rule

THE COLLAPSE OF the Ottoman Empire and the demise of Abdul Hamid as caliph coincided with a felt need on the part of many Muslims in India to have a Muslim world leader to look to at a time when the demise of the Mughal dynasty (a Muslim line of rulers) had created a power vacuum in India which had been filled by the British colonial authority there. As mentioned earlier, this left, in Indian Muslim thinking, the Ottoman Empire as a remaining vestige of Muslim power in the world. During the Young Turk period, the regime, anxious to maintain the Ottoman Empire and enhance its influence, continued to maintain the fiction of an Ottoman caliph, knowing of the enthusiasm for such a caliph in the Indian Muslim community. Although among Indian Muslims there was an intense debate as to whether, in view of their not being descendants of the Quraysh, the Turkish sultans were qualified to be caliphs, those in favor prevailed and became known as the Khilafatists, who became an organized movement that was active from 1919 to 1924.

The Mughal emperors in India were the only Sunni monarchs that rivaled the Ottoman Sultans in wealth and extent of territory during the sixteenth and seventeenth centuries. "They commonly assumed the title of Khalifah, and from the reign of Akbar onwards they called their capital *dār ul-khilāfat* (the abode of the Caliphate)."[14] However, as alluded to earlier, given the deep-rooted belief in tradition in India, a considerable number of scholars "remained faithful to the earlier doctrine that the caliphate could belong only to the Quraysh."[15] Although, the Mughal emperors were independent of the Ottoman sultans, their status "did not stand in the way of such complimentary interchange of titles."[16] In his book *The Caliphate* (1966, originally published in 1924), Sir Thomas Arnold documented such exchange of titles as in the correspondence between Muhammad I and Shah Ruhk[17] and between Muhammad II and Uzun Hasan or Sultan Husayn of Khurasan.[18] In addition,

> correspondence was opened in the name of Akbar in 1557 with Sultan Sulayman, when Akbar was only a boy of fourteen years of age; advantage was of the presence in India of the Turkish admiral, Sidi Ali Katibi, to establish relations with the Ottoman court. . . . Accordingly, Sulayman is addressed as "he who has attained the exalted rank of the Caliphate," the familiar verse (Quran, xxxv. 37) is quoted, and prayers are offered that his Caliphate may abide for ever.[19]

Following the demise of the Mughal dynasty, "the title Khalīfah had been adopted officially by the imperial home,"[20] in an attempt to win the hearts of Muslim Indians.

↪   *Sharif Hussain bin Ali (1852–1931)*

THE REVOLUTION OF Hussain bin Ali of Hijaz against the Ottoman Empire was one of the major factors that led to the defeat of the empire, at least on the Arabian Peninsula front. This was done mainly through the fact that the Hussain bin Ali revolution engaged the empire politically and militarily for an extended period of time, eventually depleting funds and efforts that could have been used on other fighting fronts. As Mutlaq al-Balawi explained, "[T]he Hussain bin Ali Revolution began modestly with limited abilities, and could not have been influential if not for the support it received from foreign powers."[21] Such support, mainly British, encouraged many of the Arabian tribes to join the revolution which strengthened it and made it more effective. With these tribes engaged in domestic fighting, the Ottoman Empire began to face an internal war, in addition to its wars against the British in Iraq, Palestine, and later Syria, the base of the fourth army unit and basis of the Ottoman Empire's power in the eastern part of Arab lands. Previously, sending the first battalion to the Suez Canal in 1915 was part of what distracted the Ottoman army, which began to weaken even before the beginning of World War I.[22] Despite the fact that the Ottomans fired Sharif Hussain bin Ali and replaced him with Sharif Ali Haidr as Amir of Mecca, Sharif Hussain bin Ali's success stemmed from the support he received from the tribes and his shrewd manner of recruiting them to his side. The fall of Mecca and Taif at the hands of Sharif Hussain bin Ali in the early days of his revolution had a negative effect on the forces defending Medina while simultaneously rendering his men more self confident.[23]

The Ottomans' total defeat in the northern Arabian Peninsula, and the British indirect control over the area, led to the emergence of the Hijaz Kingdom commanded by Sharif Hussain bin Ali, who declared himself king or caliph of that part of Arab land in November 1916 with the British blessing.[24] Hussain bin Ali's ambition, however, was not confined to Mecca and Taif. The new king had an eye to control the whole of the Arabian Peninsula, as noted by Suleiman al-Ghannam.[25] Such ambition created uneasiness on the part of King Abdul Aziz al Saud, a sentiment which led to increasing tensions between him and Hussain bin Ali in light of the political vacuum, unrest, and anarchy created by the absence of Ottomans' influence in the area, and the weakness of other local amirs.[26] Hussain bin Ali did gain some success as the allies continued supporting him until he annexed other cities including Medina. However, despite the allies' initial support of Hussain bin Ali, he began to feel that his trust in them was apparently overestimated when they did not deliver on their promise to him for full support over all Arab land. Sharif Hussain bin Ali's son, Prince Faisal, became aware of the maneuvers of European politicians during the Reconciliation Conference in Paris (resulting in the January 3, 1919, Faisal-Weizmann Agreement) and realized their ambitions in the Arabian Peninsula. This led him to believe that previous agreements with the allies would not be fulfilled. Despite all this knowledge conveyed by his son, Sharif Hussain bin Ali continued trusting Britain hoping that it would support him to counter and defeat Abdul Aziz al Saud in the Arabian Peninsula. Hussain bin Ali was quite aware that Abdul Aziz al Saud was the real and only obstacle in the Arabian Peninsula who might successfully impede the realization of his dream, which was that of total control of the area. This is further confirmed by the fact that Abdul Aziz did not recognize Hussain bin Ali as king of all Arabs. Quite aware of that fact, Hussain bin Ali was determined to get rid of Abdul Aziz, relying on his relationship with Britain with his support of them during World War I still fresh in his mind. However, when he continued his attempts to control other areas of Arab land, Abdul Aziz's forces confronted bin Ali and defeated him badly with no British support coming to help or rescue him.[27] As the British rescinded on their earlier agreement to support him against other Arab amirs, Hussain bin Ali's forces and position began to weaken considerably and his relationship with Britain clearly worsened. Eventually, he realized that the British would never deliver on their promise for him to replace the Ottoman Empire in the Arabian Peninsula and began fighting in quite a distracted manner that further weakened him (to the advantage of Abdul Aziz).

Earlier, when Abdul Aziz al Saud stood in a neutral position during World War I, neither the Ottomans' nor the allies' efforts to sway him one way or another to their side succeeded.[28] Abdul Aziz became increasingly aware that it would be in the interest of his growing state to deal wisely with both the Muslim Ottoman state (which was supporting Ibn Rashid against him), on the one hand, and with the British forces that were so close to the Arabian Gulf, which would make it easier for them to attack and harm him. The king thus continued maintaining that delicate balance until the British forces decided to appoint Abdalla bin Hussain Emir of eastern Jordan, and Faisl bin Hussain king of Iraq. At that point, Abdul Aziz wrote to the British authorities complaining that these new appointments were unjust to his interests.[29] He later clearly expressed his feelings of dissatisfaction with the British action as he maintained,

You see them plotting plots against me: they surrounded me with enemies, they established small states around me, and appointed kings out of my enemies always extending financial and political support to them . . . the Amir in Hijaz, his son Abdalla in eastern Jordan, and his son Faisal in Iraq.[30]

Following such feelings of threats, Abdul Aziz immediately took action to counter any possible attacks and thus stood on the offensive. He prepared himself and his men militarily and was soon able to annex and control many positions in the area. In the analysis of Hafiz Wahba, some of the most important reasons and factors that allowed Abdul Aziz to achieve success and supremacy in most parts of the Arabian Peninsula included, first, his wisdom and political cunning, and second, Britain's neutrality in his war against Hussain bin Ali, who was left—when they saw his rapid collapse—with no support to face his own predicament. A third factor was Abdul Aziz's reliance on the strength of the Brotherhood, loosely organized groups of men "characterized by bravery and commitment to religion to the extent of extremism."[31]

However, since the Ottoman Empire made the mistake of siding with Germany and its allies during World War I, it was quite clear that the Allies, especially Britain and France, were coordinating their policies to inherit and distribute between them the Ottoman Empire spoils after the war. The Allies dissolved the Ottoman Empire at the end of the war; however, they didn't simply grant independence to the empire's former possessions in the Middle East. The European nations of the early twentieth century still had imperialist inclinations. Moreover, after fighting the war, they were intent on "dividing the spoils." During the peace negotiations that followed, these motivations frequently put them at odds with U.S. President Woodrow Wilson, who wanted the peace agreement to embody the ideals of democracy and self-determination. Wilson's intercession prevented the Middle East from being carved into outright colonies of the victorious European powers. Instead, a system of "mandates" was created, whereby France and Britain would govern former Ottoman lands at the behest of the League of Nations. The so-called British and French mandates were distributed as follows: French Mandate: present-day Syria and Lebanon; British Mandate: present-day Israel (Palestine), Jordan, and Iraq.

In Mutlaq al-Balawi's analysis, examining the period beginning with the revolution of Sharif Hussain bin Ali and followed by subsequent events, Arabs' political short-sightedness becomes clear only in retrospect. Arab leaders supported the Allies in exchange for false promises and left their countries vulnerable to foreign interests; the reality was that Arabs were now subject to the dictates of a rekindled European colonialism. Simultaneously, maintains al-Balawi, Arabs lost their land and dignity, and fought against the Muslim Ottoman Empire, thus pursuing a mirage with the enemies' armies in goal and faith supporting them with all that they possessed of weapons, equipment, money, and men.[32]

⇨   *King Fuad I and His Interest in the Caliphate*

THE VARIOUS DECLARATIONS made by the Allies following World War I aroused hopes for independence in Egypt. Self-determination became the pre-occupation of Egyptians, especially when President Wilson made public his Fourteen Points. This is when a group of Egyptian politicians met to plan the future of Egypt as an independent country.[33] Those men formed a *wafd*, or delegation, and "in November 1918 met with Sir Reginald Wingate, the British High Commissioner, to request that they be allowed to proceed to the Paris Peace Conference and present Egypt's case."[34] The delegation was led by Saad Zaghlul, "a friend of Cromer's and a former cabinet minister . . . as well as the elected vice-president of the national assembly."[35] The *wafd* would, in later years, turn into a powerful nationalist political group bearing the same name. The request for complete independence was refused by the British government in London, which led to riots and nationalist agitation in Egypt, which was at that time governed by the sultan Prince Fuad, the youngest of the deposed Khedive Ismail's sons.[36] Zaghlul was arrested many times and exiled in Malta and Seychelles. Violence continued throughout the years to come until, in 1922, the British declared Egypt an independent country.[37] However, a number of restrictions rendered such declaration of independence void. The four points that the British reserved include the following: the defense of Egypt against foreign aggression or interference; the security of the communications of the British Empire, literally control over the Suez Canal; the protection of foreign interests and the protection of minorities; and the Sudan and its status.[38]

A descendant of the Muhammad Ali dynasty, Fuad I assumed power as king in 1922 when Egypt was technically still under British partial control following the defeat of the Ottoman Empire in World War I. Fuad inherited a constitutional parliament with a complexity of tendencies represented by conflicting parties including the nationalists and the Islamists, in addition to the army. A couple of years later, the abolition of the caliphate by Ankara in 1924 gave rise to different maneuvers,[39] including King Fuad's interest in becoming caliph in Egypt. Each of the conflicting three parties named above was a threat to Fuad's throne. The additional status of caliph was no doubt intended to bolster his own image. In weighing the three, the king apparently chose to appease the conservatives of al-Azhar. It was, in fact, during Fuad's rein that al-Azhar was stripped of its independent status as a religious authority. By according it a ministerial status, Fuad was paving the way to win al-Azhar's approval of bestowing the caliphate on him.[40] The main two tendencies that Fuad inherited have been described by Jacques Berque as he explained,

> What are we to understand of Islam at that time? There was the traditional Islam, founded on faith and the law, which appeared in such high places as al-Azhar, with all their weight of collective significance. This system gradually shed its archaicism, and derived from its very continuity methods of integrating heterogeneous elements, the boldest of which—though not the only one—had been proposed, twenty years earlier, by 'Abduh. These ideas were followed up by the somewhat less talented *Manar* school, who sought to use a technique of rationalism in the service of an ethic of "antecedence," *salafia*.[41]

The *Manar* School was established by Muhammad Rashid Rida (1865–1935). As will be detailed in the following chapter, Rida was a disciple of Imam Muhammad 'Abduh in the latter's attempts to reform Islamic thought. However, after 'Abduh's death Rida diverted from his teacher's path and returned to the Salafi textual tradition on which he had been brought up in Syria. Rida became prominent among conservatives who opposed reform. Most important, Rida's position concerning the end of the caliphate and of the Ottoman Empire following World War I was significant enough that he played a key role in calls to convene a conference in Cairo to establish King Fuad as caliph of all Muslims based in Egypt.[42]

Ironically, this was what prompted 'Abd al-Raziq, another disciple of 'Abduh, to write vigorously against the re-establishment of the caliphate in Egypt. This occurred in the midst of the same political context following the abolishment of the Ottoman caliphate, which had ruled the Arab world, spiritually as well as politically, until it was abolished in 1924 by Mustafa Kemal Ataturk in the aftermath of World War I. The British occupying power sought an alternative that could be used to manipulate the Muslim world and hoped to persuade Egypt's King Fuad to take on the title of caliph. In the midst of these preparations, 'Abd al-Raziq published his book that tried to show that neither "the Holy Quran" nor the "Prophet's Sunna" laid down the specific form that a

Muslim government should take. He asserted quite strongly that the choice of government and of political system had been left to the Muslims themselves to decide on, thus his rejection of attempts to turn a political authority into a religious symbol.[43]

Given the circumstances in which 'Abd al-Raziq's book was written and published, some critics perceived it as a political effort of the first rank, an integral part in a heated political debate. The book was thus denounced by these critics for not being an academic research, political research, or even closer to 'ilm al-Kalām as known among early intellectual Muslim thinkers. The culmination of this political debate was the Caliphate Conference convened in Cairo in 1925 to vote on the Muslim kings as caliph of all Muslims to fill the vacuum created by the Turkish regime's abolishment of the seat of the caliphate. This was evidenced by the fact that the function of the conference was not confined to Egyptian society but extended to all Muslim societies. Even those delegates from other countries who could not attend were keen to send written memorandums and authorized others in attendance to speak for them. To this effect, the Egyptian *Alahram* paper published in its May 12, 1925, issue a letter of authorization from some Indonesian islands stating the following:

> We have heard of your diligent efforts to organize the caliphate conference; and we have unanimously decided to defer to the conference and to announce our association with you and our readiness to undertake your decisions.[44]

One of King Fuad's tactics to defeat his opponents was to form a new political party, al-Ittihad (the Union), to support him in his battle against 'Abd al-Raziq's ideas on the caliphate. The party was comprised mainly of uneducated peasants and major Egyptian landowners. Al-Ittihad was formed by the palace mainly to stand against the Wafd and its leader, Saad Zaghlul, to frustrate what they believed was his plan to replace the monarchy with a modern republican system.[45]

Many instances in 'Abd al-Raziq's book explain King Fuad's frustration with the language the author used against the monarchy system. For example, unlike most earlier research conducted on the caliphate in which the terminology used by Muslim thinkers in reference to the leader was imam and imamate, 'Abd al-Raziq chose to use the terms caliph, caliphate, king, and sultan. In comparison, while imamate and imam were used about forty-nine times in his entire book, caliph and related terms were used more than two hundred times, and the terms king and sultan, in addition to other related terms, were used about a hundred and fifty times in the book.[46]

The *London Times* also wrote indicating that after the ousting of the last caliph in Turkey, it was suggested that a conference would be convened in Cairo of Sunni leaders to appoint a caliph. It is believed, the paper maintained, that the religious scholars in Egypt prefer to nominate King Fuad for the caliphate. Nothing indicates that King Fuad would reject such a great honor with all that comes with it, with a clear appreciation of his commitment to the right religious principles. However, the *Times* added, the offer of such a position to his majesty is contingent upon the consent of the 'ulama of other countries, which are more conservative about traditions than Egypt.[47]

The British position in support of King Fuad's interest in the caliphate stirred great anger among many players in the Egyptian political scene, but mainly among the Constitutionalist Liberals to whom 'Abd al-Raziq belonged. Contrary to their historical relationship with the reform movement in Egypt that dated back to the time of Muhammad 'Abduh and was now represented by the Constitutionalist Liberals, the British left their traditional friends in the cold and did not support them in the face of the palace attacks. They did not move to rescue 'Abd al-Raziq from what would turn out to be a severe attack launched against him by al-Azhar and the palace, despite the serious consequences that followed that campaign. Those consequences, which were hardly in favor of the British, included the fall of the political coalition of cabinet ministers that the British themselves had formed between the Constitutionalist Liberal party and the Ittihad party to curb the success of Saad Zaghlul and the Wafd party.[48]

The position taken by the British in support of the king was a calculated move to benefit from the caliphate system not only in Egypt through appeasing all conservative circles, but also in other parts with a Muslim majority that were under British colonial influence. An example of this was India where the caliphate system had a very good reputation among Muslim Indians. Standing against intellectual groups that opposed the renewal of the caliphate in Egypt would help the British win the hearts of Muslims in India, a move which in turn would dissuade these groups from allying with the Hindus in the Indian Nationalist Movement, which was in the making led by Ghandi and the Congress party.[49] The British justification of not supporting their old allies, the Constitutionalist Liberals, was based on their argument that this was a religious problem within the jurisprudence of the Azhar religious scholars.[50] This was the exact atmosphere that motivated Ali 'Abd al-Raziq to write his book affirming the nonvalidity of the very concept of caliphate.

NOTES

1. Sir Thomas W. Arnold, *The Caliphate* (1924; New York: Barnes and Noble, 1966), 162.

2. Stanford J. Shaw and Ezel Kural Shaw, *History of the Ottoman Empire and Modern Turkey*, vol. 2 (Cambridge: Cambridge University Press, 1988), 259.

3. Ibid.

4 Ibid., 260.

5. Ibid.

6. Turkish for Reorganization: "series of reforms promulgated in the Ottoman Empire between 1839 and 1876 under the reigns of the sultans Abdul Hamid I and Abdul Aziz. These reforms, heavily influenced by European ideas, were intended to effectuate a fundamental change of the empire from the old system based on theocratic principles to that of a modern state." Encyclopedia Britannica Online, http://www.britannica.com/eb/article-9071216/Tanzimat (accessed 2007).

7. Shaw and Shaw, 266.

8. Jamal al-Din al-Afghani, *Al-A'mal al-Kamilah li Jamal al-Din al-Afghani*, ed. Muhammad 'Imarah (Cairo: Egyptian Public Association for Publication, 1966), 245.

9. Ibid., 245–247.

10. Ibid., 247.

ما وسعني لغيظ لم أكظمه، من اهتمام السلطان بمثل هذا البهتان، وهذه الإختلافات والأراجيف المضرة في حيثية الخلافة، وعظيم خطرها، ورفعة شأنها، مع معرفتي دناءة مختلفيها و مرتبيها، وهو يدعو عليهم بشر الدعاء كالعجوز الدرديس البتراء.... الخلافة؟ كفالة الله في خلقه، فأين أحلام أولئك العجزة من مقام الإمامة، والخلافة، ما تتطلبه من الشروط والصفات؟ أين؟؟!

11. Ibid., 248.

12. Ibid.

أتيت لأستميح جلالتك أن تقيلني من بيعتي لك، لأني رجعت عنها... نعم ... بايعتك بالخلافة، والخليفة لا يصلح أن يكون غير صادق الوعد. بيد جلالتك الحل والعقد، وبإمكانك أن لا تعد، وإذا وعدت وجب عليك الوفاء، وقد رجوتك بالأمر الفلاني، ووعدت بأنك تمضيه، ولم تفعل.

13. Ibid., 248. من عجز عن إصلاح نفسه كيف يكون مصلحاً لغيره

14. Arnold, *The Caliphate*, 159.

15. Ibid., 162.

16. Ibid.

17. Ibid., 133.

18. Ibid., 135, 118.

19. Ibid., 159–160.

20. Ibid., 162.

21. Mutlaq al-Balawi, *Al-'Uthmaniun fi Shamal al-Jazira al-'Arabyiya: 1908–1923* (*The Ottomans North of the Arabian Peninsula: 1908–1923*) (Beirut: Arab Encyclopedia House, 2007), 253. Original was in Arabic, English translation of this and all subsequent references from this source are mine.

22. Ibid., 254.

23. Ibid., 256–285.

24. Fuad Hamza, *Qalb al-Jazīra al-'Arabyyīya* (*The Heart of the Arabian Peninsula*), 2nd ed. (Riyadh: al-Nasr Modern Library, 1968), 312.

25. Suleiman al-Ghannam, *Political, Regional, and International Environment in the Arabian Peninsula during the Emergence of King Abdul Aziz to Establish the Modern Saudi State* (Riaydh: Maktabat al-Ebaikan, 1999), 106.

26. al-Balawi, *Al-'Uthmānīūn fī Shamāl al-Jazīra al-'Arabyīya*, 269.

27. Ibid., 323.

28. Ibid., 231.

29. Amin al-Raihani, *The Modern History of Najd and the Biography of Abdul Aziz bin Abd al-Rahman al-Faisal al Saud, King of Hijaz and Najd and Their Supplements* (Beirut: Arabic Studies and Printing Publishing Foundation, 1980), 277.

30. Amin al-Raihani, *Arab Kings*, 2nd ed. (Beirut: Arabic Studies and Printing Publishing Foundation, 1986), 58. Also quoted in al-Balawi, *al-'Uthmāniyyūn fī Shamāl al-Jazīra al-'Arabiyya*, 334.

تراهم يدسون الدسائس علي، أحاطوني بالأعداء، أقاموا دويلات حولي، ونصبوا من أعدائي ملوكاً وهم يمدونهم دائماً بالمساعدات المالية والسياسية ... الأمير في الحجاز، وابنه عبدالله في شرق الأردن، وابنه فيصل في العراق...

31. Hafiz Wahba, *The Arabian Peninsula in the 20th Century*, 3rd ed. (Cairo: Afaq Arabic Publishing, 1956), 285–286.

32. al-Balawi, *Al-'Uthmāniyyūn fī Shamāl al-Jazīra al-'Arabiyya*, 252.

33. Afaf Lutfi Al-Sayyid Marsot, *A Short History of Modern Egypt* (Cambridge: Cambridge University Press, 1994), 80.

34. Ibid.

35. Ibid.

36. Ibid.

37. Ibid., 80–81.

38. Ibid., 82.

39. Jacque Berque, *Egypt: Imperialism and Revolution*, trans. Jean Stewart (London: Faber and Faber, 1972), 274–275.

40. See Rif'at al-Sa'īd, *Al-Irhāb al-Muta'aslam: Limādha wa Matā wa ilā Ayn?* (*Islamized Terrorism: Why, When, and to Where?*) (Cairo: Amal Publishing, 2004), 63–64; 82–83.

41. Ibid., 272–273.

42. For full details on the thought of Rida in this section, I refer to Youssef al-Sayed, *Rashid Rida wa-al-'Awda ila Manhaj al-Salaf* (*Rashid Rida and the Return to the Salaf Manhaj [Approach/Methodology]*) (Cairo: Mirette, 2000), 160. Also, http://weekly.ahram.org.eg/2000/499/books7.htm (accessed July 14, 2007).

43. Ibid.

44. *Alahram*, May 12, 1925, quoted in 'Imarah, *Al-Islām wa Usūl al-Ḥukm* (1972), 9.

45. Ibid., 15.

46. Ibid., 10.

47. *Alahram*, September 14, 1925, quoted in 'Imarah, *Al-Islām wa Usūl al-Ḥukm* (1972), 13.

48. 'Imarah, *Al-Islām wa Usūl al-Ḥukm* (1972), 36.

49. Ibid., 37.

50. Ibid., 39.

4

Ali 'Abd al-Raziq's Intellectual Formation and His Place among the Disciples of Muhammad 'Abduh

*A*N EXAMINATION OF the influential forces that were instrumental in shaping the political thought of 'Abd al-Raziq, in concert with an overview of the intellectual and political climate present in Egypt during his young adulthood, provides the necessary background for understanding his intellectual formation. This chapter seeks to situate 'Abd al-Raziq's development against the backdrop of wider events and trends of political thought in Egypt and the Islamic world, an orientation particularly helpful for the general reader. This period is defined by two opposing trends, that of an Islamist tendency in tension with that of a secular-nationalist tendency. 'Abd al-Raziq's thought is shaped by exposure to these dual tendencies at work in Egypt and his engagement with the intellectual elite at al-Azhar, and developed against a backdrop of political uprisings in Egypt and across the greater umma. The ideas of Muhammad 'Abduh will be introduced at some length, and the two main branches of thought that emerge among his disciples will provide support for the contention that 'Abd al-Raziq's research and findings constituted a singular departure in this field of study. Additionally, 'Abd al-Raziq's place among the disciples of Muhammad 'Abduh will be outlined, with an emphasis on the importance of 'Abd al-Raziq's unique contribution to any discussion concerning the relationship between religion and politics within Islam, an argument for political secularism advanced in the language of Islam.

The question of what constitutes a proper Islamic position with respect to the secularization of government and politics has been a subject of heated debate among Muslim intellectuals for nearly a century. The central issue in this debate has been whether or not political secularism has a defensible place within Islam and, by implication, within the politics of countries with a Muslim majority. Different schools of political and religious thought throughout the Arab and Muslim worlds have been actively engaged in this debate. With the publication of Ali 'Abd al-Raziq's book *Al-Islām wa Usūl al-Ḥukm: Baḥth fil Khilāfah wal Ḥukūmah fil Islām* (*Islam and the Foundations of Rule: Research on the Caliphate and Government in Islam*)[1] in 1925, along with the author's call for the abolition of the caliphate as an Islamic institution, this debate suddenly took a new turn. The importance and danger of 'Abd al-Raziq's book stemmed not so much from its call for political secularism and the separation of religion and state as from the fact that this call was now coming from a denizen of al-Azhar, Islam's most venerable institution of learning. The book represented, in the judgment of some critics, the first attempt by an Azharite 'Ālim to "Islamize secularism"—that is to say, to found a claim that Islam fosters a secularist view of the state and politics on arguments based on Islam's authoritative sources (usūl), the Qurān, the Sunna, Ijmāʿ (consensus), and Qiyās (reasoning by way of analogy), contending that these sources indicated that Islam is "religion, *not* state" (dīn lā dawlah), not "religion *and* state" (dīn wa dawlah).[2] The immediate and decisive response to 'Abd al-Raziq's book by al-Azhar's Supreme Council was total condemnation, termination of his membership in al-Azhar Council, and dismissal from the body of the 'ulama.

Ali 'Abd al-Raziq lived in a complex intellectual setting that emerged out of the intellectual and cultural renaissance (*nahDah*) associated with Muhammad 'Abduh (1849–1905) and those influenced by his teachings. As the movement developed, it came to be marked by interaction between two broad tendencies: an Islamist tendency represented by people such as Hasan al-Banna (1906–1949) and a secular-nationalist tendency represented by 'Abd al-Raziq himself and others. Although entirely different in their approaches and beliefs, both of these tendencies shared the belief that the Islamic world was in a state of weakness and deterioration, exacerbated by the domination of European colonialism, and in urgent need of intellectual and cultural rejuvenation. The major differences between the two approaches centered on Islam's encounter with modernity. The Islamist view, as articulated by Hasan al-Banna and others, was that Egypt would be able to find solutions to its economic, political, and cultural problems only through a return to "true" Islam as a governing ideology. In the Islamist view, Islam was a comprehensive order influencing all aspects of human life.[3]

Al-Banna founded in 1928 the Muslim Brothers' Society with the intention of promoting "true" Islam and launching resistance to foreign colonization. In 1932 when the Egyptian ministry of education transferred al-Banna to Cairo, his society began to grow into a nationwide movement.[4] Around 1936, al-Banna became actively involved in politics and began to address the king and members of the Egyptian government in published letters, calling on them to adopt an Islamic political order and to dissolve corrupt political parties. When several Egyptian groups waged a nationalistic campaign against the British occupation after the Second World War, the Muslim Brothers were an integral part of that campaign. But in 1948 the Brothers' hostility was directed at their own Egyptian opponents, and soon after in December 1948 a member of the Muslim Brothers assassinated the Egyptian prime minister, Mahmoud Fahmi Nokrashi. A few months later, in February 1949, the Egyptian secret police retaliated and assassinated al-Banna.[5] But al-Banna's political thought did not die with him; his ideas and his advocacy of an Islamic political system were kept alive by his followers. Islamists throughout the Arab world as well as in non-Arab Muslim countries have right up to the present time been replicating the Egyptian Muslim Brothers' methods and their constant call for an Islamic state. In the analysis of Nazih Ayoub, "The movement's leaders may be considered the main initiators of the early formulations of a concept of political Islam in the Arab world."[6]

This advocacy of an Islamic state stood in sharp contrast to the liberal secular-nationalist tendency that was predominant in Egypt at the time. The rise and development of Egyptian nationalism emerged as part of Egypt's struggle for independence. The liberal aspect of the secular-nationalist movement was represented by people such as Muhammad 'Abduh, who has been considered one of the most forceful advocates of Islamic liberalism in modern times. 'Abduh was a student and close colleague of Jamāl al-Din al-Afghani (1839–1897), who was a pioneer of Islamic reform. Both 'Abduh and 'Abd al-Raziq were influenced by al-Afghani's thoughts on reforming Islam. Al-Afghani rejected the idea of closing the gate of ijtihād [7] (independent inquiry) and, conversely, believed that it would be in the best interest of Islam that it should remain open. He posed a series of very important questions that displayed his suspicion of the validity of closing ijtihād. Some of the questions that he posed in this regard include the following: "What is the meaning that the gate of ijtihād is closed? What is the text that indicates such closure? And who is the Imam that said no Muslim should continue ijtihād and independent inquiry in Islam after me?"[8] Al-Afghani elucidated further that Muslims have the right to find guidance in the Quran and the authentic Hadith narrative, and continue their efforts and ijtihād to expand their understanding of them. Not only that, he also believed that Muslims should continue inferring answers to their questions based on reasoned analogy drawing from what is applicable in the modern sciences while taking into consideration the concerns and needs of the period at hand, inasmuch as the conclusions do not conflict with the essence of the original texts. Al-Afghani went further to assume that if the founders of Islamic jurisprudence, Abu Hanifa, Malik, al-Shaf'i, and Ahmed Ibn Hanbal, were alive today, they would have continued their ijtihād, creatively extrapolating rules for all issues from the Quran and Hadith, because, he maintained, the more these Imams contemplated deeply in these sciences, the better enabled and meticulous they would have become in understanding them. Despite the fact those prominent imams made ijtihād and did well on their independent inquiries, it would be incorrect to assume that they discovered all secrets of the Quran, or that they were able to include them in their books. In fact, al-Afghani asserted, for all the fine and dedicated scholarship of these four men, the wealth of their efforts in communicating what the Quran and Hadith contained was but a small drop in a sea of knowledge, a second of the total hours of a whole year.[9]

Inspired by al-Afghani's thinking, the reform movement in Egypt began as a reaction to European colonialism in Arab lands in the 1870s and beyond. Al-Afghani's discursive style was designed to stir up a sense of solidarity and activism among Muslims and to call Muslims to a renewal of ijtihād. "Islam was constructed as a force that can unfold its high civilizational potential and challenge the encroaching West, if cleansed of the forces of backwardness."[10]

As articulated by Robert Bellah, the two basic components of 'Abduh's thought are, first, his assertion that Islam is a religious ideology wholly appropriate to the needs of the modern world and, second, his belief that whatever good in the modern world that is not already included in Islam is not in conflict with it.[11] 'Abduh and many of his disciples, maintains Bellah, argued further that Islam is a religion that gives profound dignity to the individual, aspires to bring about a better social order in this world, demands the full inclusion of every Muslim in a functioning community, and grants high status and protection to women within the family. Underlying all of 'Abduh's thought is his ever-present conviction that Islam and modernity are compatible.[12] Convinced that Islam is indeed a rational religion that can serve as the basis of life in the modern world, he saw no conflict between it and the principles of modern civilization.[13]

'Abduh's influence produced diverse results among his followers, some of whom moved in a conservative direction and others down a more liberal path. Ironically, as Albert Hourani explains, while 'Abduh's purpose was to prove that Islam and modern civilization are compatible, the more conservative of his disciples carried his insistence on the unchanging nature and absolute claims of the essential Islam toward a strict Hanbali fundamentalism, while those with a more liberal bent took 'Abduh's views on civilization as their start-ing point and tended to dissolve the relationship 'Abduh created between Is-lam and modern civilization, supplanting it with "a *de facto* division of spheres of influence."[14] The first group is represented pre-eminently by Muhammad Rashid Rida (1865–1935) and the second group by a number of writers includ-ing Qasim Amin (1863–1908), Ahmad Lutfi al-Sayyid (1872–1963) and Ali 'Abd al-Raziq. Although 'Abd al-Raziq "has been influenced, to a certain extent, by 'Abduh's ideas, he has advanced beyond them in many essential respects,"[15] as will be discussed within the course of this chapter.

The view of Islam held by Rida was initially in line with that expounded by al-Afghani and 'Abduh, addressing the same question of the backwardness of Muslim countries and blaming this backwardness on Muslim deviation from "true" Islam.[16] As his thinking about Islam developed, Rida came to be influ-enced by a strict Hanbali thought that led him in later years to enthusiastically support the Wahhabi movement in central Arabia and its policy. In his defense of their conquest of the Hijaz, Rida declared that the Wahhabi doctrine was that of original Muslims. He also shared the Wahhabis' contempt of Sufism, which he considered as having been corrupted in its later development so that one had to draw a clear distinction between a true (i.e., earlier) Islamic mysti-cism and a false (i.e., later) one.[17] On the subject of the *salaf* (pious Muslim of the first three generations of Islam), Rida's views differed from the teachings of 'Abduh. While 'Abduh focused on the creators of the central tradition of Muslim thought and devotion up to the time of al-Ghazali, Rida was much more focused on a strict adherence to the salaf, hence his eventual closeness to the Hanbali thought.[18]

Rida also departed from the teachings of his mentor, 'Abduh, on the sub-ject of the caliphate. Throughout the first half of his career—that is to say, prior to the abolition of the caliphate by the Turkish government in 1924—he did not oppose its existence as a Turkish institution and thought that it was neces-sary for Muslim and Arab unity and strength in the face of foreign pressure. However, in his opinion, this caliphate could be accepted only as a "caliph-ate of necessity," not as an authentic or ideal caliphate. This attitude seems to have been based on the notion that the Ottoman sultans did not have one of ijtihād's essential conditions: knowledge of the Arabic language. Given that Arabic was the language of Islam's basic texts, the Ottoman sultans' nonmas-tery of Arabic rendered them incapable of ijtihād.[19] Rashid Rida later took part in the great debate over Ali 'Abd al-Raziq's *Al-Islām wa-Uṣūl al-Ḥukm*, which he denounced vigorously in his journal, *al-Manar*. He saw the danger of 'Abd al-Raziq's book in the possibility of its being used by the enemies of Islam. His criticism of it found expression in a lengthy treatise on the caliphate, published when it had become clear that the caliph had become a mere figurehead without real power. In his attempt to restore the caliphate, Rida suggested that this could be done only in two stages: the establishment of a "caliphate of necessity," to unify the efforts of Muslim countries against foreign dangers, then the restoration of a genuine caliphate possessing qualifications for ijtihād when the time was ripe.[20]

On the opposite end of the spectrum of 'Abduh's disciples stands Ali 'Abd al-Raziq. Before introducing his book, however, it is important to shed light on his background—his life, his upbringing, his career, and his writings. Ali 'Abd al-Raziq was born into a highly educated, wealthy, and influential Egyptian family. He was born in 1887 in the Abu Jarj village, in the al-Minia province. After memorizing the Quran, he joined the al-Azhar University in Cairo where the house of his father, Bayt Āl 'Abd al-Raziq, was the meeting place of the Egyptian elite and intellectuals, such as Imam Muhammad 'Abduh and his disciples, including Muhammad Rashid Rida, in addition to politicians such as Ahmed Lutfi al-Sayyid, the leader of the Egyptian Umma Party, among many others. The 'Abd al-Raziq family was also an important pillar of the Egyptian Umma Party, then later the al-Ahrār al-Dustūriyyūn (Constitutionalist Liberals) Party. After the establishment of the Egyptian University in Cairo in 1908, 'Abd al-Raziq joined it, where he studied other disciplines of Western civilization while simultaneously attending al-Azhar. In 1912, he graduated with distinction from al-Azhar and was awarded its highest certificate in Islamic Law. He then traveled to England, at the expense of his family, and enrolled at Oxford University intending to study economics, but the outbreak of World War I forced him to return to Egypt in 1915. He was soon appointed as a Shari'a Qādī (judge), and he continued in that position until he wrote Al-Islām wa Usūl al-Ḥukm in 1925. Shortly after, when many including his own colleagues in al-Azhar received the book with strong opposition, 'Abd al-Raziq was fired from his position and his tenure on al-Azhar Supreme Council was immediately terminated. 'Abd al-Raziq's ideas were perceived as secular, and the fact that his argument that the Islamic khilāfah (caliphate) system should be abolished was utterly rejected. However, he eventually regained his position at al-Azhar when his brother, Mustafa 'Abd al-Raziq Pasha (1885–1946), assumed the respected position of grand sheikh (rector) of al-Azhar in 1945. During this time, 'Abd al-Raziq was also appointed as a cabinet minister of al-Awqāf (Endowment) between December 1948 and July 1949 under Prime Minister

Ibrahim 'Abdel Hadi Pasha (1898–1981). He also enjoyed membership in the Egyptian Parliament and Senate (*Majlis al-Nuwwāb* and *Majlis al-Shuyūkh*, respectively) and was appointed as a member of the Arabic Language Academy Council, *Majama' al-Lughah al-'Arabiyyah.*

Ali 'Abd al-Raziq's other books include *Al-Ijmā' fī al-Sharī'a al-Islāmiyya* (*Consensus in Islamic Law*), 1947; *Amālī 'Abd al-Raziq* (a collection of lectures that he delivered to the students of the Cairo University College of Law); and *Min Āthār al-Sheikh Mustafa 'Abd al-Raziq* (an edited version of the works of his brother, Mustafa 'Abd al-Raziq, with a foreword by Taha Husayn), 1957. Sheikh Ali 'Abd al-Raziq died on September 23, 1966.[21]

⮑   *The Controversy over the Book*

THE PUBLICATION OF *Al-Islām wa Usūl al-Ḥukm* in 1925 precipitated a stormy intellectual debate whose dust did not settle for quite a long time. As noted, the main reason for the intensity of the controversy was that Ali 'Abd al-Raziq was the first sheikh with the standing of an Azharite 'ālim ever to declare that "Islam is a religion not a state, a message not a government." As was also previously noted, when the book was first published, its danger was seen as lying not so much in the fact that it was calling for a secular state and a separation between religion and the state as in the fact that this idea was being propounded by an Azharite on the basis of the traditional Islamic type of argumentation based on the notion of the four sources (*usūl*): the Quran, Sunna, Consensus, and reasoned analogy. Those sources, the book was arguing, gave no indication that Islam was "a religion *and* a state," but only that it was a "religion *not* a state." In advancing this kind of argument the study represents an attempt, on the part of an author who was a member of al-Azhar's Supreme Council and a Shari'a jurist and judge, to "Islamize secularism." This Islamization project was, furthermore, reflected in the fact that the word "Islam" appeared twice in the book's full title *Al-Islām wa Usūl al-Ḥukm: Baḥth fī Khilāfah wal Hukūmah fī Islām.*[22] All these factors contributed to intensification of the controversy over the ideas expressed in the book, a controversy whose lingering effect is evidenced by the many accounts that have been written in Arabic about the book.

The seriousness of the situation in which 'Abd al-Raziq found himself is underscored by the fact that al-Azhar Supreme Council itself condemned and denounced 'Abd al-Raziq's book, expelled him from the circle of 'ulamā, and terminated his membership in the council. The action has been perceived by many, including Muhammad 'Imarah who thinks 'Abd al-Raziq had the right to express his opinion, as a case of partisan political decision-making carried out under the pretext of religion. What was at issue, 'Imarah maintains, is "the statement contained in al-Azhar Supreme Council's declaration to the effect that 'the religious government' is an inseparable part of the Islamic Shari'a."[23]

'Abd al-Raziq did not anticipate that his book would turn into a virtual bomb that would cause explosions within many Egyptian political parties and cabinet ministries. Neither did he expect that those controversial ideas would lead to his expulsion from al-Azhar circle of scholars. The main question that al-Azhar Supreme Council posed in its indictment of the content of the book revolved around whether 'Abd al-Raziq was able to divide the religion of Islam into two, religion and state, to eliminate the aḥkam (rules) pertinent to life, and to disregard the verses of the Quran and the Sunna of the Prophet.[24] In self defense, 'Abd al-Raziq denied that he meant any of that, and explained further that the prophet came with basics and principles and general rules that touched widely on different aspects of life and nations. These, he maintained, included systems of punishment, organization of the army, jihad, commercial transactions, and general rules of behavior. However, 'Abd al-Raziq was quick to add that "if you contemplated all this, you would find that all that Islam stipulated and that Muslims adopted of systems, basics, and principles did not have anything to do with methods of governing."[25] To support his argument further, 'Abd al-Raziq quoted the Hadith, "If life in the sight of God were to weigh a wing of a mosquito, the non-believer would not have enjoyed a mouthful of water of it." Then he went further to use another Hadith reminder of the prophet's saying, "You are more cognizant of your life affairs," which, in his view, clearly meant that Muslims should be better informed and more knowledgeable of the type of government that is more suitable to their time. However, 'Abd al-Raziq's defense did not change the Azhar Supreme Council's decision to expel him from the circle of religious scholars as stated in their following verdict:

> We, the Rector of al-Azhar and twenty four 'ulama of the [Azhar] Supreme Council, have unanimously ruled to expel Sheikh Ali 'Abd al-Raziq—one of al-Azhar 'ulamā, and the Shari'a Judge of the al-Mansura Elementary Court, author of the book *Islam and the Foundations of Rule*—out of the council of 'ulamā. This Verdict was issued on Wednesday 22 Muḥarram 1344 H. (12 August 1925) with the signature of the al-Azhar Rector.[26]

After the verdict was officially issued, King Fuad ordered the termination of 'Abd al-Raziq's tenure as a judge of the judiciary. This could be viewed in the context of the allegation that the Azhar decision was motivated by the palace in order to frustrate any attempts that might stand in the king's way to become caliph of all Muslims.

In the midst of that boiling political scene, the controversy of Ali ʿAbd al-Raziq's book in the Egyptian media in fact began, before the Azhar issued its verdict, when ʿAbd al-Raziq gave a copy of the book to his friend Muhammad Husayn Haykal, then editor-in-chief of the Constitutionalist Liberals' Party's paper, *al-Siyāsa*. On May 24, 1925, the paper announced the publication of the book, emphasized ʿAbd al-Raziq's effort, and recommended the book for its readers.[27] Soon after, on June 8, Rashid Rida wrote an article that appeared on the front page of *al-Liwāʾ al-Misrī wa-al-Akhbār* newspaper. It was in that article that Rida alluded to the danger of the call adopted by the book and, most specifically, what he saw as the danger inherent in his argument that such "an innovation" was coming from a Shariʿa judge and a denizen of al-Azhar. Thus, came Rashid's warning for the Azhar Supreme Council to condemn the book and its author.[28]

Before proceeding, a brief overview of the contents of *Al-Islām wa Usūl al-Hukm* is in order (an extended overview and a detailed analysis of the book are provided in chapter 5). The book is divided into three main parts, each of which is further divided into short chapters. The overall structure of the book is as follows:

PART I: The Caliphate and Islam

    Chapter 1: The Caliphate and Its Nature

    Chapter 2: The Legal Categorization of the Caliphate (Obligatory or Not)

    Chapter 3: The Caliphate from a Sociological Perspective

PART II: Government and the Caliphate

    Chapter 1: The Ruling System in the Time of the Prophet

    Chapter 2: Messengership and Rule

    Chapter 3: Messengership, not Rulership; Religion, not State

PART III: The Caliphate and Government in History

    Chapter 1: Religious Unity and the Arabs

    Chapter 2: The Arab State

    Chapter 3: The Islamic Caliphate

ʿAbd al-Raziq discusses the term *khilāfah*, its meaning in language, how the khalīfah receives his instructions, etc. Most important, however, is his discussion of the issue of whether the caliphate is an obligatory institution, one that the Muslim community is obliged to have (*hukm al-Khilāfah*). He devotes part of the discussion to Ibn Khaldun's argument in his *Muqaddimah* that appointing the caliph is indeed obligatory and that if Muslims were to renounce it, they would be punished collectively. Ali 'Abd al-Raziq then takes note of the disagreement among Muslim scholars as to whether the obligatory character of the caliphate is based on revelation or reason. This disagreement, he points out, is of as much interest to him as what the two sides in the debate had in common, namely the conviction that the caliphate is an obligatory institution. In other words, Muslim scholars have come close to reaching a consensus on this fundamental point, a consensus noted by Ibn Khaldun.[29] An important exception was the *Khawārij* movement, which took exception to the common view. 'Abd al-Raziq maintains, however, that none of the scholars who affirmed the obligatory character of the caliphate had been able to present evidence from the Quran to support this position. He adds that if there were one single evidence in the Quran, these scholars would have never hesitated to refer to it and praise God for it. Or even if there were in the Quran anything resembling evidence for *wujūb al-Imāmah*, it would have come to the notice of the scholars. Failing to find clear-cut evidence (hujja) in favor of their position, the scholars turned from scripture and looked for evidence in the consensus of the community of scholars at times, and arguments based on analogy at other times.[30] 'Abd al-Raziq further argues that the Quran is not alone in neglecting to mention anything about the khilāfah, but the Sunna also never mentioned it. This is confirmed by the failure of the scholars to provide any evidence from the Sunna to support their position. However, he discusses such recent works on the subject as *al-Khilāfah al-'Uzhmah* (*The Grand Caliphate*) by Muhammad Rashid Rida in which Rida claims that both the Quran and the Sunnah affirm the obligatory character of the caliphate, citing the Quranic verse, "Obey God, Obey the Messenger, and those in authority among you" (4:59), in addition to some narratives of *Hadith Sahīh,* purporting that they confirm the claim of *wujūb al-khilafah*.[31] 'Abd al-Raziq further argues that a close look at what Rida and other scholars have presented in the way of evidence from the Quran and Sunna does not in fact constitute genuine evidence, but consists merely of references to the imāmate or bay'ah (oath of allegiance), none of which qualifies as bona fide evidence for their position.[32] As previously noted, chapter 5 provides full details of the content of *Al-Islām wa Usūl al-Hukm*.

The content of the book and its language clearly show 'Abd al-Raziq's uniqueness among 'Abduh's disciples. Unlike most liberals, whose arguments were couched in secular language, 'Abd al-Raziq phrased his in the language of traditional Islam, the language of al-Azhar, which made it somewhat difficult for his detractors to refute his argument. In fact, 'Abd al-Raziq became a star following the controversy that the book created in the Egyptian society when his ideas drew the spotlight of journalistic and political discussion. Most importantly, the Constitutionalist Liberals' Party stood firmly in support of 'Abd al-Raziq, whose prominent family represented some of the founding members of the party.[33]

Within the controversy surrounding the book, there has been at least one claim that 'Abd al-Raziq might have not been the real author of the book. This, however, is an extreme claim that cannot be taken seriously.[34] Based on what he understood from 'Abd al-Raziq's introduction, Muhammad Diyā al-Dīn al-Rayyis charged that the book was authored during World War I, between 1915 and 1917, and not in 1925, as was widely known (and evidenced by the date of the original edition).[35] Conversely, what 'Abd al-Raziq actually mentioned in the book's introduction is the following: "I was put in charge of Egypt's Shari'a Courts since 1915, which motivated me to research the history of Shari'a Law, and the law with its different kinds is a branch of government given that its history relates largely to the history of law."[36] Diyā al-Dīn al-Rayyis goes further in doubting the authenticity of 'Abd al-Raziq's authorship of the book, maintaining that "it is proved based on texts from the book that 'Abd al-Raziq mentions sultan Muhammad V, the Ottoman caliph in name and attacks him, [despite the fact that] the end of the sultanate was in 1918.[37] There can certainly be no logical fallacy or weaker point to support the claim that the book was authored before 1918. In fact, the same flawed logic can be used to claim that the book was authored in 632 because 'Abd al-Raziq also mentions Abubakr, the first "Guided Caliph," by name.

Another controversy centered on whether 'Abd al-Raziq renounced his ideas before his death. However, such claims were mainly attributed to 'Abd al-Raziq's sons, alleging that they said he had written articles refuting his earlier ideas, but that he died before he published them.[38] This also defies any logic because if this were true, the sons, who were faced with heated debates hardly in favor of their father in a boiling Egyptian political atmosphere, would have certainly been keen enough to publish those articles instead of claiming they were lost. This allegation has also recently been refuted by the revelation of a letter that 'Abd al-Raziq wrote at the age of seventy-five to his nephew reaffirming his beliefs, as he maintained, "What we desire is the safety of government of the evils and corruption of tyranny."[39] Thus, the fact remains that, tracing the issue through its original sources of the Quran, Sunna and Ijmāʿ (consensus), Ali ʿAbd al-Raziq refuted in his book all claims calling for a religious government in Islam. He concluded that those advocating the necessity of the Islamic government, based on these sources exaggerated in their illusion, were far from accurate, and fell back on erroneous assumptions and confusion.

One of those who called for the necessity of the caliphate was Ibn Khaldun. Despite his critique of Ibn Khaldun's position in support of the caliphate, ʿAbd al-Raziq shared many aspects of his vision on the importance of political science. As will be shown in subsequent chapters, in light of ʿAbd al-Raziq's analysis that Muslims neglected this aspect of science, it is important here to mention his critique that, of all the wealth of their translation from Greek sciences, cultures, and philosophies, early Muslims did not translate Aristotle's book *Politics*. In refutation of the accusation that he adopted a Western approach in his critique of the caliphate, ʿAbd al-Raziq in fact concentrated solely on using the Islamic heritage of the Quran, Sunna, and Ijmāʿ. Such a critical analytical method clearly demonstrates the influence of Ibn Khaldun on ʿAbd al-Raziq.

ʿAbd al-Raziq's book thus continued the efforts of the NahDa pioneers in Egypt beginning with al-Afghani, Muhammad ʿAbduh, Rashid Rida, and others. While ʿAbd al-Raziq's detractors considered his ideas a rejection of what Islam advocated in political matters, supporters of ʿAbd al-Raziq's thought perceived the book as one of the most remarkable efforts in the path of developing Arab/Islamic thinking. "It is truly one prominent aspect of our modern intellectual life, a dear chapter of our heritage and struggle for freedom."[40] Irrespective of these differing reactions to his ideas, this study emphasizes the urgent need for scholars to understand ʿAbd al-Raziq's thought as a major contribution to the debate over Islam and politics.

The intensification of the effect of ʿAbd al-Raziq's book is clearly attributed to the political atmosphere in the Islamic world during that specific time. It was one year after the caliphate was abolished in Turkey and when King Fuad, supported by the British, was aspiring to become the new caliph of all Muslims. Fuad was motivated by the fact that the abolishment of the caliphate left the Sunni Muslim world without a caliph or sultan for the first time in more than four hundred years. This prompted a feeling of Muslims around the world of the necessity of renewing the caliphate. Those in favor of re-establishing the caliphate seat had different reasons in mind. While some thought of it as a necessity for uniting Muslims in their struggle against the ambitions of colonial powers, others believed it was an Islamic symbol that should be preserved, and yet a third group believed it was a religious duty and one of the fundamentals of Islam, a belief which made abandoning the institution of the caliphate equivalent to choosing a state of sin.[41]

NOTES

1. 'Abd al-Raziq, *Al-Islām wa Usūl al-Ḥukm* (1925).

2. Muhammad 'Imarah, *Ma'rikat Al-Islām wa Usūl al-Ḥukm* (*The Battle of Islam and the Foundations of Rule*) (Cairo, Beirut: Dar al-Shurūq, 1989/1410), 9.

3. Hasan al-Banna, *Majmu'at Rasa'il al-Imam al-Shahīd Hasan al-Banna* (*A Collection of Imam Hasan al-Banna's Messages*) (Beirut: Dar al-Andalus, 1965), 341, 347.

4. Hasan al-Banna, *Memoirs of Hasan al-Banna Shaheed* (Karachi: International Islamic Publishers, 1981), 141–142, 178–180. See also *Majmu'at Rasa'il al-Imam al-Shahīd Hasan al-Banna*, 264–265.

5. Richard P. Mitchell, *The Society of the Muslim Brothers* (London: Oxford University Press, 1969), 35–72.

6. Nazih Ayoub, *Political Islam: Religion and Politics in the Arab World* (London: Routledge, 1991), 130.

7. Ijtihād was a unique Islamic research method of independent inquiry that resulted in the emergence of different schools of Islamic jurisprudence. However, the gate of ijtihād was officially declared closed at the end of the eleventh century by early conservative Muslim jurists. Modern Muslim reformist thinkers such as al-Afghani and 'Abduh, among others, continued ijtihād, which they believed is an inherent part of the Islamic spirit of reform.

8. Jamāl al-Din al-Afghani, *Al-A'māl Al-Kāmilah li-Jamāl al-Dīn al-Afghānī* (*The Complete Works of Jamal al-Din al-Afghani*), ed. Muhammad 'Imarah (Cairo: Egypt Association of Printing and Publishing, and Arab House of Print and Publication, 1968), 329.

9. Ibid. For a comprehensive coverage of al-Afghani's thoughts on the reform movements, see previous reference, 327–330.

10. Armando Salvatore, *Islam and the Political Discourse of Modernity* (Reading, U.K.: Ithaca Press, 1997), 85.

11. Robert N. Bellah, *Beyond Belief: Essays on Religion in a Post-Traditional World* (Berkeley: University of California Press, 1991), 160, 165.

12. Ibid.

13. Yvonne Haddad, "Muhammad 'Abduh: Pioneer of Islamic Reform," in *Pioneers of Islamic Revival*, ed. Rahema Ali (London: Zed Books, 1994), 44.

14. Albert Hourani, *Arabic Thought in the Liberal Age: 1798–1939* (Oxford: Oxford University Press, 1962), 169.

15. Adams, *Islam and Modernism in Egypt*, 259.

16. Hourani, *Arabic Thought in the Liberal Age*, 226–228.

17. Ibid., 231–232.

18. Ibid., 230.

19. Ibid., 240.

20. Ibid., 241.

21. This is a synthesis of a detailed biography of Ali ʿAbd al-Raziq included in ʿImarah, *Maʿrikat Al-Islām*, 23–24. The original text was in Arabic; English translation of this and other references to ʿImarah are mine unless otherwise indicated.

22. ʿImarah, *Maʿrikat al-Islām*, 8.

23. Ibid.

24. Refer to the Arabic text of al-Azhar's seven points of indictment of ʿAbd al-Raziq's book in ʿImarah, *Al-Islām wa Usūl al-Ḥukm* (1972), 21.

25. Nashawi al-Deeb, "Muḥakamat Sheikh Azharī Asbaḥa Wazīran lil Awqāf," (A Trial of an Azharite Scholar Who Became a Minister of Endowment), *al-ʿAraby* 11, no. 884 (November 9, 2003). Original was in Arabic. English translation is mine: http://www.al-araby.com/articles/884/031109_011_000884_spc03.htm (accessed July 12, 2007).

26. Quoted in Muhammad ʿImarah, *Al-Islām wa Usūl al-Ḥukm* (1972), 91. Original was in Arabic; English translation is mine. Exact original Arabic text reads:

حكمنا نحن شيخ الجامع الأزهر بإجماع أربعة وعشرين عالمًا معنا من هيئة كبار العلماء بإخراج الشيخ علي عبد الرازق أحد علماء الجامع الازهر ، والقاضي الشرعي بمحكمة المنصورة الابتدائية الشرعية ومؤلف كتاب « الإسلام وأصول الحكم » من زمرة العلماء . صدر هذا الحكم في يوم الأربعاء ٢٢ المحرم سنة ١٣٤٤ هـ (١٢ اغسطس سنة ١٩٢٥ م) بتوقيع شيخ الأزهر.

27.

قام الشيخ "علي عبد الرازق" بإهداء نسخة من كتابه "الإسلام وأصول الحكم" إلى صديقه الدكتور محمد حسين هيكل رئيس تحرير جريدة "السياسة" لسان حال حزب الأحرار الدستوريين، وكانت أسرة "عبد الرازق" من قادة الحزب ورجاله المبرزين فأعلنت الجريدة في ٢٤ مايو ١٩٢٥ عن صدور الكتاب وجهود الشيخ علي عبد الرازق المبذولة فيه.

28. Yasir Hijazi, "*Al-Islām wa Usūl al-Ḥukm*: Maʿrikat al-Dīn wal Siyāsa" (*Islam and the Foundations of Rule*: The Battle of Religion and Politics), http://www.thenewlibya.com/october25/Asalaamhkm.htm accessed 2007. Original was in Arabic; English translation is mine.

29. Ali ʿAbd al-Raziq, *Al-Islām wa Usūl al-Ḥukm: Baḥth fil Khilāfah wal Ḥukūmah fil Islam* (*Islam and the Foundations of Rule: Research of the Caliphate and Government in Islam*) (Beirut: Dar Maktabat al-Hayat, 1966), 37.

30. Ibid., 39.

31. Ibid., 43.

32. Ibid., 44.

33. al-Deeb, "Muḥakamat Sheikh Azharī," http://www.al-araby.com/articles/884/031109_011_000884_spc03.htm (accessed August 2007).

34. For the claim, see Muhammad Diyaʾ al-Dīn al-Rayyis, *Al-Islām wa-al-Khilāfa fī al-ʿAsr al-Ḥadīth: Naqd Kitāb al-Islām wa-Usūl al-Ḥukm* (Beirut: Al-ʿAsr al-Ḥadīth lil-Nashr, 1973).

35. Ibid.

36. Ali 'Abd al-Raziq, *Al-Islām wa Usul al-Ḥukm* (*Islam and the Foundations of Rule*) (Cairo: Al-Ma'arif House for Print and Publications, 2001), 5.

37. Hijazi, "Al-Islām wa Usūl al-Ḥukm" (The Battle of Religion and Politics). Original was in Arabic; English translation is mine. http://www.thenewlibya.com/october25/ Asalaamhkm.htm (accessed August 2007).

38. Ibid.

39. Sādiq al-Balādī, "75 'Āman 'alā Sudūr *Al-Islām wa Usūl al-Ḥukm*," (75 Years after the Publication of *Islam and the Foundations of Rule*), http://www.althakafaaljadeda. com/296/sadik.htm, accessed 2007. Original was in Arabic; English translation is mine.

40. Ahmed Amin al-Alim quoted in al-Balādī, *Al-'Uthmāniyyūn fī Shamāl al-Jazīra al-'Arabiyya*.

41. 'Imarah, *Al-Islām wa Usūl al-Ḥukm* (1972), 7–8.

5

The Central Argument

IN *AL-ISLĀM WA USŪL AL ḤUKM*, 'Ali 'Abd al-Raziq's argument that Islam is a "religion, not a state; a message, not a government" was a major departure from the traditional view that the religious and political spheres are intertwined and inseparable in Islam. In fact, 'Abd al-Raziq's argument was so far afield from traditional Muslim thought, that many contended his position was a foreign corruption imported from the West and thus incompatible with Islam. However, careful scholarly examination of 'Abd al-Raziq's book reveals that his arguments are not at all rooted in Western thought, but rather sit firmly within the dictates of Islam's sacred texts, namely the Quran and Hadith, and enjoys considerable support from the historical record. The following analysis provides a careful overview of the three main sections of 'Abd al-Raziq's controversial book and analyzes his methodology and arguments, as well as his engagement of those scholars whose conclusions he refutes, while emphasizing the uniquely Islamic roots of his thinking on the subject.

The central message of *Al-Islām wa Usūl al-Ḥukm* is thus 'Abd al-Raziq's repudiation of the caliphate (khilāfah) as a political institution, his call for its abolition, and his insistence that Islam is a spiritual message having no necessary connection with politics or government. "Islam is a religion, not a state; a message, not a government," he asserts throughout his book. In arguing for this point of view, the book stands at variance with the main current of Muslim thought, which has always considered the Prophet Muhammad the founder of a state as well as of a religion. Thus, most Muslim religious scholars of 'Abd al-Raziq's time saw his call for separation of religion and state as an intrusion of a secularism alien to the spirit of Islam. In 'Abd al-Raziq's opinion, the prophet never established or headed a government; nor did he call for such, since he was merely a messenger assigned with the task of proclaiming a religious message.[1] He argues that given the lack of political content in its scriptural texts, we cannot construct an Islamic doctrine regarding the kind of government or rule that Muslims should follow. As a worldwide umma or *umam* (plural of umma), Muslims should seek a good government suited to their needs and particular circumstances, utilizing the intellectual resources with which they have been endowed and disregarding those calling for "an Islamic government" or who claim that the "Islamic government" is the khilāfah in particular. 'Abd al-Raziq maintains that if the *fuqahā'* (jurists) meant by the caliphate and imamate what political scientists meant by government, thus shifting to a secular and scientific mode of argument, then much of what they have said could, in that context, have some validity. For example, their assertion that the performance of the five pillars and the welfare of the community depend on the existence of an effective government is certainly valid, quite apart from the question of what shape that government should have, whether free or oppressive, totalitarian or constitutional, socialist or fascist. But if by the caliphate they meant the particular institution that historically has born that name and no other, then their evidence falls short of their claim, and their justification is not sound.[2] 'Abd al-Raziq elucidates further:

> The practical reality that is supported by rationality and witnessed by history—ancient or modern—is that God's *sha'āir* [principles] and the characteristics of his glorious religion do not depend on such a type of government that the *Fuqahā* or jurists call *Khilāfah* or those called *Khulafā*. The reality is that the welfare of Muslims in this world does not stop at that. Thus, we do not need such a *Khilāfah* for our religious or worldly affairs.[3]

'Abd al-Raziq further claims that the caliphate was a disaster for Islam and Muslims, a source of tyranny and corruption which the religion of Islam and our world are better off without.[4]

'Abd al-Raziq condemns the view of some Muslim scholars who believe in the religious *wujūb* (necessity) of the khilāfah and the imamate, adding that these 'ulama, and with them the predominant majority of Muslims, assume that the caliph is an absolute ruler receiving his sultan (right to rule) from God and possessing absolute authority over people's religion and life. However, 'Abd al-Raziq maintains, if Islam was a religion, not a state, and if the prophet was a messenger, not a ruler, then Islam never prescribed a certain type of government, nor did it demand a specific political system, let alone suggesting such a system as the khilāfah. As previously discussed in chapter 2 of this analysis, it is clear that 'Abd al-Raziq's views on the khilāfah contrast deeply with Muhammad al-Mawardi's (974/364–1058/450) theory of the imamate. The main point of al-Mawardi's theory is that the imamate is wājib (obligatory)—necessary based on revelation. As this chapter will reveal, Ali 'Abd al-Raziq's book is a direct deconstruction of al-Mawardi's theory and indeed of classical Muslim thought on the khilāfah.

Although I have alluded to the book structure in a previous chapter, it is important to emphasize that 'Abd al-Raziq's book is divided into three main sections, called *kutub* (volumes or books), which I have translated here as "parts," each of which is further divided into sections that he referred to as *abwāb* (doors or gates) that I have translated as "chapters."

The first part, "Al-Khilāfah wal Islam" (The Caliphate and Islam), is divided into three smaller chapters: "The Caliphate and Its Nature"; "The Legal Categorization of the Caliphate"; and "The Caliphate from a Sociological Perspective." The second part, "Al-Hukūmah wal Islam" (Government and Islam), is similarly divided into three chapters: "The Ruling System in the Time of the Prophet" (or, The Government System in the Prophet's Time); "Message and Government"; and "Message, not Government, Religion, not State." The third part, "Al-Khilāfah wa al-Hukūmah fil Tārīkh" (The Caliphate and Government in History), consists also of three chapters: "Religious Unity and the Arabs"; "The Arab State"; and "The Islamic Caliphate." The following section of this analysis presents the overall structure of the book and the discussion pertinent to each of the book's three parts.

❧   *Part 1: The Caliphate and Islam*

THE FIRST CHAPTER of part 1, "The Caliphate and Its Nature," includes a detailed discussion covering such issues as the meaning and connotation of the khilāfah in the Arabic language, what people mean when they talk about the successor of the prophet, the reasons behind the name of the khilāfah, the rights of the khilāfah from the scholars' perspective, the khilāfah seen as bound by Shari'a, the khilāfah and the kingdom, from where does the khalīfah receive his *wilāyah* (authority to govern), generating his wilāyah from Allah, generating his wilāyah from the umma, and the emergence of such a debate among Western scholars.

Although the author discusses the khilāfah subject, its meaning in language, and how the khalīfah (caliph) receives his instructions in chapter 1 of part 1, the most important aspect of this chapter is his analysis of the scholars' debate on whether or not the caliphate is a necessity. He refers to Ibn Khaldun's *Muqaddimah* (*Introduction to History*), in which the latter argues that appointing the caliph is a wājib, a necessity, and if Muslims renounce the caliph they will be punished collectively. Yet, 'Abd al-Raziq argues that Muslim scholars disagree among themselves whether this wujūb is *shar'ī* (Sharī'a-based) or *'aqlī* (reason-based). He maintains that he is concerned not with this disagreement but with the fact that Muslim scholars did not have a disagreement regarding their firm belief that the khilāfah falls within the wājib or necessary "to the extent that Ibn Khaldun assumed that there had been Ijmā' (consensus) among Muslims on this.[5] There were, however, a few deviations when some, including the khawārij, did not agree on the wujūb of al-Ijmā'. 'Abd al-Raziq maintains that none of the scholars who asserted wujūb al-Khilāfah had been able to present evidence from the Quran to support his argument. He adds:

> If there were one single evidence in the Quran, these scholars would have never hesitated to refer to and praise it. Or even if there were in the Noble Book what resembled an evidence for *wujūb al-Imāmah*, someone among the supporters of the *Khilāfah* would have tried to turn any such resemblance into evidence. However, the fair scholars failed to find *ḥujjah* or evidence in favor of their opinion in God's Book. Thus, they left the Book and went to find evidence in the claim of *Ijmā'* [consensus among legal scholars or jurists] at times, and *Qiyās* (reasoning by way of analogy), at other times.[6]

The author elucidates that the Quran is not alone in neglecting mentioning anything about the khilāfah—the Sunna also never mentioned it. This is confirmed by the failure of the scholars to provide any evidence from the Sunna to support their claim bi wujūb al-khilāfah (of the necessity of the caliphate). 'Abd al-Raziq does discuss such recent works on the subject as *Al-Khilāfah al-'Uzhmah* (*The Grand Caliphate*) by Muhammad Rashid Rida in which Rida claims that both the Quran and the Sunna referred to wujūb al-khilāfah, citing the Quranic verse, "Obey Allah, the Prophet, and those of authority among you,"[7] in addition to some *Hadith sahīh* (authentic Hadith narratives), purporting that they confirm the claim of wujūb al-khilāfah.[8] However, 'Abd al-Raziq argues, a close look at these claims affirms that these Quranic verses and the Hadith used do not amount to necessity or wujūb al-khilāfah, but are merely references to the imamate or bay'ah (oath of allegiance), nothing that qualifies as evidence of wujūb al-khilāfah.[9] 'Abd al-Raziq concludes chapter 1 of part 1 by briefly referring to an earlier similar debate between Europeans including such political thinkers as Hobbes and Locke. He compares the argument of those Muslim scholars who advocate the necessity of the caliphate with Hobbes's argument that the authority of kings is a sacred and God-given right, and associates the opposing argument with Locke's mode of thinking.[10]

Issues covered by the second chapter include those qualified to elect the caliph, those in opposition, evidence of those who are in favor of the caliphate, the Quran and the khilāfah, uncovering the shubhah (ambiguity) of some verses, the Sunnah and the caliphate, and uncovering the shubhah of anyone who assumes evidence in the Sunnah. Perhaps the most important aspect of this chapter is the author's reference to what scholars such as Ibn Khaldun pointed out as evidence for the necessity of the caliphate, which 'Abd al-Raziq summarizes as follows.

First, consensus among the prophet's companions who, upon the prophet's death, took the initiative to give Abu Bakr the Bay'ah (oath of allegiance), deferring all of their affairs to him (as caliph) during that time and all times after him so that people were not left in a vacuum or anarchy at any age or time. This was considered Ijmā' (consensus), taken as evidence to prove and justify the necessity of the imam.[11] Second, appointing the imam is contingent upon the practicing of the religious pillars and promoting the welfare of the community—this includes *al-amr bi-al-ma'rūf wa-al-nahy 'an al-munkar* (ordering what is right and forbidding what is wrong), which is no doubt an obligation (*farD*). Thus, without appointing an imam, this obligation cannot be carried out, which might result in the spread of anarchy, injustice, and unresolved disputes. It is evident that an obligation is contingent upon an obligation, hence the necessity of appointing an imam.[12] However, 'Abd al-Raziq refutes these scholars' claims of the necessity of the caliphate and argues that none of these scholars tried to provide Quranic evidence to prove the necessity of the caliphate.

The third chapter of part 1, "The Caliphate from a Sociological Perspective," is the longest and covers such issues as subjecting the Ijmā' claim to scrutiny; the deterioration of political science in the Muslim community; the Muslim revolution against the khilāfah; the khilāfah's dependency on power and oppression; Islam as the religion of equality and glory; the khilāfah, injustice, and tyranny; why the Ijmā' claim should not be valid; the last evidence on khilāfah; the necessity of a form of rule or government; how religion acknowledges government; the contention that neither dīn (religion) nor dunyā (world) needs the khilāfah; the extension of khilāfah in Islam; and the pseudo-khilāfah in Egypt. While the author discusses the issue of Ijmā' (consensus) and Muslims' disagreements on it, he also argues that Muslims have had bad luck with regard to political science and politics, maintaining:

> It is quite noticeable in the history of scientific movement of Muslims that the chance of political science among them was the worst compared to other sciences. Its existence among them was the weakest, for we don't know any of their political writers or translators, nor do we know any works by them on anything to do with the systems of government or the principles of politics, save a few to which no importance can be attached when compared with their scholarly activity in scientific areas other than politics.[13]

In answering the question as to why, with regard to politics, this was the case with Muslims, 'Abd al-Raziq blames this "deficiency" on the caliphate based on absolute power and oppression. The author cites historical events in which kings were oppressive to their people with regard to academic freedom and arrogant in monopolizing teaching institutions. Accordingly, 'Abd al-Raziq concludes that such imposed restraints were the reason behind the limited Islamic renaissance in the field of politics, in addition to the scholars' *nukūs* (withdrawal) from addressing those fields. He then comes back to the issue of consensus, arguing that there was no consensus among religious scholars regarding appointing an imam. 'Abd al-Raziq's ultimate conclusion is that there is no scriptural evidence confirming the necessity of the caliphate.

⤙   *Part 2: Government and Islam (the Caliphate)*

IN THE FIRST chapter of part 2, "Nizhām al-Ḥukm fī 'Asr al-Nubuwwa" (The Ruling System in the Time of the Prophet), 'Abd al-Raziq discusses the legal system in the time of the Prophet Muhammad, arguing that it was characterized by ambiguity and vagueness that "makes researching it quite difficult."[14] However, he acknowledges that jurisprudence regarding settling disputes was very much present during the prophet's time, as it was among the Arabs and others before Islam. Within this context, the prophet of Islam ruled on many conflicts brought to his attention. 'Abd al-Raziq then refers to three of the prophet's companions regarded as judges by the majority of Muslim scholars. These include 'Ali ibn Abi Talib, the prophet's cousin and son-in-law, who later became the fourth guided caliph in the aftermath of the prophet's death; 'Umar ibn al-Khattab, the second guided caliph after the prophet; and Mu'āzh ibn Jabal, who was sent to Yemen as a judge by the prophet. 'Abd al-Raziq argues that, in researching the legal system during the prophet's time, he could not find clear references to basic governmental functions. He maintains that the material remaining from that period only reflects that the Prophet Muhammad appointed a leader for the army, an imam to lead the prayer, an educator to teach the Quran, a preacher to call people to Islam, etc. Even this, 'Abd al-Raziq explains, was not done in a consistent manner but was executed intermittently. He concludes this chapter by emphasizing the point he mentioned earlier—the deeper he tried to research this subject of jurisprudence in the prophet's time, the more ambiguous it appeared to him.

The essence of 'Abd al-Raziq's argument is reflected in the second and third chapters of part 2, "Message and Government" and "Message, Not Government; Religion, Not State." He argues that there is nothing wrong with Muslims' questioning whether or not the Prophet Muhammad was a king. He maintains that people might hesitate to make such an inquiry because of the prophethood status, but it is nonetheless a legitimate inquiry. The fear to question may stem from the fact that this subject had not been discussed clearly before and the 'ulama have not come to an agreement in this regard. However, discussing such an issue should not be considered as bid'ah (innovation), for the difference between a prophet and a king is very clear. Nonetheless, the Muslim layperson tends to think that the Prophet Muhammad was a king simultaneously and that by establishing Islam, he established a civil and political state in which he was its king and sovereign. Even Ibn Khaldun, in his *Muqaddimah* (*Introduction*), leans in this direction, for he made the khilāfah exclusive to the king and his kingship. Ironically, 'Abd al-Raziq maintains that the Prophet's *ḥukūmah* (government)[15] has some similarities with and shares characteristics of the political government along with features of the sultanate and monarchy. In this respect, he argues that *jihād* is the one specific thing similar to monarchy that emerged during the prophet's time. However, though at first glance the jihād might be interpreted as aiming to expand the "Islamic state" and consolidate its power, the truth is that the jihād was meant to spread the message, not the sultan or power of the state. It was features such as the jihād that made people think that the prophet did establish an Islamic kingdom with the prophet as king. However, such a claim does not find justification anywhere in the Quran or the Sunna; not only that, but it negates the very meaning of the message of Islam, which was spiritual in nature.[16]

In the next chapter, "Risālah la Ḥukm, Dīn lā Dawlah" (Message Not Government, Religion Not State), 'Abd al-Raziq maintains that the Prophet Muhammad was thus only a messenger who had received a purely religious call, untainted by a desire for monarchy or government, which explains why he did not establish a kingdom in the political meaning in which it is understood today. What might have been confusing to people throughout the years since the *risālah* (message) is that the message itself required a kind of *za'āmah* or leadership for the prophet—but this leadership has nothing to do with the kind of leadership enjoyed by kings in their power over their subjects. Hence, people need to distinguish between the leadership of the messenger, on the one hand, and the king's leadership, on the other, for the difference between these two kinds of leadership almost amounts to opposition. He draws an analogy between the Prophet Muhammad's religious leadership and the leadership of Moses and Jesus, which was not *za'āmah mulūkiyyah* (a royal leadership), but a religious call. This religious leadership is the za'āmah of most messengers, save a few exceptions. Religious leadership necessitates some kind of social distinction and power among the messenger's community so that his word carries a powerful weight. Although the messenger might deal with his umma the way a king does, the messenger has a function that nobody shares with him—the sultan (power or authority) that comes to him directly from heaven through God's revelation (*Wahy*). This is a holy power (*quwwah qudusiyyah*) that God made exclusive to his messengers; it is a holy power that has nothing to do with the connotations of kingdom or monarchy—even the power of a present-day king of kings or sultan of sultans does not come close to it.

'Abd al-Raziq then delves into arguing that the Quran "supports the argument that the Prophet Muhammad—*salla Allahu 'Alihi wa sallam* [peace be upon him]—had nothing to do with monarchy or politics."[17] Other verses further confirm that the prophet's mission did not exceed the limits of conveyance and proclamation that is stripped of all sultan associations. In other words, the Quran confirms that the heavenly mission, which is spiritual in nature, does not have any associations with royal power. Such Quranic verses used by the writer to illustrate his point include:

He who obeys the Messenger, obeys Allah: but if any turn away, we have not sent thee to watch over them.[18]

But thy people reject this, though it is the Truth. Say "not mine is the responsibility for arranging your affairs." For every Prophecy is a limit of time and soon shall ye know.[19]

Say: "O ye people, now Truth hath reached you from your Lord. Those who accept guidance, do so for the good of their own souls; those who stray do so for their own loss: and I am not set over you to arrange your affairs."[20]

Verily we have revealed the Book to thee in Truth, for (instructing) humankind. He, then that receives guidance benefits his own soul: but he that strays injures his own soul. Nor art thou set a custodian over them.[21]

If then they rejected [the Faith], We have not sent thee as a guard over them. Thy duty is but to convey.[22]

Therefore, do thou remind for thou art one to remind, not to manage (their) affairs.[23]

These Quranic verses, among others, are cited by 'Abd al-Raziq to support his argument that the Quran makes it crystal clear that the Prophet Muhammad did not have any rights over his umma, apart from the right to proclaim the spiritual message. If he were a king, he would have had the right to preside over his umma as kings do, for the rights of the king are different from the rights of the messenger, just as the right of government is different from the right of the message.[24] He maintains that this is confirmed by further Quranic scriptures affirming the role of the prophet as merely a *muballigh* (conveyor, transmitter, or communicator) of God's message: *wa mā 'alā al-rasūli illā al-balāghu al-mubīnu* (the messenger's task is only to convey clearly) (Quran 24:54). 'Abd al-Raziq's focus on this highlights the Quran's specific statements on the prophet's role and status as a muballigh, a transmitter, as the following verses illustrate:

The Messenger's duty is to proclaim (the Message). But Allah knows all that ye reveal and ye conceal.[25] "And We sent down the book to thee so that you make clear to them what they had disputed about, and it should be a guide and a mercy to those who believe." "But if they turn away, thy duty is only to convey the clear Message."[26] "Say: 'Obey Allah and obey the Messenger. But if ye turn away, he is only responsible for the duty placed on him and ye for that placed on you. If you obey him, ye shall be on right guidance. The Messenger's duty is only to convey clearly [God's Message]".[27]

Another aspect of the prophet's mission is that he is concurrently sent as a *mubashshir* (one who gives glad tidings) and *nadhīr* (one who warns against sin): "We sent It down [the Quran] in Truth, and in Truth has It descended. And We sent thee only to give glad tidings and to warn."[28] "We have sent thee but as (Messenger) to all humankind, giving them glad tidings, and warning them (against sin), but most people know not."[29]

↦   *Part 3: The Caliphate and Government in History*

AS BRIEFLY MENTIONED above, part 3, "The Caliphate and Government in History," focuses on such issues as the religious unity and the Arabs, the political state of the Arabs after the prophet, and the Islamic Caliphate. 'Abd al-Raziq argues that since Islam was a religion sent to the entire world (east and west, Arabs and non-Arabs, men and women, rich and poor, learned and ignorant), its message was thus for a religious unity through which God intended to unify the world with its entire continents and countries. He notes that, in spite of the fact that the Prophet Muhammad was an Arab and that the Quran was revealed in Arabic, Islam has never been only an Arab call, unity, or religion because it has never acknowledged the merits of one nation, language, country, time, or generation over another. It was a universal religion sent to the entire world. The only thing meriting preference in God's sight, according to Islam, is *taqwah* (righteousness or piousness).[30]

The author maintains that not only was the prophet a spiritual leader who never established or headed a government, but he also never named a successor before his death.[31] Thus, the prophet's religious leadership, which came through his message, ended with his death, and nobody could have succeeded him in his capacity as a religious leader as much as nobody would have been able to succeed him as a prophet with a divine message. Accordingly, if there must have been a leadership after the prophet from among his followers, then that was a new leadership unlike the one that we knew with the prophet. This was natural and obvious because the new leadership was not related to the prophet's message and was not based on religion. Thus, it was "*naw' lā dīnī*"[32] (a non-religious type)—a civil political leadership, nothing more and nothing less. In other words, it was the leadership of government and power, not the leadership of religion; "and this is what took place,"[33] as 'Abd al-Raziq noted. Thus, he lays the foundation for his advocacy of separation of religion and state. He discusses the influence of Islam on Arab nations and its role in laying the foundation for preparing them to establish a political state based on religious unity.[34] He discusses the Bay'ah (oath of allegiance or the voting of) Abu Bakr al-Siddiq to succeed the Prophet Muhammad, claiming that the voting was political, characterized by all that characterizes a modern state, and the new state emerged like all governments based on power and the sword. Thus, it was an Arab state with an Arab rule where Islam, on the other hand, is the religion of all humankind—neither Arab nor non-Arab. 'Abd al-Raziq asserts that the state established by Abu Bakr was an Arab state based on a religious call, a state that had a marked, undeniable influence in the transformation and development of Islam. Nonetheless, it was still an Arab state supporting Arab authority and promoting Arab interests. Eventually, it was that Arab state that made Arabs at that time well suited around the globe to colonize many countries the same way powerful nations do during times of invasion and colonialism.[35] However, many factors contributed to labeling Abu Bakr as a religious leader that made people imagine that he was undertaking his duties religiously on behalf of the Prophet Muhammad. This is how, 'Abd al-Raziq concludes, the notion of the Muslim leadership as a religious position came into existence. One of the reasons for such a claim was the title given to Abu Bakr as "successor of the Prophet of God" (*Khalīfat Rasūl Allah*).[36]

In his last chapter of part 3, "The Islamic Caliphate," 'Abd al-Raziq discusses the implications of the caliphate system that emerged after the death of the Prophet Muhammad. He maintains that "we couldn't confirm who invented for Abu Bakr [al-Siddiq] the title of Caliph of the Prophet, but we knew that Abu Bakr approved of it and accepted it."[37] It is not strange that Abu Bakr chose to accept the title, for it is a title that has power, glamour, and attraction, especially as it helped him to control a new emerging state in the midst of stormy discords, which were part of the life of a community deeply influenced by tribal allegiances, a community that barely came out of the jāhiliyya (the Age of Ignorance). It was their contact with the Prophet Muhammad—their submitting to his religious message—that helped them to totally accept his (Muhammad's) leadership. Given these circumstances, Abu Bakr must have thought such a title would be strong enough to ease the difficulty and tension of dealing with the tribal community and help him control them, and perhaps it did.[38]

However, 'Abd al-Raziq argues, the problem with this title is that some of these people thought of the caliphate of Abu Bakr as a true caliphate of the Prophet Muhammad with all the meanings and duties implied by such a title. The danger came from the claim that "since Abu Bakr is *Khalīfat Rasūl-Allah*, and since Muhammad was *Khalīfat Allah*, it follows that Abu Bakr is, by implication, also *Khalīfat Allah*." This latter title, however, angered Abu Bakr, who had to make a statement refuting such a title, maintaining that "I am no Caliph of God, but the Caliph of God's Prophet."[39] Nonetheless, this declaration did not stop a group of Arabs and Muslims from following Abu Bakr's caliphate religiously, the same way they did with the Prophet Muhammad's religious leadership. This group then considered opposing Abu Bakr a violation of the religion and *irtidād* (literally, going back on or renouncing one's faith). 'Abd al-Raziq believes that this was apparently the basis and beginning of the wars of apostasy (*ridda*).[40] In 'Abd al-Raziq's view, this is where the problem began because those who opposed Abu Bakr were not necessarily *murtaddūn* (apostates), as were largely perceived, but only people who did not want to lend Abu Bakr their religious allegiance. He provides an interesting analysis regarding the situation of the so-called murtaddūn as he maintains:

> There were, of course, those few who left Islam immediately following the Prophet's death—those were legitimately called *murtaddūn*. However, it was not right to fight those who [later] merely rejected Abu Bakr as their religious leader, without renouncing their faith, as *murtaddūn*.[41]

He elucidates that fighting such people was motivated by politics in defense of Arab unity and the protection of their state. His conclusion in this respect is that many of those who refused to offer the bay'ah (oath of allegiance) to Abu Bakr as caliph were called murtaddīn when they should never have been considered as such. For example, 'Abd al-Raziq maintains that such people as 'Ali ibn Abi Talib and Sa'ad ibn 'Ubada were not treated nor spoken of as murtaddīn[42] despite the fact that they refused to acknowledge the caliphate of Abu Bakr. Hence, 'Abd al-Raziq also believes that Abu Bakr's war against those who refused to pay *zakāt* (almsgiving) was not justified. He explains that the decision not to pay zakāt was dictated by this group's rejection of Abu Bakr as caliph. Accordingly, they felt no obligation to recognize his rule or submit to his sultan. This was by no means a case of renouncing one's faith or religion; this was a statement against the ruler. This, 'Abd al-Raziq further maintains, was an unjust historical era because those who refused to recognize Abū Bakr's authority were falsely labeled "apostates" and the war launched against them was misleadingly labeled "wars of apostasy," as noted above.

'Abd al-Raziq also finds justification in history when he cites from the Hadīth collection of al-Bukhārī that 'Umar ibn al-Khattāb, the second caliph, denounced Abu Bakr's war against the alleged murtaddūn, cautioning and reminding him:

> How dare you fight people when the Prophet of Allah (Peace Be Upon Him) said: "I have been ordered to fight people until they say 'There is no

God but God,' and whoever said it has protected himself and his wealth from me, and it is Allah that takes care of him."[43]

This, 'Abd al-Raziq maintains—in addition to many other historical incidents—encourages us "to not hesitate for a moment to declare that what was labeled as *ḥarb al-murtaddīn* in the first days of the Abu Bakr *Khilāfah* was not a religious war but purely a political war which laypeople assumed was religious. It was not at all for religion."[44] In his analysis, 'Abd al-Raziq is more inclined to believe that some Muslims might have actually apostatized after the prophet's death, during the early days of Abu Bakr's caliphate, in addition to those who falsely claimed the prophecy. This is why Abu Bakr's first action was to step up his attack on the apostates and liars until he defeated them. However, 'Abd al-Raziq explains:

> We do not want to indulge into whether or not Abu Bakr had a purely religious authority that made him responsible for taking care of those who retreated back from Islam. Also, we do not want to research whether or not there were non-religious reasons that provoked Abu Bakr to launch those wars. Yet, there was no doubt that Abu Bakr began his career in the new state by fighting those apostates. This is actually when the title *murtaddūn* emerged for describing real apostates; however, it was used after that to describe all those Arabs that Abu Bakr fought, whether they were religious opponents that were real *murtaddīn*, or political opponents who were not *murtaddīn*.[45]

For this reason, 'Abd al-Raziq further explains, Abu Bakr's wars in their totality had a religious characteristic and were considered to be launched in the name of Islam—people believed that to join Abu Bakr was to join the flag of Islam, and to abandon him was, by implication, to abandon Islam.[46] There might have been other reasons related to Abu Bakr that helped people's misconception and made it easy for them to give Abu Bakr's rule a religious connotation. Abu Bakr enjoyed an excellent high status with the prophet of Islam during his lifetime, and kept that status with all Muslims following the prophet's death. Furthermore, if Abu Bakr walked in the footsteps of the prophet in his own personal life, no doubt he also followed the prophet's teachings in dealing with state affairs, handling them through a religious path as much as he could. It is thus quite understandable that Abu Bakr gave all possible religious characteristics to his position as king, or caliph, in the new state.[47]

It should become clear from the above discussion that the title *Khalīfat Rasūl Allah*, despite all of the considerations that had surrounded it, was one of the reasons behind the inaccuracy that was passed on to the general Muslim population, driving them to erroneously believe that the khilāfah was a religious seat, and that whoever was in charge of Muslims affairs necessarily occupied the same seat of power as the prophet, who received his revelation from God. In ʿAbd al-Raziq's analysis, it was in the interest of the sultans or rulers to make popular that inaccuracy among people so they could use and manipulate religion to justify and protect their thrones and keep away their dissidents. This attitude was deliberately used to make people believe that obedience to caliphs, imams, and sultans is part of obedience to God and, by implication, disobedience to them is disobedience to God. He adds, "The sultans were not even confined to what Abu Bakr had accepted and were not angry for what had made him angry" (when he was described as Khalīfat Allah and made clear that he was not), but "instead they made the sultan God's Caliph on earth over his servants, Glory be to Him of what they associate with him."[48] Not only that, but the caliphate began to be associated with religious research and became part of monotheistic beliefs learned by Muslims alongside their learning of God's attributes as well as His messengers' attributes, even alongside their learning of the *Shahādah*: the creed, the first pillar of Islam, that there is no God but God and that Muhammad is the messenger of God.[49] This, ʿAbd al-Raziq sadly explains, is the guilt of kings and sultans and their tyranny over Muslims—that they deviated from the right path and guidance and kept their citizens blindfolded to the truth and concealed from them the paths to illumination in the name of religion. It is also in the name of religion that these leaders became despotic and oppressive toward their people. They humiliated them, deprived them of studying the political sciences in order for them to know for themselves, and deceived them. In the name of religion, they further became narrow-minded and dulled their mental faculties until they became unable to see beyond religion in what should be matters of pure administration and politics. They also limited the people's understanding of religion, blocked their access to its essence, and deprived them of all educational doors that would touch the khilāfah. All this ended in the death of the avenues for research and intellectual activity among Muslims until they suffered a state of paralysis in their political thought and in all things relating to the caliphate and caliphs.[50]

ʿAbd al-Raziq does maintain that the religion of Islam is innocent of this notion of khilāfah that Muslims have known, it is also innocent of all the tyranny, lust for power, dictatorship, wealth and sultan with which they associated it. Not only that, but the caliphate has nothing to do with religious planning, nor the judiciary, nor any other state affairs or government seats. All these fall within the category of pure politics which have nothing to do with religion—for religion neither knew nor denied these political characteristics; neither ordered nor forbade them—it has been left for people to decide how to use their minds, other nations' experiences, and the principles and fundamentals of politics in organizing their governments. The building and organization of Muslim armies, the building and architecture of cities and ports, and the systemization of government offices all have nothing to do with religion because they are domains of experts and specialists in their fields. Nothing in religion prevents Muslims from racing with other nations in all areas of politics and social sciences. Nothing prevents them from destroying this old ancient system of khilāfah that oppresses and humiliates them. It is high time for Muslims to build the basis of their nations, the system of their governments, using the most modern products of the human mind and the best of nations' experiences that have proven to be the best fundamentals of rule.[51]

In Albert Hourani's analysis, it becomes clear that 'Abd al-Raziq's assertion that the Prophet Muhammad's only function was prophetic preaching implies that the prophet really did not have any role by way of which to exercise political authority. The prophet's mission, thus, is purely spiritual, as 'Abd al-Raziq clarifies in the following:

> The prophet can have, in the political direction of the nation, a role similar to that of the ruler, but he has a role special to himself and which he shares with no one. It is his function also to touch the souls which inhabit the bodies of men, and to rend the veil [in order] to perceive the hearts within their breasts. He has the right, or rather the duty, to open the hearts of his followers so as to touch the sources of love and hatred, of good and evil, the course of their inmost thoughts, the hiding places of temptation, the springs of purpose and the foundations of their moral character. . . . Prophecy, which is all this and still more, implies that the prophet has the right to unite himself with men's souls by a communion of care and protection, and also to dispose of their hearts freely and without obstacle.[52]

Thus, 'Abd al-Raziq maintains, the prophet's sultan or authority was based on his message; his is a general authority whose order is to be obeyed by Muslims, and his "rule" comprehensive.[53] This is one of the areas specified by some critics, such as Muhammad 'Imarah (1989), as contradictory in 'Abd al-Raziq's thoughts. For example, when he attempts to evaluate the nature of the system established by Islam during the time of the Prophet Muhammad and his experience in the Arabian Peninsula, 'Abd al-Raziq denies in many instances that such an experience was political, constituted a political system, or even remotely related to ruling, government, or the state. Accordingly, 'Abd al-Raziq's assertion in this regard is that such an experience was merely religious and spiritual and had nothing to do with politics. To confirm this, he often repeats this argument:

> The Arab unity found during the time of the Prophet was never a political unity by any means and never had the meaning of government or the state, but was merely a religious unity exclusive of any political connotations, a unity of faith and religious denomination, not that of the state or monarchy.[54]

To draw what he saw as contradiction, 'Imarah also cites 'Abd al-Raziq's argument that the prophet's authority was more powerful than the authority of kings and governments in that it encompassed spiritual aspects of human life (which fall within the messenger's domain) and civic aspects of human life (which fall within the realm of governments). This means that politics, the state, and government, in their civil meaning, were implied in and part of the nature of the system established by the prophet.[55] 'Imarah's full discussion on this and other areas he perceived as contradictory in 'Abd al-Raziq's book will be discussed as part of chapter 7 of this analysis, "Critiques of Abd al-Raziq's Position."

At this point, however, it is important to note that a close reading of 'Abd al-Raziq's argument in this respect reveals 'Imarah's negligence of an important clarification made by 'Abd al-Raziq when he cautioned the reader against "confusing between the leadership of the message, and the leadership of a king," arguing that the difference between them amounts to being a conflict.[56] For example, he maintains that the leadership of Moses and Jesus was not a political or royal leadership, nor was the leadership of most messengers. The status of the message requires an authority far larger and wider for the messenger than the authority that exists between rulers and ruled—an authority even wider than that between father and children. Thus, while 'Abd al-Raziq admits that "the Prophet might deal with the nation's politics the way kings do," he maintains that the messenger alone has a function not shared by others, including communicating spiritual aspects of human life.[57] As stated above, in the seventh chapter of this analysis I provide an in-depth discussion on 'Imarah's critique of specific aspects of 'Abd al-Raziq's book, which he alleges are contradictions.

Apparently, 'Abd al-Raziq anticipated such criticism and tried to address it within his book. He argues that a great deal of what took place during the prophet's time can be considered as having some state characteristics and government features, and whoever perceives it in such a way may conclude that the prophet was both a messenger and a political king. Yet, such a perception would be challenged by another problem worthy of consideration. Following this assumption, the question that should be asked here is: was the prophet's establishment of an Islamic kingdom and his conduct in that regard something that fell outside of the boundaries of his message as a prophet, or was it part of what God had revealed to him to profess as a messenger? In answering this question, 'Abd al-Raziq elucidates that it is important to consider the prophetic kingdom either as separate of the Islamic message—as falling outside of the boundaries of the message—or as part of the prophetic message and complementary to it.[58] This question will be dealt with more elaborately in chapter 6 of this analysis, The Ruling System in the Time of the Prophet.

'Abd al-Raziq's core argument in *Al-Islām wa Usūl al-Ḥukm* is that Islam is a code of disciplinary and religious precepts binding upon the individual conscience without any relation to power or politics. After studying the career of the Prophet Muhammad, 'Abd al-Raziq concluded that the prophet had never envisioned the establishment of any specific political institution, such as the caliphate. Any political or military activities that took place during the prophet's time had nothing to do with religion and were conducted merely for the protection of the community and for its immediate material welfare in the dangerous tribal world of seventh-century Arabia.[59] As such, the traditional view that the prophet had ordered the formation of a particular political institution (i.e., the caliphate) that Muslims are religiously obligated to follow, even in the modern era, is deeply tenuous. It should be clear to the reader from the above analysis that the ideas of 'Abd al-Raziq are not, as some of his detractors have contended, the foreign import of Western thought. On the contrary, they are deeply rooted in Islamic thought. 'Abd al-Raziq engaged in a new critical examination of Islam's history and sacred texts, especially the Quran, in keeping with the active revivalist spirit of the early twentieth century Muslim world. In so doing, he, like Muhammad 'Abduh before him, sought to restore prosperity and prestige to the Islamic world amid the trauma of European colonialism.

NOTES

1. 'Abd al-Raziq, *Al-Islām wa Usūl al-Hukm* (1925), 64. (All English translations from 'Abd al-Raziq's original Arabic text, *Al-Islām wa Usūl al-Hukm*, are mine, unless otherwise indicated.)

2. Ibid., 35.

3. Ibid., 35–36.

الواقع المحسوس الذي يؤيده العقل، ويشهد به التاريخ قديماً وحديثاً، أن شعائر الله تعالى ومظاهر دينه الكريم لا تتوقف على ذلك النوع من الحكومة يسميه الفقهاء خلافة. ولا على أولئك الذين يلقبهم الناس خلفاء. والواقع أيضاً أن صلاح المسلمين في دنياهم لا يتوقف على شئ من ذلك. فليس بنا حاجة إلى تلك الخلافة لأمور ديننا ولا لأمور دنيانا. ولو شئنا لقلنا أكثر من ذلك، فإنما كانت الخلافة ولم تزل نكبة على الإسلام وعلى المسلمين، وينبوع شر وفساد.

4. Ibid., 36.

5. 'Abd al-Raziq, *Al-Islām wa Usūl al-Hukm* (1966), 37. Although all other references to 'Abd al-Raziq's argument are from the first Cairo edition of his book (1925), my references to this part on the meaning of the Khilāfah are derived from the *Dār Maktabat al-Hayāt*, Beirut edition (1966).

6. 'Abd al-Raziq, *Al-Islām wa Usūl al-Hukm* (1966), 39.

7. Quran 4:59. "وأطيعوا الله وأطيعوا الرسول وأولي الأمر منكم"

8. 'Abd al-Raziq, *Al-Islām wa Usūl al-Hukm* (1966), 43.

9. Ibid., 44.

10. 'Abd al-Raziq, *Al-Islām wa Usūl al-Hukm* (1925), 11.

11. Ibid., 12–13.

12. Ibid., 13.

13. Ibid., 22.

من الملاحظ البيّن في تاريخ الحركة العلمية عند المسلمين أن حظ العلوم السياسية فيهم كان بالنسبة لغيرها من العلوم الأخرى أسوأ حظ، وأن وجودها بينهم كان أضعف وجود، فلسنا نعرف لهم مؤلفاً في السياسة ولا مترجماً. ولا نعرف لهم بحثاً في شئ من أنظمة الحكم ولا أصول السياسة، اللهم إلا قليلاً لا يقام له وزن إزاء حركتهم العلمية في غير السياسة من الفنون.

14. Ibid., 39.

15. Although it can be argued that 'Abd al-Raziq uses the expression "the Prophet's *Hukūmah*" in what might be some contradiction of his claim that the prophet never established a government, his use of the term is a reflection of what was largely perceived.

16. 'Abd al-Raziq, *Al-Islām wa Usūl al-Hukm* (1925), 48–63.

17. Ibid.

18. Quran, 4:80.

19. Quran, 6:66–67.

20. Quran, 10:108.

21. Quran, 39:41.

22. Quran, 42:48.

23. Quran, 88:21–22.

24. 'Abd al-Raziq, *Al-Islām wa Usūl al-Ḥukm* (1925), 72–73.

القرآن الكريم صريح في أن محمداً صلى اللّه عليه وسلّم لم يكن له من الحق على أمته غير حق
الرسالة. ولو كان صلى اللّه عليه وسلّم ملكاً لكان له على أمته حق الملك أيضاً. وأن للملك حقاً
غير حق الرسالة، وفضل غير فضلها، وأثراً غير أثرها.

25. Quran, 5:99.

26. Quran, 16:64, 82.

27. Quran, 24:54.

28. Quran, 17:105.

29. Quran, 34:28.

30. 'Abd al-Raziq, *Al-Islām wa Usūl al-Ḥukm* (1925), 81.

31. Ibid., 87.

32. This was the point that al-Azhar Supreme Council found extremely offensive and which, among other points, influenced their conviction of 'Abd al-Raziq.

33. 'Abd al-Raziq, *Al-Islām wa Usūl al-Ḥukm* (1925), 90.

34. Ibid., 91.

35. Ibid., 92.

36. Ibid., 94.

37. Ibid., 95.

38. Ibid., 96.

39. Ibid. "لستُ خليفة الله، ولكني خليفة رسول الله"

40. Ibid., 97.

41. Ibid.

42. Ibid.

43. Ibid., 99. These were Umar's exact words:

"كيف تقاتل الناس وقد قال رسول الله صلى الله عليه وسلّم، أُمرت أن أقاتل الناس حتى يقولوا،
لا إله إلّا الله، فمن قالها عصم مني ماله ونفسه إلّا بحقه، وحسابه على الله."

44. Ibid.

45. Ibid., 100.

46. Ibid., 100–101.

47. Ibid., 101.

48. Ibid., 102.

49. Ibid.

50. Ibid., 102–103.

51. Ibid., 102.

52. Ibid., 67 (Hourani's translation, 186–187).

قد يتناول الرسول من سياسة الأمة مثل ما يتناول الملوك. ولكن للرسول وحده وظيفة لا شريك له
فيها. من وظيفته أيضاً أن يتصل بالأرواح التي في الأجساد، وينزع الحجب ليطلع على قلوب
أتباعه، ليصل إلى مجامع الحب والضغينة، ومنابت الحسنة والسيئة، ومجاري الخواطر، ومكامن
الوساوس، ومنابع النيات، ومستودع الأخلاق.... الرسالة تقتضي لصاحبها، وهي كما ترى، حق
الإتصال بكل نفس أتصال رعاية وتدبير، وحق التصريف لكل قلب تصريفاً غير محدود.

53. 'Abd al-Raziq, *Al-Islām wa Usūl al-Ḥukm* (1925), 68.

54. 'Abd al-Raziq, *Al-Islām wa Usūl al-Ḥukm* (2001), 99, quoted in 'Imarah, *Ma'rikat al-Islām wa-Usūl al-Ḥukm*, 153.

55. Ibid., 153.

56. 'Abd al-Raziq, *Al-Islām wa Usūl al-Ḥukm* (1925), 65.

57. Ibid., 67.

58. Ibid., 55–56.

59. Nadav Safran, *Egypt in Search of Political Community: An Analysis of the Intellectual and Political Revolution of Egypt, 1804–1952* (Cambridge, Mass.: Harvard University Press, 1961), 141–142.

6

The Ruling System in the Time of the Prophet

*I*N ORDER TO understand how 'Abd al-Raziq arrived at his conception of political secularism, we must examine his supporting arguments and acknowledge the sources from which his evidence is drawn and how the argument is constructed. 'Abd al-Raziq begins with the premise that all functional societies require mediation and some form of judicial authority. These roles were performed during the Prophet Muhammad's time, and individuals such as Abu Bakr, 'Umar, and the prophet himself were among those who served the community in a judicial capacity. 'Abd al-Raziq does not argue against the necessity of governmental roles, nor against the historical indications of the interplay between religion and government in the prophet's time, but asserts that the absence or ambiguity of the details should serve to give pause to those seeking to offer well-reasoned conclusions concerning the relationship intended between Islam and the state. 'Abd al-Raziq maintains, if the intention was for Islam to be the framework for governance, this guidance would have been provided in a clearly defined and accessible way, rather than a puzzle of missing pieces which can be reconstructed in a myriad of patterns, none possible to cross-check or confirm for accuracy.

'Abd al-Raziq consistently argued that it was difficult to research the history of the state of the judiciary during the time of the Prophet Muhammad. In his view, such difficulty stems from the ambiguity that characterized the state of the judiciary at that time, which mystified any attempt to reach a mature, scientific, and satisfying conclusion in this regard.[1] Nonetheless, 'Abd al-Raziq never denied that the judiciary—within its purview of ruling on and settling disputes—did exist during the time of the prophet as it had previously existed among Arabs and other nations before Islam. As noted earlier, the Prophet Muhammad himself ruled on many disputes brought before him. However, 'Abd al-Raziq's main point revolves around his contention that, if we wanted to deduce or infer anything from the prophet's judiciary system, we would find such inference to be difficult, if not impossible. This is because what was transmitted to us of Hadith narrative related to the prophetic judiciary ruling does not indicate a clear picture of what that judiciary system looked like.

Despite the fact that such ambiguity about the judiciary system during the prophet's time made it difficult to research the subject, 'Abd al-Raziq discusses three of the prophet's companions who were considered by the 'ulama as having been appointed judges by the prophet. These include 'Umar ibn al-Khattab, Ali ibn Abi Talib, and Mu'adh ibn Jabal, in addition to Abu Musa al-Ash'ari. By displaying and exposing these cases, 'Abd al-Raziq's strategy is to lay the groundwork for refuting the notion that appointing these judges implied in any way the existence of a complete concept of government during the prophet's time.

The first of the cases discussed is that of 'Umar ibn al-Khattab in relation to the judiciary. 'Abd al-Raziq describes accounts in this regard as strange from a historical point of view. He further believes that what reached us of those accounts were most probably mere assumptions. In the *Sunnan al-Tirmidhi*, by Abu 'Isa Muhammad al-Tirmidhi (d. 892), one of the six canonical collections of Hadith, 'Uthman said to 'Abdullahi ibn 'Umar, "go and rule between people." 'Abdullahi said, "would you excuse me from doing so?" 'Uthman asked him, "what do you fear, did your father not rule between people?" 'Abdullahi replied, "[but also] Abu Bakr ruled [between people, and yet] if he had a problem, he asked the Prophet, and if the Prophet had a problem, he asked Jibril [the Archangel Gabriel], but I will not find anyone to ask [if faced by a problem in ruling]."[2] What can be deduced from this Hadith is that both the first and second Rightly Guided Caliphs, Abubakr and 'Umar, were engaged in a judiciary system as judges.

The second example 'Abd al-Raziq provides relates to Ali ibn Abi Talib, who eventually became the fourth Rightly Guided Caliph. According to this Hadith, Ali was sent as a young man by the Prophet Muhammad to Yemen to rule between people. Abu Dā'ūd[3] quoted Ali as saying,

The Prophet sent me to Yemen as a judge and I was young and did not have knowledge about the judiciary. He [the Prophet] said, "God will guide your heart, stable your speech, and when the two conflicting parties sit before you, do not rule until you hear from the last person as you had heard from the first; this will be more appropriate to help you rule [accurately]."[4]

After following these instructions, Ali said, "I have been a judge and never suspected ruling after that."[5]

The third example provided by 'Abd al-Raziq concerns Mu'adh ibn Jabal. Al-Bukhari[6] relates that the Prophet Muhammad sent Mu'adh as a judge to Janad in Yemen to teach people the Quran and Islamic rules. He also assigned him to rule between them and to collect the almsgiving from workers in Yemen.[7] Al-Bukhari also mentioned in relation to this issue that the Prophet Muhammad sent Abu Musa and Mu'adh to Yemen, each to a different part, as Yemen was comprised of two parts. The prophet instructed them to "be lenient, not difficult; persuade and do not dissuade."[8] In a different Hadith narrative by al-Bukhari, 'Abd al-Raziq maintains, the prophet said to Mu'adh ibn Jabal,

> You will encounter a nation of the people of the Book, when you get there ask them to say, "there is no God but God and Muhammad is the Messenger of God." If they obey you on that, tell them that God prescribed for them five prayers every day and night. If they obey you on that, then tell them that God prescribed for them Zakat[9] (almsgiving), that will be taken from their rich and given back to their poor. If they obey you on that, then never touch their precious possessions, and beware of the one who has been treated unjustly because there is no veil between him and God.[10]

This story, 'Abd al-Raziq observes, is similar to another related by Ahmad Zaynī Dahlān in al-Sīra al-Nabawiyya (Life of the Prophet). The Prophet Muhammad, the story goes, sent Abu Musa al-Ash'ari and Mu'adh ibn Jabal to Yemen before the farewell pilgrimage, in the tenth Hijri year (in another version it was the ninth). Mu'adh headed to the upper Yemen toward 'Adan, his mission including Janad, whereas Abu Musa was assigned to lower Yemen. In addition, 'Abd al-Raziq further elucidates, Ahmad, Abu Daūd, and al-Tirmidhi, among others, related the Hadith narrative of al-Harith ibn 'Amr. He said some friends of Mu'adh's told us about him, that when the Prophet Muhammad sent him to Yemen he asked him, how would you rule if you are assigned a case?; he said, by Allah's Book. The Prophet continued, asking what if you didn't find the answer in Allah's Book? He answered, by his Prophet's Sunna. What if you didn't find an answer neither in the Prophet's sunna nor in Allah's Book? the Prophet continued asking. Mu'adh said, I will exercise my independent judgment (ajtahidu).[11] Mu'adh further explains that, at that point, "the Prophet struck his chest [with his hand] and said, 'Thank God who helped the messenger of his Prophet to do what pleases God's Prophet.'"[12]

These are some of the different stories that 'Abd al-Raziq included to highlight what he had previously mentioned of the difficulty of conducting comprehensive research on the judiciary system during the prophet's time. The complexity of this situation resides in the fact that those who believe that Islam is both religion and state will not hesitate to use these same stories to validate their argument based on their own interpretation. However, 'Abd al-Raziq insists that the more deeply he researched the judiciary system during the prophet's time, the more he realized that other basic aspects of government functions were absent or not described in a clear manner. Accounts regarding countries opened by Muslims during that time, in 'Abd al-Raziq's opinion, only indicate that the prophet appointed leaders of the army, secretary of the treasury, prayer imam, Quran teacher, or a preacher to preach about Islam. Even this was done intermittently for short periods of time. Accordingly, 'Abd al-Raziq maintains, if we excluded the work of the judiciary (in addition to delegating people to serve as judges) and other elements without which the concept of a state is incomplete, we would definitely "not find in what was transmitted to us in this regard anything clear that might enable us to say in a satisfying manner that this was the system of the Prophetic government."[13]

In his attempt to find answers for his own questions regarding this issue, 'Abd al-Raziq further draws an interesting comparison between accounts provided by historians regarding the state of affairs during the prophet's time on the one hand, and governance during the time of caliphs or kings who ruled in the aftermath of the prophet's death and beyond. He observes that when such authors write about a caliph or a king, they provide detailed accounts of his governors, judges, and workers in a way that reflects their understanding of the value of such scientific research. This led those writers to exert meticulous efforts for their important research. In contrast, he maintains, in examining such research in the history of the prophet, what can be observed is that writers injected information about matters of governance into their accounts in an unclear and scattered manner that did not match their research on other eras. Thus, the deeper one researched into the judiciary system during the prophet's time, the more ambiguous the research findings were. Not only that, but "the perplexity of the mind takes us from one ambiguity to another then returns us to one research after another, until we reach the climax of such a confusing issue" with no definitive result.[14] 'Abd al-Raziq believes that the absence of clarity is not merely indicative of something, but constitutes the basic concern of this perplexity. Other aspects of ambiguity are branches of this issue which is the mother of all issues. And thus, without God's help, "there is no hope to reach the truth" in this matter.[15] 'Abd al-Raziq then delves into criticizing rigid thinking in Islam, maintaining that the adventure of researching such a complicated issue might be reason for creating what can metaphorically be described as a "bomb" whose war would be ignited by those who know religion only as a fossil, a frozen rigidity that the rational mind should not come close to, or that rationality itself should not deal with. This unbending way of thinking, in 'Abd al-Raziq's opinion, only justifies his assertion that the Prophet Muhammad was a spiritual leader who came with a religious message that had no connection to politics.

'Abd al-Raziq's description of the state of affairs during the prophet's time is clearly at variance with commonly accepted traditional accounts on this issue. The majority of such accounts agree that the prophet before the Hijra to Medina was only concerned with proclaiming the religious message, without paying any attention to politics in Mecca or the Arabian Peninsula. However, after he migrated to Medina to avoid persecution, the prophet began to organize Muslims and signed a treaty with the Medina dignitaries. Most early writers of Islamic history consider that to be the basis of an emergent Islamic government whose first goal was to unite all Muslims (all Arabs at that point) into one nation. A look at the nature of the situation in Arabia before Islam is necessary for this discussion. In the era that the Quran labels as jāhiliyya (ignorance), Arabs were nomadic Bedouins divided into conflicting tribes that lacked any kind of government or organized political institutions. This was reflected in that they had no organized army to protect their territories, no police to ensure their security and to keep things in order, and no organized treasury as the concept of taxation had not yet taken root. In short, history does not delineate any type of organized government or laws that Arabs had in the pre-Islamic era. They were merely tribes characterized with 'asabiyyāt (tribalism) and revenge in the incident of any attack. Although it was common to have an appointed leader during war times with an enemy, such a function ended with the close of the war itself, then blood and tribal ties quickly replaced the position during peace times.[16]

Arabs were thus tribes that spread during the pre-Islamic era throughout the Arabian Peninsula. Although each tribe had its independent status, these tribes were not unified politically and were often in conflict with each other. It was Islam that aimed at unifying these tribes to form one nation. Thus, after Islam succeeded in doing so, the concept of tribalism began to lose prominence because all tribes chose to be fused into the larger Islamic context of the umma (a nation or group of nations).[17]

'Abd al-Raziq believes that because the prophet succeeded, through spreading the religious message, in unifying the conflicting Arab tribes into one nation under Islam, there was an assumption that he was a political leader. However, what 'Abd al-Raziq intends to clarify here is his argument that the religious message with which the prophet was sent to lead Muslims was different from political leadership. He maintains that, because preaching a message is quite different from political leadership, there are many kings who are not messengers just as there were messengers who were not kings. He draws yet another comparison between Islam and Christianity, arguing that, although Jesus was a messenger for the Christian call and leader of Christians, he called for submitting to Caesar (give unto Caesar what belongs to him and to God what belongs to God).[18] Save a few, 'Abd al-Raziq further explains, we do not know any in the history of monotheistic messengers in whom God combined both religious and political leaderships. Then he poses his key question: was the Prophet Muhammad among those few, or was he merely a messenger with no royalty bestowed on him? Despite the fact that this seems a rhetorical question, 'Abd al-Raziq will come back to address it in the course of his book as this chapter will demonstrate.

Although quite satisfied with his conviction that the Prophet Muhammad was only a religious leader and that Islam is a religion not a state, 'Abd al-Raziq makes an attempt to reflect on the perspective of a Muslim layperson in this regard. He maintains that such laypeople lean toward assuming that the prophet was both messenger and king, that he established a civil political state based on Islam for which he was leader and master. This kind of thinking, 'Abd al-Raziq argues, is not only what goes with Muslims' general taste, but is perhaps also the opinion of the crowds of 'ulama who tend to consider Islam as a political unity and a state that the prophet established.[19] Ibn Khaldun among other jurists also made the caliphate inclusive of royalty. To reflect further on what has been perceived in this respect, 'Abd al-Raziq discusses the Egyptian writer Rifaʿa Rafiʿ al-Tahtawi's (1801–1873) work on the function of what was perceived to be government during the prophet's time. Al-Tahtawi details his perception of the Islamic government system during the prophet's time including what is found in the "Grand Imamate's" basic functions such as cabinet ministries, secretaries, writing or documenting, in addition to juristic work that included teaching the Quran, Islamic law, writing, prayer, the function of the imam, and the *muʾadhdhin* (one who calls for prayer). Al-Tahtawi also mentions other functions such as translation, documentation of the army work, bids, debts, and confirming that a debt system had an origin in the prophet's time. Not only that, but Tahtawi discusses other functions that took place during the prophet's time including leadership, the judiciary, and all that related to it such as witnesses, writing conditions and contracts, inheritance, and expenditure. Al-Tahtawi concluded the list by mentioning chief builders, city guards and spies, prison guards, and those who executed ḥudūd. After reviewing Tahtawi's full account, ʿAbd al-Raziq acknowledges that al-Tahtawi detailed all government functions one by one without leaving anything out.[20] In explaining this contradiction, ʿAbd al-Raziq argues that "the prophetic government" no doubt had some characteristics of the political government and some of the sultanate or royalty vestige. The first of these is the concept of jihād, which appeared during the prophet's time. In ʿAbd al-Raziq's view, all the battles that the prophet fought were purely to spread the message of Islam. Yet, because for some the apparent meaning of jihād is not only for spreading God's word and religion, but to establish sultan and expand the kingdom, there was the confusion and assumption that the prophet was also a political leader. Then, as was the case with the previous section, ʿAbd al-Raziq poses another question, asking: "But, wasn't the call for religion a call for God not for government?"[21]

To answer his own rhetorical question, in the context of his thought about government as an institution distinct from religion, ʿAbd al-Raziq explains that the call for religion is exclusively a call for God that is based on peaceful persuasion and heart-winning methods. Force and coercion are not appropriate for a call aimed at guiding the hearts and purifying the beliefs. The prophet, he maintains, followed the same line of messengers before him who did not have any history of forcing people into belief by the sword or invading a nation in order to convince them to believe in his religion. The prophet was inspired by what the Quran taught him: "Let there be no coercion in religion";[22] and "Call on people to go on your God's path by wisdom, good advice, and argue with them with the best method."[23] ʿAbd al-Raziq also quotes the Quranic verse instructing the prophet to "remind, you are only a reminder, not a controller over them."[24]

In ʿAbd al-Raziq's analysis, these are clear principles demonstrating that the prophet's message was based on advising, mentoring, and persuading, not using force or imposing tyranny, methods that are characteristics of the rules of kings. If he were to fall back on force and coercion, that would not be for the purpose of conveying his religious message to the world because these methods belong to monarchies and kingdoms. This, in ʿAbd al-Raziq's view, is where the confusion resides and is what contributed to how people understood the meaning of prophetic jihād, hence their perplexity.[25]

Within the context of his expanded explanation of the confusion about jihād, 'Abd al-Raziq relates another example arguing that indeed the time of the prophet witnessed major work related to financial affairs that included expenditure, zakat, spoils, *jizya* (poll tax), etc. Further, the prophet had collectors and helpers who undertook these tasks for him. While admitting that organizing all these financial functions is part of the work of the state, if not the most important pillar of government, 'Abd al-Raziq is quick to note that such function falls outside of the realm of the religious message and is remote to messengers' work given that they were exclusively messengers, not rulers. To support his point, 'Abd al-Raziq uses an example from al-Tabari (838–923)[26] to show that the prophet appointed several Muslim Arab dignitaries to undertake these functions. All this was found during the time of the prophet, which can be reflective of the state features and what can be perceived as government characteristics. Accordingly, he maintains, whoever sees it through this lens can certainly say that the Prophet Muhammad was both prophet of God as well as a political king. However, 'Abd al-Raziq argues, believers in this notion will be faced with the following question that is worthy of contemplation: was the prophet's establishment of an Islamic kingdom and his behavior in that regard considered outside the limits of his message, or was it part of what God sent him for and what He revealed to him? In dealing with this question 'Abd al-Raziq first emphasizes the argument that the prophetic kingdom is a separate enterprise of the Islamic call and hence falls outside the boundaries of the message. He maintains that his opinion does not have an equivalent in Islamic schools of thought nor do we remember anything in the sayings of the founding fathers of these schools indicating it. Nonetheless, he further asserts, it is a valid opinion and that believing in it should not amount to being in a state of disbelief or atheism. 'Abd al-Raziq is aware of his opponents' claim that his denial of the caliphate system altogether is based on his advocacy of such strange views.[27]

With respect to his analysis of the other contrasting opinion that the prophetic kingdom is part of the message function that it is complementary of it, 'Abd al-Raziq maintains that this is the opinion that is accepted by Muslims, heart and soul, because it is the opinion that their principles and schools of thought support. However, he argues that it is crystal clear that this opinion cannot be intellectually fathomed, unless it is proven that it is inherent in the message that the prophet should, after conveying the divine call, undertake the executive function of implementing it practically. This means that the prophet is a conveyor and an executive simultaneously.[28] Looking at those who did research on the meaning of the message, 'Abd al-Raziq found out that they mostly neglected to consider implementation as part of the essence of the message, with the exception of Ibn Khaldun who indicated that Islam is the only religion, of all other religions, that is unique in combining the religious call and actually implementing it. This is clear in many subjects that Ibn Khaldun discussed in his *Introduction to History*.[29] In summary, Ibn Khaldun argues that Islam is shar'ī (law-based), *tablīghī* (message-based), and *tatbīqī* (practice-based), that it is a religion in which religious authority and political authority are combined, unlike all other religions.

'Abd al-Raziq, however, does not find evidence or support for such a claim. Not only that, but he argues that it negates the meaning of the message and does not correspond to what the nature of the religious call requires. But even if the claim is true, there is an additional problem for which people need to find a response as well as an egress. To characterize the nature of such a problem, 'Abd al-Raziq then poses a series of questions including the following: if the prophet did establish a religious state, or embarked on establishing one, why did his state lack many aspects of the fundamentals of a state or the pillars of government? why didn't his system allow for the process of appointing judges (in a clear, not scattered, manner)? why didn't he talk to his people about the ruling system and basics of Shūrā? why did he leave the 'ulama in a state of bewilderment and perplexity with regard to the government system during his time? What 'Abd al-Raziq is trying to explore is the origin of what appears as ambiguity, confusion, shortcoming, or perplexity in the construction of government at the time of the prophet. He discusses those who insist that the prophet, in addition to bringing a new religion, also established a new state complete with rules, functions, and positions, and that the organization of its affairs were guided by God's revelation. Based on this, these people had to believe that the government system during the prophet's time reached the ultimate state of perfection. However, 'Abd al-Raziq maintains that if these same people were asked the secret of what appeared to be shortcomings in the state systems or confusion in the basis of such systems, they might try to find answers in the writings of such people as al-Tahtawi and others[30] who assumed that the prophet's government included all that was required of works, workers, systems, limited fundamentals, and detailed patterns,[31] as previously noted. Others who support this view might go further to say that nothing prevents them from assuming that the state system in the prophet's time was solid, meticulous, and complete. However, 'Abd al-Raziq insists that he was not able to find any real or actual details of such a system of the prophetic government as they described. He cites two reasons for such lack of details:

either because those who made the assumptions left the aspect of transferring those details for us to research, or because they did convey it but we do not have sufficient knowledge of it.[32] Then, immediately following, he quotes the Quranic verse (17:85), "you have been given only a little amount of knowledge" to support such lack of knowledge. Or yet, it could be for another reason that we don't know about yet.[33]

Based on this last point he mentioned, ʿAbd al-Raziq delves into making an interesting argument on the human being's limited knowledge of all things. This, he maintains, requires that learned people should always believe that many facts are concealed from them. Given this, they should begin searching and continue researching to try to reveal what is hidden and infer what is new because in this lies the essence and development of learning. However, ʿAbd al-Raziq is quick to add that the possibility of such ignorance of some facts should not deter us from confirming what we have knowledge about and consider such knowledge scientific facts on which we can base rules, construct schools of thought, clarify reasons, and deduce results until it is proven otherwise through scientific evidence.[34] Based on this, we can say that it is quite possible that information about the government system in the time of the Prophet Muhammad has been concealed from us, that days to come might reveal to us that it was the highest role model in ruling. Nonetheless, such a possibility should not deter us from investigating anew, until we know for sure, the origin of the ambiguity and perplexity in what was believed to be the prophetic government system, its secret, and meaning.

Another intriguing point ʿAbd al-Raziq discusses to address some of the earlier questions relates to what is today called the first principles of government (*arkān al-hukūma*), state systems (*Tanzhimat al-dawla*), and the basis of government (*asās al-ḥukm*). These he believes are general terminologies and constructed situations that are not in reality necessary for a state system if what is meant is a simple state, an "instinctive" government that refuses all exaggerations and that rejects all that simple *fitra* (natural disposition) does not need or require. He further explains that all that can be observed about the prophetic state in contemplation goes back to one meaning, that it lacked all these phenomena that have become today, in the view of political scientists, part of the basis of a civil government. While these are in fact not obligatory, they do not necessarily amount to being shortcomings of a government or a characteristic of anarchy and disorder.[35]

ʿAbd al-Raziq then dedicates a section to focusing on the prophet's personality, especially with regard to his being a humble man. He maintains,

The Prophet Muhammad, peace be upon him, used to like modesty/humility [things simple] and hated exaggeration. His private and public lives were based on pure modesty that was not tainted with anything. He used to call for modesty in speech and deed, as [reflected] in his conversation with Jarir ibn 'Abdalla al-Bajali [when he told him], "Jarir, if you talked be concise, and if you reached your goal do not burden yourself."[36]

'Abd al-Raziq goes on to relate many Hadith narratives to support his point of the simple lifestyle that the prophet led. This included how the prophet dealt with people modestly, how he did not like to be distinguished among his companions, that whenever he was given a choice between two things he decided on the simple one, provided it did not entail sin. Then 'Abd al-Raziq correlates all these characteristics of the prophet's personality to the main line of his argument, arguing that this, which appears to us to be ambiguity or perplexity or shortcoming in the system of the prophetic "government," could just be this very modesty and fitra (basic instinct). After relaying all these possibilities of what might be the reason for the ambiguities surrounding the prophetic "government," 'Abd al-Raziq declares that it would be very easy for him to choose one of these possibilities he hypothesized. However, he explains that he could not make a decision on these possibilities because it would be inappropriate and incorrect to do so.

In summary, in his analysis of what was perceived to be government during the time of the Prophet Muhammad, 'Abd al-Raziq argues that, although what had existed might have had the characteristics of government, it lacked many features that constitute the concept of government as largely known. One of the most important features that he highlighted in this respect is the judiciary system, acknowledging that it did exist during the time of the Prophet. He used Hadith narratives corroborating that even the Prophet himself ruled on cases brought before him, and that both 'Umar and Ali functioned as judges during their caliphate reins. Nonetheless, as previously detailed, after researching the issue thoroughly, 'Abd al-Raziq's ultimate conclusion is that the Prophet Muhammad never established or headed a government and that he was merely a messenger assigned the task of conveying and proclaiming a religious message that had no connection with politics. Given this, modern-day Muslims have no obligation to follow the caliphate political model of government. They are free to develop any form of political rule that is most suited to their time as well as their respective political and socioeconomic needs.

NOTES

1. Ali 'Abd al-Raziq, *Al-Islām wa Usūl al-Ḥukm* (Sousa, Tunisia: Ma'arif Publishing, 2001), 51. All references to 'Abd al-Raziq in this chapter are from the 2001 edition of his book. The original text was in Arabic, English translation of this and all other passages referred to in this chapter are mine, unless otherwise indicated.

2. Quoted in 'Abd al-Raziq, *Al-Islām wa Usūl al-Ḥukm* (2001), 52–53.

3. Abu Daūd (d. 889).

4. 'Abd al-Raziq, *Al-Islām wa Usūl al-Ḥukm* (2001), 53.

روى ابن داؤرد ، رحمه الله، عن علي بن أبي طالب، رضي الله عنه، وقال بعثني رسول الله، صلى الله عليه وسلم، إلى اليمن قاضياً ، وأنا حديث السن، ولا علم لي بالقضاء ، وقال إن الله سيهدي قلبك، ويثبّت لسانك، فإذا جلس بين يديك الخصمان فلا تقضي حتى تسمع من الآخر ، كما سمعت من الأول، فإنه أحرى أن يتبيّن لك القضاء. قال فمازلت قاضياً ، وما شككت في قضاء بعد."

5. Ibid.

6. Al-Bukhari (d. 870).

7. Ibid., Sahih al-Bukhari, vol 5, 161–163 qtd. in 'Abd al-Raziq, *Al-Islām wa Usūl al-Ḥukm* (2001), 54.

8. Ibid.

9. *Zakāt* (almsgiving) is one of the Five Pillars of Islam, the other four being Prayer (*Salāt*), Fasting (*Sawm*), Pilgrimage to Mecca (*Hajj*), and primarily the declaration of Faith (*Shahādā*).

10. 'Abd al-Raziq, *Al-Islām wa Usūl al-Ḥukm* (2001), 55.

11. *Ajtahid* is the first-person conjugation of the present tense of the Arabic root *jahd* from which also comes the Arabic noun *ijtihād* (independent inquiry).

12. 'Abd al-Raziq, *Al-Islām wa Usūl al-Ḥukm* (2001), 55–56.

الحمد لله الذي وفق رسول رسول الله لما يرضاه رسول الله

13. Ibid., 57.

14. Ibid., 58.

15. Ibid., 57.

16. Ahmad Amīn, *Fajr al-Islam*, quoted in Muhammad Hassan al-Wazzani, *Al-Islam wa-al-Dawala* (*Islam and the State*) (Fez, Morocco: Alwazzani Association, 1987), 7.

17. Ahmed Muhammad 'Owf, "Al-Arab fī Jāhiliyya" (Arabs in the Jāhiliyya), online version of *Minbar al-Islam* magazine. Original was in Arabic; English translation is mine. http://www.islammemo.cc/article1.aspx?id=26493, accessed 2007.

18. 'Abd al-Raziq, *Al-Islām wa Usūl al-Ḥukm* (2001), 62.

19. Ibid., 63.

20. Ibid., 64–65.

21. Ibid., 65.

22. Quran, 2:256.

23. Quran, 16:124.

24. Quran, 88:21, 22.

25. 'Abd al-Raziq, *Al-Islām wa Usūl al-Ḥukm* (2001), 66.

26. Abu Jafar Muhammad ibn Jarir al-Tabari (838–923), theologian, historian, and most famous for his Quranic commentary and his *History of Prophets and Kings*.

27. ʿAbd al-Raziq, *Al-Islām wa Usūl al-Ḥukm* (2001), 68.

فأما أن المملكة النبوية عمل منفصل عن دعوة الإسلام، وخارج عن حدود الرسالة، فذلك رأي لا
نعرف في مذاهب المسلمين ما يشاكله، ولا نذكر في كلامهم ما يدل عليه، وهو على ذلك رأي
صالح لأنْ يذهب إليه، ولا نرى القول به كفراً أو إلحاداً، وربما كان محمولاً على هذا المذهب ما
يراه بعض الفرق الإسلامية من إنكار الخلافة في الإسلام مرة واحدة.

28. Ibid., 68–69.

29. Ibid., 69.

30. In reference to Rufāʿa al-Tahtāwī, quoted in ʿAbd al-Raziq, *Al-Islām wa Usūl al-Ḥukm* (2001).

31. Ibid., 71.

32. Ibid., 71–72.

33. Ibid., 72.

34. Ibid.

35. Ibid., 73.

36. Ibid.

كان محمد صلّى الله عليه وسلّم يحب البساطة، ويكره التكليف. وعلى البساطة الخالصة التي لا
شائبة فيها قامت حياته الخاصة والعامة، كما يدعو للبساطة في القول والعمل، كما في حديثه
مع جرير بن عبدالله البجلي «يا جرير إذا قلت فأوجز، وإذا بلغت حاجتك فلا تتكلّف.»

7

Critiques of 'Abd al-Raziq's Position

*A*BD AL-RAZIQ'S BOOK *Al-Islām wa Usūl al-Ḥukm* prompted admiration and outrage, but above all strong reaction, upon its publication in Egypt. The controversy thrust the issue of separation of religion and state to the forefront, and the work compelled engagement, drawing responses from across the intellectual community in Egypt and beyond. Positive responses of secular scholars who either supported the author's contention about the desirability of separation of religion and state in Islam or his right to express his opinions in the intellectual space will be addressed in this chapter, then a detailed analysis of the rancorous attacks from religious traditionalists is offered. Several contemporary responses to 'Abd al-Raziq's book will also be briefly introduced. An overview of the responses, both positive and negative, offer valuable counterweights by which to evaluate the arguments put forth in 'Abd al-Raziq's controversial book.

'Ali 'Abd al-Raziq's study created quite a stir among the scholars of Egypt, compelling them to grapple with the issue of whether the caliphate was a necessary part of an Islamic order. As noted, responses to and critiques of 'Abd al-Raziq's book have been written by both detractors and supporters of the author's argument. On the one hand, the rage that 'Abd al-Raziq's book aroused led to the immediate publication of several contentious books and responses that bitterly assailed the author and his ideas. On the other hand, secular intellectuals publicly defended the author's right to exercise freedom of expression. This chapter's main concern will be to examine in detail the attack on 'Ali 'Abd al-Raziq's book by traditionalist 'ulamā such as Muhammad al-Khidr Husayn, Mamdouh Haqqi, and Muhammad al-Bakhit al-Muti'i. However, before delving into a discussion of these scholars' criticisms, brief mention must be made of the responses of the secular scholars who agreed with and supported 'Abd al-Raziq's views.

Taha Husayn defended 'Abd al-Raziq's thesis enthusiastically, arguing that
for many years Muslims have understood the distinction between religion and
state, that religion is one thing while state and culture are quite another thing.[1]
In his book *Waladī* (*My Son*), Muhammad Husayn Haykal spoke in favor of
separation of religion and state in Turkey as one of the "necessary foundations
for any true democracy, a healthy social life, and for the upsurge of civilization."[2] But Haykal's strongest defense of 'Abd al-Raziq's book was reflected
in many articles and editorials that he wrote in 1926 as editor-in-chief of the
Constitutionalist Liberals Party's official paper, *Elsiyasa*. Haykal wrote articles
for *Elsiyasa*, vigorously defending freedom of thought and 'Abd al-Raziq's
right to free speech, especially after al-Azhar Supreme Council issued its verdict against 'Abd al-Raziq. Furthermore, within his discussion and study of
the social and cultural history of Islam, Ahmed Amin used, in different words,
aspects of 'Abd al-Raziq's argument for separation of religion and state.[3]

In spite of such manifestations of support for 'Abd al-Raziq, it was the
negative critiques of his book that had the greatest impact on the Egyptian
political scene, creating an uproar against the book and the position it took on
the relationship between religion and state. Undoubtedly the most coherent
of these negative critiques of the book have been formulated in three main
publications: (1) *NaqD Kitāb Al-Islām wa Usūl al-Ḥukm* (*Refuting the Book
Islam and the Foundations of Rule*), a book written by Sheikh Muhammad
al-Khidr Husayn (1875–1958) and published in Cairo in 1926—one year after
'Abd al-Raziq's book had been published; (2) *Ḥaqīqat Al-Islām wa Usūl al-
Ḥukm* (*The Truth about Islam and the Foundations of Rule*), written by Sheikh
Muhammad al-Bakhit al-Muti'i (1854–1935), Mufti al-Diyār al-Misriyyah, the
former Grand Mufti of Egypt, also published in Cairo in 1926; and (3) *Naqd
wa Ta'līq* (*Commentary and Criticism*), written later by Mamdouh Haqqi and
published, along with the *Dar al-Ḥayat* edition of 'Abd al-Raziq's book, in
Beirut in 1966. In addition to these major works, a short response to 'Abd
al-Raziq's book has recently been published in an interview format by the Tunisian historian and intellectual Muhammad al-Talbi in his book *'Iyāl Allah:
Afkār Jadīdah fī 'Alāqat al-Muslim bi Nafsihī wa bil Ākharīn* (*Children of God:
New Ideas on the Muslim's Relationship with Himself and Others*)[4] (1992). More
recently, Muhammad 'Imarah (1995) also wrote *Mulāhadhāt Intiqādiyya 'Aala
al-Kitāb* (*Critical Observations on the Book*) in which he pinpointed what he
saw as some weak points in 'Abd al-Raziq's book, especially what he described
as its "negativity" and "flawed intellectual methodology." 'Imarah's critique focuses on four contradictions that he sees in the book and will be discussed

later in this chapter. As noted in previous chapters, other responses to 'Abd al-Raziq's book include references to *Al-Islām wa Usūl al-Ḥukm* written by Albert Hourani[5] and Charles C. Adams[6] who discuss 'Abd al-Raziq as part of a comprehensive study of Muhammad 'Abduh's disciples and students. As also previously noted, Adams explores 'Abduh's influence on 'Abd al-Raziq and examines whether his liberal views are related to the modern reform movement inaugurated by 'Abduh.[7] In his study of 'Abduh and his disciples, Albert Hourani places 'Ali 'Abd al-Raziq among those who did accept Islam as principles, yet believed that secular norms should regulate life in society.[8] It was, however, the key critiques that fueled the controversy surrounding 'Abd al-Raziq's work and, along with all of the responses to the book, remain fundamental to any contemporary examination of his thesis.

This section discusses the full arguments of the different critiques of and responses to 'Abd al-Raziq's book with special emphasis on the critiques of Muhammad al-Khidr Husayn, Mamdouh Haqqi, and Sheikh Muhammad al-Bakhit al-Muti'i. The focus on these three critiques stems from the fact that each one of them tried categorically to refute 'Abd al-Raziq's main thesis, that Islam is *dīn lā dawlah* (religion, not state) and that the Prophet Muhammad was sent as a spiritual leader, not as a political leader.

↬   *Muhammad al-Khidr Husayn*

HUSAYN BEGINS HIS critique by claiming that 'Abd al-Raziq is not *mujadid*[9] or a modernist as some have assumed, but he should more aptly be described as an estranged, Westernized person who has been fascinated by the West, its theorists, philosophers, and Orientalists. Husayn believed such influence is what caused 'Abd al-Raziq to look at Islam and the issue of state and religion through the same lens through which the European Renaissance saw Catholic Christianity. Hence, he saw the khilāfah as divinely sanctioned tyranny, which makes the caliph an agent of God whom nobody should question. It is also through this same Western lens that 'Abd al-Raziq saw Islam as only a religion and not a state, a spiritual message that is not related to politics or the organization of society.[10] Further, Husayn maintains:

When 'Abd al-Raziq relies on the Orientalist Sir [Thomas] Arnold[11] [1864–1930] with regard to *"taqrīr aḥkām shar'iyyah"* [deciding on lawful rules] pertinent to the Imamate and Caliphate, he demonstrates his fascination with the West and the influences of the hegemony practiced by Western civilization on the minds of some to the extent that they began to borrow, not only its social and historical tools of research, but also *Aḥkām al-Shar' wal Dīn* [*Rules on Law and Religion*].[12]

With respect to 'Abd al-Raziq's referral of his readers to Sir Arnold's book on a matter of *ḥukm shar'ī* (lawful rule), Husayn declares, "He probably confused serious matters with funny things[13], or at best he intended to take *Akhām al-Sharī'a* outside the circle of those who have mastered its science."[14] If 'Abd al-Raziq knows that the *Sharī'a* has fundamentals and aims (*maqāsid wa usūl*) that Sir Arnold had not studied well, then referring the reader to the latter's book "is nothing but an obstacle in the path of research that distracts the naïve and leads them to hesitation and suspicion."[15]

In his attempt to refute 'Abd al-Raziq's claim that neither the Quran nor the prophetic Sunna mentioned anything about the caliphate, and that the Ijmā' was not all in favor of it, Husayn argues that the judgment of the caliphate is based on practicality and not on religious belief. He further explains what he sees as the difference between "practical *aḥkām*" and religious belief, maintaining that in practical aḥkām it is sufficient to employ useful proofs, whereas beliefs must be based on solid and undisputable evidence.[16] Husayn also cautions that Arabic terms must be understood within the context of their meaningful Arabic style, reminding the reader that linguistic terminologies in all languages can mean what is not intended. However, in his discussion of 'Abd al-Raziq's claim of the absence of the caliphate from the Quran, Husayn does not present a convincing argument given the fact that his response to this point appears to be more of a personal attack on 'Abd al-Raziq. Rather, Husayn focuses most of his discussion on detailing different Hadīth narratives mentioning or dealing with the caliphate and calling for obeying the caliph. He maintains that if these narratives fell in the hands of a mujtahid (an independent inquirer) exploring their wisdom, he would not hesitate to agree that the issue of appointing the imam is an established lawful wājib (duty). Thus, "'Abd al-Raziq's argument that the prophetic Sunna makes no mention of the caliphate is a daring position that will be assumed only by a person intending to dispute facts."[17] With regard to the Ijmā' and 'Abd al-Raziq's argument that it does not constitute evidence amounting to establishing the necessity of the caliphate, Husayn conversely believes that it does constitute a decisive ḥujja or evidence of the necessity of the caliphate. Husayn's main argument here is that the mere fact that the prophet's companions did not have any disagreement on appointing a caliphate as successor of the prophet stands as evidence of Ijmā'.

Their only disagreement, he maintains, was on who the most appropriate or suitable person to assume the position of the caliph was, and they soon chose Abu Bakr as caliph. Those who refused to pay Abu Bakr the bay'ah (oath of allegiance), Husayn explains, did not dispute the necessity of the caliphate.[18] However, in Hourani's analysis, 'Abd al-Raziq insists that there was no real Ijmāʿ on the caliphate issue. The lack of opposition to the caliph's claim to authority does not constitute a tacit Ijmāʿ; for the caliph's authority did not allow for free expression of opinion,[19] an argument that 'Abd al-Raziq makes clear in the original edition of his book.[20]

In addressing 'Abd al-Raziq's argument that the Prophet Muhammad was a messenger of a religious message which was purely spiritual and tainted neither by a tendency to govern or rule, nor by a call for a religious state—and that the Prophet Muhammad never established a kingdom within the meaning that can be understood politically—Husayn argues that such an opinion was not based on scientific research or on Islamic law. Rather, "it was a perception influenced by fascination of Western life, which tends to distort facts."[21]

However, it is worth mentioning that despite the fact that Husayn's aggressive book might have followed a scientific approach to criticism, it is marred by some hasty conclusions—such as his accusing 'Abd al-Raziq of *al-wuqū' fi ham'at al-ilhād* (falling into atheism).[22] In addition, many, including Muhammad 'Imarah, have also criticized Husayn for dedicating his book to King Fuad I of Egypt (1917–1936), an attempt that was largely perceived as appeasing the palace at a time when it exerted relentless effort aimed primarily at controlling al-Azhar as an academic institution of unique religious status and depriving it of its independence.[23]

⮑ *Mamdouh Haqqi*

ANOTHER CRITICAL ANALYSIS of 'Abd al-Raziq's book appeared in 1966 with the publication of Mamdouh Haqqi's *Naqd wa Ta'līq* (*Commentary and Criticism*),[24] contained in the Beirut edition of 'Abd al-Raziq's book. In his critique, Mamdouh Haqqi argues against 'Abd al-Raziq's questioning of the legitimacy of the Prophet Muhammad as a messenger and head of state simultaneously. He asks: "Should the Prophet be less than Moses, David and Solomon?" The prophet's work and role in building a state, Haqqi maintains, does not at all deviate from his mission as a messenger. This is because Islam not only is a religion, like Christianity, but is a religion and state at the same time.[25] While the Bible clearly states: "Render therefore unto Caesar the things which are

Caesar's, and unto God the things which are God's,"[26] in Islam the state and religion are inseparable.[27]

Haqqi maintains that Islam is not only a religion that connects the individual with God, it is dīn and dunyā simultaneously, an important point of departure that makes the Islamic religion distinctly different from other religions in that it is also a unique system of rule. It is a system that should not be compared to or measured with reference to other political systems, for it is not an absolute monarchy, constitutional, parliamentary, communist, or socialist system. It is a special system that should be studied within its own Islamic terms. Thus, all those who have tried to see Islam through the lenses of other ideologies advocating such theories as "Democracy in Islam," "Socialism in Islam," and so on are at fault.[28] Haqqi then proceeds to explain the concept of the caliphate as he explains the idea that the khilāfah in Islam is not similar to a monarchy or republic because the caliph represents the umma in two capacities: "He represents both religion and state, I insist on saying 'represents' (*yumaththil*) instead of 'govern' or 'rule' (*yaḥkum*), because his authority is not absolute, being limited within the general *dastūr* or constitution that is based on the Quran and the Sunna."[29] If some developments later take place in the Muslim community through time, given the fact that international relations and societies emerge as new organizations, the caliph should go back to *Ijma' al-Muslimīn* (consensus of Muslims) or *Qiyās* (reasoning by way of analogy). He should not be a tyrant over Muslims in their dīn *or* dunyā because he is controlled by the Shūrā system and the general dastūr, which is *al-Quran al-Karīm*.[30] Haqqi cites the following Quranic scripture from *Sūrat al-Shūrā* to support his point: "Those who respond to their Lord, and perform regular prayer, who [conduct] their affairs through mutual consultation and spend out of what we bestow on them for sustenance."[31] He also includes the following verse from *Sūrat Āl-'Imrān* to support his point that the caliph should not be a tyrant (the address in the Quran, in the second person, is to the Prophet Muhammad):

> It is part of Allah's Mercy that you deal gently with them. If you were severe or harsh-hearted [*wa law kunta fazan ghalīz al-qalb*], they would have broken away from about you; so pass over [their faults] and ask for Allah's forgiveness for them and consult them in affairs [of moment]. Then, when you have made a decision, put your trust in Allah [*fa tawakkal 'ala Allah*].[32]

In Haqqi's analysis of the above-mentioned Quranic scriptures, the first is based on four pillars: (1) responding to God's order (*amr*) without hesitation; (2) thanking God for his blessings through prayer and worship; (3) consultation in worldly affairs; and (4) establishing good human relationships based on love and kindness. The second verse, maintains Haqqi, vividly explains the relationship between the ruler and the ruled as it indicates the following: (1) the person who has taken the state leadership responsibility, entrusted to govern Muslim affairs, must be kind, merciful, friendly, and not cruel or a tyrant; (2) the verse instructs him to forgive and ask God's forgiveness for those who need it; (3) it also orders the ruler to consult with those around him to expand his own individual experience by acquiring their expertise before he makes his decision; and (4) if, after all this, the right path has become clear to him, he should close the door of doubt and hesitation and continue in implementing what he has decided, putting his trust in Allah.[33]

Both verses, Haqqi claims, limit the scope in which the ruler may move in handling state affairs; they curb his tyranny and put him forth on the right path. This, further explains Haqqi,

> is the basis for *Usūl al-Ḥukm*, there is no other basis. Relying on his ['Abd al-Raziq's] *tafsīr* on people's opinions—no matter what they are—or on some eccentric examples (such as the tyranny and dictatorship of some caliphs in the name of religion) does not negate the truth, that such tyrants' conduct does not apply to *usūl al-Dīn al-sarīhah* [the clear fundamentals of religion and message], and that religion has nothing to do with what they do.[34]

In particular, Haqqi questions what he refers to as 'Abd al-Raziq's "selective" reference to the 'Abbasid Caliph, al-Mansour, as an example of a corrupt and violent imam, arguing that the reference to a caliph should instead be to Abu Bakr al-Siddiq—who was the first who carried the title caliph—because Abu Bakr was elected by the Muslim community, whereas al-Mansour jumped (*qafadh*) to the caliphate with a sword in his hand, using it to cut off people's heads until he assumed the throne.[35] In reality, 'Abd al-Raziq in fact referred to both Abu Bakr and al-Mansour and thus Haqqi has clearly mischaracterized 'Abd al-Raziq's argument. In fact 'Abd al-Raziq dedicates an important section of his book to discussing the caliphate of Abu Bakr whereas reference to al-Mansour is brief in comparison. However, Haqqi also explains the duty of the caliph in the Islamic concept as that of a servant of the people, not their master or tyrant. "If he followed the right path, he is commended by the Muslim community, and if he deviated from that path of the Ḥaqq (truth; the right path) and turned into a dictator, they voted him out and isolated him."[36] As to those that 'Abd al-Raziq used as examples of unjust tyrants, such as the 'Abbasid Caliph al-Mansour and his companions, these are not *Khulafā Rasul-Allah*, but despotic kings who stole the *burdat al-khilāfah* (the caliphate garment) unjustly and tried to protect themselves with it when they were bare naked.[37]

However, it is important to note that while Haqqi's reflection on the Islamic ideal—that the Muslim community (in a given state) can vote a tyrant out of power—has remained true in theory, this ideal is far from the reality of dictatorial regimes in recent times. The political system in some Arab/Islamic countries serves as the best example of 'Abd al-Raziq's argument regarding the exploitation and manipulation of religious authority to advance not what the Quran says, but the ruling government's own misinterpretation of Islam. Almost all regimes that we have witnessed in our lifetime thus far (of those who claim to have established an Islamic state, though not strictly the khilāfah) fit 'Abd al-Raziq's argument of the exploitation of religious authority to serve the ruling elite, not the people or the masses. Contrary to what Haqqi has claimed, none of these allegedly religious leaders has been voted out of power in a peaceful manner, if at all, simply because they assumed power through dictatorial means. The Taliban in Afghanistan and the current military government of the Sudan (1989–present) are but two examples of such pseudo-Islamic rulers who assumed power by force. Chapter 8 will elaborate further on these two examples.

It is clear that 'Abd al-Raziq's book was met with such opposition because of its advocacy of a new historical theory about "matters of which accepted historical views had something of the nature of religious doctrine," as Albert Hourani has noted. Such theory was drawn "more from non-Muslim writers on Islam, who might be accused of trying to weaken its holds on its adherents, than from the fundamental Islamic sources, the sciences of Quranic interpretation and *Hadith*."[38] This premise as followed by 'Abd al-Raziq was therefore perceived by other critics of the book, such as Muhammad Rashid Rida, as "the latest attempt by the enemies of Islam to weaken it from within," as noted several times for emphasis.[39]

Yet, one of the strongest manifestations of opposition to the book came earlier from the former Grand Mufti of Egypt, Muhammad al-Bakhit al-Muti'i.

↔   *Muhammad al-Bakhit al-Muti'i*

MUHAMMAD AL-BAKHIT AL-MUTI'I (largely known as al-Bakhit) published his book *Ḥaqīqat Al-Islām wa Usūl al-Ḥukm* (*The Truth about Islam and the Foundations of Rule*) the year following the publication of 'Abd al-Raziq's book.[40] In his preface, al-Bakhit emphasizes that 'Abd al-Raziq's book did not mention any positive opinion nor did it provide evidence for what its author claimed. Al-Bakhit maintains:

> All that 'Abd al-Raziq said were negative issues and mere denial of what Muslims had consensus on, or had been clearly stated in the Quran or the Prophetic Sunna. 'Abd al-Raziq depended in his denial on intellectual sophistry, assumed suppositions, and poetic proof. However, all these matters that 'Abd al-Raziq denied are issues of jurisprudence and *shar'* (law) that cannot simply be dealt with merely using the intellect, for it must be proven by texts from the Quran, the Prophetic Sunna, *Ijmā'* or *Qiyās*.[41]

Hence the need al-Bakhit felt to respond to these denials and to correct them, which prompted the choice of the title of his book, *Ḥaqīqat Al-Islām wa Usūl al-Ḥukm*. In his refutation of 'Abd al-Raziq's claim that the Prophet Muhammad's leadership was merely religious, not political, and that Arab unity during the prophet's time was Islamic, not political, al-Bakhit argues that such an "erroneous evaluation" of the prophet's role contradicts the Quranic verses and Hadith narratives that state clearly that the prophet's leadership was both religious and civil, that Arab unity was both Islamic and political, and that Arabs' submission to the prophet's authority was submission of belief and faith as well as submission of government and sultan.[42] Al-Bakhit argues that 'Abd al-Raziq's claims constitute a denial of a matter upon which all Muslims historically agree; Islam is *shar'* that is meant to be both theoretical and practical, and that unlike other religions, religious and political authority are inseparable in Islam. He further emphasizes that 'Abd al-Raziq could not find evidence to support his denials of the political nature of Islam. To confirm his point further, al-Bakhit emphasizes that anybody who carefully studies and refers to the Quran or the Hadith will have no doubt that the prophet was ordered to rule between people with rules derived from what was revealed to him in the Quran and that Islam is a religion of legislative and executive authority and should be preached as such.[43]

Al-Bakhit also rails against 'Abd al-Raziq's allowing himself to be influenced by non-Muslim thinkers and thinks that he should not accept their

evaluation of the caliphate. He maintains that there is a major difference between Islam and Christianity and that "'Abd al-Raziq seemed confused between the two, as evidenced by his argument on page fifty-three of his book
[discussed below]."[44] However, on the page that al-Bakhit referenced, 'Abd al-
Raziq quotes a number of Quranic verses including the following:

> "Let there be no compulsion in religion"; "Invite (all) to the Way of thy
> Lord with wisdom and beautiful preaching; and argue with them in ways
> that are best and most gracious"; and "Therefore do remind, for you are
> only a reminder. You are not a watcher over them."[45]

'Abd al-Raziq then maintains that all these are clear principles that show
that the message of the Prophet Muhammad, like the previous messages of his
brothers (a reference to pre-Islamic prophets), depended on persuasion and
advice. He could not depend on force and oppression, for if he did he would
not be faithful to his calling as a prophet charged with guiding people on the
right path. 'Abd al-Raziq used the above mentioned verses from the Quran to
support his argument.[46]

In fact, this is exactly where al-Bakhit critiques what he perceives as 'Abd
al-Raziq's thesis of denial and the latter's attack on the whole theory of prophecy on which Islam depends. As al-Bakhit puts it:

> The religion of Islam is based on the pursuit of control, strength, might,
> and the refusal of any law that is contrary to the Shari'a and its divine law,
> and the rejection of any authority the wielder of which is not charged with
> execution of its ethics.[47]

Sheikh al-Bakhit argues that to follow 'Abd al-Raziq's claim that the
Prophet Muhammad was a spiritual messenger who never headed a political
state would mean denying the existence of both the umma and the prophet
himself, an argument that negates the very essence of Islam. This is where
al-Bakhit perceives 'Abd al-Raziq as relying on intellectual sophistry and sup-
positions, as we saw earlier. The only alternative for 'Abd al-Raziq to see these
matters correctly is to interpret such matters of jurisprudence through relying
on Islam's four sources: the Quran, the Sunna, Ijmā' (consensus of the community of scholars), and Qiyās (reasoning by way of analogy).

Hourani observes that, in al-Bakhit's view, the danger is not only theoretical, because in the final analysis 'Abd al-Raziq was actually saying that there

is no such thing as the Shari'a, a theory which, if accepted, would mean that there was no political society in the true sense, which would cause the umma to disintegrate into chaos and anarchy. People cannot be left free to manage their worldly affairs by their own reason and knowledge—by their own interests and desire—because this would simply mean the domination of the strong over the weak, which would ultimately cause insecurity in the society. Hence, al-Bakhit argues, the need for a regulator and governor who will keep people within their due limits, prevent oppression, and do justice ruling by the law that is accepted by all. If people are left to manage their own affairs according to their power and desires, this will lead to the domination of the strong over the poor, according to al-Bakhit.[48] Al-Bakhit explains the kind of political law that can be deduced from the principles of Islam in the following words:

> The origin of the Caliph's power is the umma [nation] from which he obtains his sultan. Muslims were the first umma who asserted that the umma is the source of all authorities, before other nations said so. The Islamic government headed by the Caliph and the general Imam is a democratic, liberal, consultative government. The Constitution for such government is God's book and the Sunna of his Prophet.[49]

Hourani makes an interesting observation here, arguing that al-Bakhit's claim above implies that the political institutions of Islam and the advantages of modern political institutions are essentially the same. He maintains that al-Bakhit "seems unaware that he has opened the door to that very invasion of Islam by the ideas of western rationalism for which he reproaches his opponent."[50] However, Leonard Binder argues that the difficulty with Hourani's easy conclusion is that it "centers on the question of the proper form of Islamic government . . . as opposed to the question of whether the *umma* is a democratic, political community."[51] Binder further expounds on Hourani's treatment of al-Bakhit's above statement:

> Regarding Hourani's quotation of what is taken as Shaykh Bakhit's concessionary statement, we see that while the caliph derives *his* authority from the umma, the umma is not the constituent power in the sense of originating the constitution. The constitution of a Government of Muslims is the Qur'an and the Sunna. Bakhit's position appears to be compatible with the contemporary Muslim consensus that an Islamic government is one which maintains the Shari'a for any group of Muslims.[52]

Binder maintains that, while this position probably owes more to Ibn Khaldun than it does to al-Mawardi and the jurists, "it is still fundamentally different from the Western idea of liberal constitutional democracy."[53]

⊶   *Muhammad 'Imarah's Four Points*

IN HIS BOOK *The Battle over Islam and the Foundations of Rule*, Muhammad 'Imarah critically addresses what he describes as four major points in 'Abd al-Raziq's book in a chapter titled "Critical Observations on the Book." These four points include what 'Imarah saw as (1) "contradiction in evaluating the Islamic experience during the Messenger's time"; (2) "contradiction in evaluating the [Islamic] experience in the aftermath of the Messenger's time"; (3) "the author's [justification of his] testimony with that which does not justify it"; and (4) "neglecting the bright side of Islamic thought."[54]

On the first point, "contradiction in evaluating the Islamic experience during the Messenger's time," 'Imarah argues that 'Abd al-Raziq often falls in contradiction when he evaluates the nature of some periods of Islamic history, and when he judges and issues rules on the nature of the Islamic experience and Islamic systems that prevailed during those periods of time.[55] Although the very succinct writing style that 'Abd al-Raziq chose in writing his book helped a great deal in concealing this contradiction, maintains 'Imarah, the author's precise choice of words—which well express his intention—helped the vigilant reader to discover many of the contradictory points the author has made. For example, when he attempts to evaluate the nature of the system established by Islam during the time of the Prophet Muhammad and his experience in the Arabian Peninsula, 'Abd al-Raziq denies in many instances that such an experience was political, constituted a political system, or was even remotely related to ruling, government, or the state. Accordingly, 'Abd al-Raziq's assertion in this regard is that such an experience was merely religious and spiritual and had nothing to do with politics. To confirm this, 'Abd al-Raziq often repeats his argument that

> the Arab unity found during the time of the Prophet, peace be upon him, was never a political unity by any means, never had the meaning of government or the state, but was merely a religious unity exclusive of any political connotations, a unity of faith and religious denomination, not that of the state or monarchy.[56]

However, 'Imarah claims that 'Abd al-Raziq's evaluation of the Islamic experience is not consistent throughout the book based on what he sees as another contradictory evaluation of the same Islamic experience during the prophet's time existing side by side with the first evaluation explained above. To illustrate his point further, 'Imarah cites 'Abd al-Raziq's argument that the prophet's authority was more powerful than the authority of kings and governments in that it encompassed spiritual aspects of human life (which fall within the messenger's domain) and sensual aspects of human life (which fall within the realm of governments). This means that politics, the state, and government in their civil meaning were implied in and part of the nature of the system established by the prophet.[57]

A close reading of 'Abd al-Raziq's argument in this respect, however, reveals 'Imarah's negligence of an important clarification made by 'Abd al-Raziq when he cautioned the reader against "confusing between the leadership of the message, and the leadership of a king," arguing that the difference between them amounts to a conflict.[58] For example, he maintains that the leadership of neither Moses nor Jesus was a political or royal leadership, nor was the leadership of most messengers. The status of the message requires an authority far larger and broader for the messenger than the authority that exists between rulers and ruled, even wider than that between father and children. Thus, while 'Abd al-Raziq admits that "the Prophet might deal with the nation's politics the way kings do, yet the Messenger alone has a function not shared by others. This includes communicating spiritual aspects of human life."[59]

Another point that 'Imarah sees as a discrepancy in 'Abd al-Raziq's book is what he calls a "contradiction in evaluating the experience in the aftermath of the Prophet's time."[60] He argues that 'Abd al-Raziq's method of thinking, which fails to note the relationship between "religion" and "politics" or between "the Quran" and "government," caused him to fall into another contradiction when evaluating the experience of and the system established by Muslims and Arabs in the period following the prophet's death. Such contradiction, maintains 'Imarah, can be seen in 'Abd al-Raziq's evaluation of the experience of the first caliph, Abu Bakr al-Siddiq. While he does not deny its religious association and argues that Abu Bakr followed the footsteps of the Prophet Muhammad, 'Abd al-Raziq comes to contradict himself by describing Abu Bakr's leadership as "nonreligious," or that it was a "nonreligious kind."[61]

The third point of contradiction discussed by 'Imarah relates to his argument that 'Abd al-Raziq tries to justify his testimony with that which does not justify it. He gives several examples to illustrate his point, including his reference to 'Abd al-Raziq's attempts to refute that the prophet's experience had any relation to politics, the state, or government, relying on his belief that the prophet's mission was a religious call to convey God's revelation, and that it was not of an authoritative or executive nature. 'Imarah's main point here is that the Quranic references used by 'Abd al-Raziq to justify his point do not justify it. Such references include a Quranic verse from Surat *Qāf* that states: "We well know what they say. You shall not use coercion with them. Remind with the Quran whoever fears my warning."[62] That means, according to al-Baidawi's interpretation, "you are not appointed to force them into faith, or to do whatever you please with them, you are only to call them into religion [without coercion]."[63] In 'Imarah's analysis, this Quranic verse deals with the call for belief; it does not speak of the political or civil aspects of the system of people's lives in the Islamic society then. In addition, the refutation that the prophet was not a "coercer" does not mean in any sense that he was not a ruler or that he did not establish a state.[64] 'Imarah uses many other verses from the Quran used by 'Abd al-Raziq as justification of his argument that such references to the Quran do not in fact justify the author's analysis, given other interpretations that can be derived from these same verses.

The fourth and last point that 'Imarah focuses on to draw out what he perceived as "another contradiction" in 'Abd al-Raziq's book is what 'Imarah refers to as "neglecting the bright side of Islamic thought." The reason behind this contradiction, he maintains, is 'Abd al-Raziq's "confusion" between Islamic thought and Islamic history and the divide between theory and practice. While Islamic "thought" includes many very admirable aspects of the ruler, the imam and their descriptions and conditions—save a few exceptions—we find 'Abd al-Raziq totally ignoring these admirable aspects and focusing only on negative examples.[65] The picture that 'Abd al-Raziq draws throughout the book of the caliph and the imam describes their absolute power and authority (derived from God), and their unlimited jurisdiction (authority) is an image foreign to the spirit of Islam. Such an image, maintains 'Imarah, came into practice in Islamic political life either through the Shi'a thinking on the imamate—which derives from or is an extension of Persian feudal theories—or through the Umayyad dynasty, which was characterized since Mu'awiya ibn Abu Sufiyaan (603–680 A.D.) by a Byzantine, Caesarean-type of throne whose tradition had prevailed in Damascus since before the rise of Islam.[66] Conversely, 'Imarah maintains, the line of Islamic thinking that truly expressed the spirit of Islam, its complete teachings, and general laws in this regard, is the Mu'tazilla[67] thinking. It was such thinking that determined that the way to choosing the

imam is through "contract, choice, and bay'ah" from the umma to the imam.
In addition, voting the imam out is the responsibility of the umma and within
its mandate. Thus, the position of the imam is political, although it is not unrelated to the totality of religious teachings.[68] 'Abd al-Raziq, argues 'Imarah,
not only neglects showing this bright aspect of Islamic thinking, but places the
advocates of this line of thinking among "*ahl al-ahwa*" (the moody/opportun-
ists) when he refers only briefly to some of their opinions in his book.[69]

Another example that indicates how 'Abd al-Raziq ignored presenting the
bright aspect in the history of Islamic thought, 'Imarah continues, is reflected
clearly in his following argument on the place and weight of such thinking in
Islamic heritage:

> It is quite noticeable in the history of Muslims' scientific movement that
> their contribution in [the field of] political science was the worst com-
> pared to other sciences. And that its existence among them was the weak-
> est, for we don't know any of their political writers or translators, nor do
> we know any research made by them on political thinking or the origins
> of politics save a few that does not have a real weight among their other
> scientific movement in . . . arts.[70]

In his response to 'Abd al-Raziq's above claim, Sheikh Muhammad al-
Khidr Husayn provides a detailed refutation where he presents the titles of a
number of books authored by Arabs and Muslims on politics and its arts, as
well as governance and its origins.[71] Husayn maintains:

> Muslims' contribution to politics/political science was not bad, and the
> existence of such sciences among them was not the weakest. We know of
> several books authored by them on politics. . . . Al-Kindi authored twelve
> books on politics including his Grand Thesis and his Public Thesis. . . . Abu
> Nasr al-Farabi authored eight books on politics including Civil Politics.[72]

Though these are the four critical points of contradiction that Muhammad
'Imarah sees as the weakest aspects of 'Abd al-Raziq's book, 'Imarah is quick
to add that such points do not reduce the book's importance as an intellectual
work that stirs debates and battles no other work has caused in Egypt from the
appearance of the printed book until the present day (1995). 'Imarah is obvi-
ously referring to the heated debate that 'Abd al-Raziq's book stirred in the
Egyptian political scene, a debate whose dust has yet to settle.

Quite a different view of 'Abd al-Raziq's book has been articulated by the Tunisian historian and intellectual Muhammad al-Talbi in his book *'Iyāl Allah: Afkār Jadīdah fī 'Alāqat al-Muslim bi Nafsihī wa bil Ākharīn* (*Children of God: New Ideas on the Muslim's Relationship with Himself and Others*).[73] Commenting on 'Abd al-Raziq's political thought, al-Talbi wrote:

> We see that the political movements that speak of Islam as a state and religion have been challenged by many such as the Egyptian thinker 'Ali 'Abd al-Raziq who tried to rebel against the idea that Islam is a state and religion. He considers that religion is religion and state is state, that there is no connection between them. However, he did not succeed in his revolution despite the fact that he had many supporters who have been spreading his ideas until this day, and despite the fact that his thought has become implicitly implemented in the Islamic world given the reality [of the prevailing circumstances].[74]

Al-Talbi further believes that the failure of 'Abd al-Raziq's ideas at the time he introduced them was due to historical circumstances—that people were neither ready nor prepared to adopt the thesis of separating religion from state. Such an idea was considered at the time bid'ah (an innovation) and *Dalālah* (profanity) that was violently opposed by al-Azhar 'ulamā.[75]

It is clear that 'Abd al-Raziq's ideas have evidently been a subject of relentless criticism and challenge since the early days of the book's publication in 1925. Based on the above discussion, within the context of these critiques, it can be said that the situation involves different political and religious underpinnings. Political and religious evaluations of 'Abd al-Raziq's ideas followed similar strategies in that they both tried to discredit the historical and juristic foundation of 'Abd al-Raziq's argument. Other scholars who tried to deem the book's argument irrelevant by attempting to prove that its author's ideas stemmed from Western ideologies, rather than Islamic thought, were not dissimilar to those who tried to discredit the religious foundation of 'Abd al-Raziq's reasoning. It is obvious that the fierce opposition that 'Abd al-Raziq's ideas received reflects the challenge his book posed to the traditional Muslim beliefs on not only the caliphate but the whole political theory of Islam perceived by many as an integral part of the Islamic message preached by the Prophet Muhammad in the seventh century.

NOTES

1. Taha Husayn, *Mustaqbal al-Thaqāfah fī Misr* (*The Future of Culture in Egypt*), trans. S. Glazer (Washington, D.C.: American Council on Learned Societies, 1954), 5.

2. Muhammad Husayn Haykal, *Waladī* (*My Son*) (Cairo: n.p., 1931), 207–211.

3. Ahmed Amin, *Duhā al-Islam* (*The Forenoon of Islam*) (Cairo: n.p., 1936), 4–5.

4. Muhammad al-Talbi, *'Iyāl Allah: Afkār Jadidah fī 'Alāqat al-Muslim bi Nafsihi wa bil Ākharīn* (*Children of God: New Ideas on the Muslim's Relationship with Himself and Others*) (Tunis: Sras Publisher, 1992). Original text was in Arabic. English translation of this and all subsequent references are mine.

5. See Hourani, *Arabic Thought in the Liberal Age.*

6. See Adams, *Islam and Modernism in Egypt.*

7. Ibid., preface.

8. Hourani, *Arabic Thought in the Liberal Age*, vi.

9. Although the Arabic term *tajdīd* literally denotes renewal, a person who is *mujaddid* might also be perceived as a modernist even though the Arabic word *hadāthah* is the literal equivalent of the English "modernity."

10. See 'Imarah, *Ma'rikat Al-Islām wa Usūl al-Hukm*, 189.

11. In reference to Sir Thomas W. Arnold's book, *The Caliphate* (Oxford: Clarendon Press, 1924) that 'Abd al-Raziq mentioned on page 15 of the original edition of *Al-Islam wa Usūl al-Hukm* (1925).

12. In 'Imarah, *Ma'rikat Al-Islām wa Usūl al-Hukm*, 190; the original was in Arabic; English translation of this and all subsequent references to Husayn are mine.

عندما يستند علي عبدالرازق إلى آراء المستشرق السير أرنولد 1864–1930 م في تقرير أحكام شرعية خاصة بالأمامة والخلافة، يظهر أثر إفتتانه بالغرب وتأثيرات الهيمنة التي تمارسها الحضارة الغربية على عقول البعض إلى الحد الذي جعلهم يأخذون عنها، لا المباحث التاريخية والإجتماعية فحسب، بل وأحكام الشرع والدين.

13. لعله أراد خلط الجد بالهزل

14. In 'Imarah, *Ma'rikat Al-Islām wa Usūl al-Hukm*, 190.

15. Ibid.

16. Ibid., 280.

17. Ibid., 282.

18. Ibid., 282–283.

19. Hourani, *Arabic Thought in the Liberal Age*, 185.

20. 'Abd al-Raziq, *Al-Islām wa Usūl al-Hukm* (1925), 18.

21. Hourani, *Arabic Thought in the Liberal Age*, 355.

22. Ibid., 204. الوقوع في حمأة الإلحاد

23. Ibid., 206–207.

24. Mamdouh Haqqi, *Naqd wa Ta'līq* (*Comments and Criticism*), published as part of the 1966 edition of 'Abd al-Raziq, *Al-Islām wa Usūl al-Hukm.*

25. Ibid., 30.

26. Gospel of Matthew 22:21.

27. 'Abd al-Raziq, *Al-Islām wa Usūl al-Hukm* (1966), 30.

28. Ibid., 26.

الدين الإسلامي يختلف إختلافاً بيّناً عن سائر الأديان، إنه نظام من الحكم الفريد، لا يصح أن نقيسه بسائر النظم الموضوعة أو نشبهه بها. فلا هو ملكي مطلق ولا دستوري ولا نيابي ولا شيوعي ولا إشتراكي.... أنه لا شئ من ذلك كله، بل هو نظام خاص: إسمه الإسلام فيجب أن يدرس على هذا الأساس. والذين حاولوا أي يشبهوه بنظام معيّن معروف فقالوا: الديمقراطية في الإسلام، والإشتراكية في الإسلام... وما شاكل ذلك، كلهم مخطئون.

29. Ibid.

والخلافة فيه (الإسلام) لا تشبه الملكية ولا الجمهورية، فالخليفة يمثل الأمة في وجهتين، أنه يمثل الدين والدنيا معاً. واصر على قول يمثل ولا أقول يحكم، لأنه ليس مطلق التصرّف، بل هو محدود ضمن أطار الدستور العام الذي يقوم على ركيزتين هما القرآن والسنة. فأذا أستجدّ على المجتمع الإسلامي مع تطور الزمن والمجتمعات والعلاقات الدولية والإنسانية أمر جديد، رجع الخليفة إلى إجماع المسلمين أو لجأ إلى القياس أو ما شابه ما يعرفه الأصوليون. وليس له أن يستبد بأمر المسلمين، لا في دينهم ولا في دنياهم، لأنه مقيّد بنظام الشورى بالدستور العام، الذي هو القرآن الكريم. قال الله تعالى: والذين استجابوا لربَّهم، وأقاموا الصلاة، وأمرهم شورى بينهم، ومما رزقناهم ينفقون.

30. Ibid.

31. Quran, 42:38.

32. Quran, 3:159.

33. 'Abd al-Raziq, *Al-Islām wa Usūl al-Hukm* (1966), 27.

34. Ibid., 28.

ذلك هو الأساس الديني في أصول الحكم، لا أساس سواه. أما اللإستناد في تفسيره إلى آراء الناس — مهما كان شأنهم — أو إلى بعض الوقائع الشاذة، كاستبداد بعض الخلفاء باسم الدين، فإنّ هذا لا ينفي الحقيقة، وهي أن عملهم لا ينطبق على أصول الدين الصريحة، وأن الدين لا علاقة له بما يفعلون.

35. Ibid., 29.

36. Ibid., 36.

37. Ibid.

38. Hourani, *Arabic Thought in the Liberal Age*, 189.

39. Ibid.

40. Sheikh Muhammad al-Bakhit al-Muti'i, *Haqīqat Al-Islām wa Usūl al-Hukm* (*The Truth about Islam and the Foundations of Rule*) (Cairo: The *Salafiyya* Publication, 1926).

41. Al-Bakhit, *Haqīqat Al-Islām wa Usūl al-Hukm*, preface.

كل ما قاله (عبدالرازق) في هذا الكتاب قضايا سالبة وإنكار محض لما أجمع عليه المسلمون أو نُص عليه صريحاً في الكتاب العزيز أو السنه النبوية، واستند في إنكارها على السفسطة والآراء الظنية والأدلة الشعرية، مع أن تلك المسائل التي أنكرها وأنكر أدلتها مسائل فقهية شرعية لا يجوز الخوض فيها بمجرد العقل، بل لابد من الإستناد فيها إلى النص من الكتاب أو السنه أو الإجماع أو القياس.

42. Ibid, 386–387.

43. Ibid, 295.

والذي يرجع إلى آيات الإحكام التي نزلت في القرآن وما اشتملت عليه من أمر النبي صلّى الله عليه وسلم بالحكم بين الناس بما أنزل الله إليه ومن بيان الأحكام المتعلقة بأمور الدين وأمور الدنيا معاً لا يشك ولا يرتاب في أن شرع الإسلام شرع تبليغي وتطبيقي وتنفيذي.

44. Ibid., 50.

45. Quran, 2:256; 16:125; 88:21–22:

لا إكراه في الدِّين قد تبيَّنَ الرُشد من الغيّ.
أدعُ إلى سبيلِ ربِّك بالحكمة والموعظة الحسنة، وجادلهم بالتي هي أحسن.
فذكِّر إنما أنتَ مُذكِّر، لستَ عَليهم بِمُصَيْطِر،

46. 'Abd al-Raziq, *Al-Islām wa Usūl al-Ḥukm* (1925), 53.

47. Ibid., 94 (Hourani's translation).

أما الديانة الإسلامية فقد وضُع أساسها على طلب الغلبة والشوكة والقوة والعزة ورفض كل قانون يخالف شريعتها وقانونها الإلهي، ونبذ كل سلطة لا يكون القائم بها صاحب الولاية على تنفيذها.

48. Hourani, *Arabic Thought in the Liberal Age*, 191.

49. Al-Bakhit, *Ḥaqīqat Al-Islām wa Usūl al-Ḥukm*, 30.

إن مصدر قوة الخليفة هي الأمة وأنه إنما يستمد سلطانه منها وأن المسلمين هم أول أمة قالت بأن الأمة هي مصدر السلطات كلها قبل أن يقول ذلك غيرها من الأمم وأن الحكومة الإسلامية التي يرأسها الخليفة والإمام العام حكومة ديمقراطية حرّة شورية دستورها كتاب الله وسنة رسول الله صلى الله عليه وسلم الذي لا يأتيه الباطل من بين يديه ولا من خلفه.

50. Hourani, *Arabic Thought in the Liberal Age*, 191–192.

51. Leonard Binder, *Islamic Liberalism: A Critique of Development Ideologies* (Chicago: University of Chicago Press, 1988), 130.

52. Ibid.

53. Ibid.

54. 'Imarah, *Ma'rikat Al-Islām wa Usūl al-Ḥukm*, 152.

55. Ibid.

56. 'Abd al-Raziq quoted in 'Imarah, *Ma'rikat Al-Islām wa Usūl al-Ḥukm*, 153.

57. Ibid.

58. 'Abd al-Raziq, *Al-Islām wa Usūl al-Ḥukm* (1925), 65.

59. Ibid., 67.

60. 'Imarah, *Ma'rikat Al-Islām wa Usūl al-Ḥukm*, 155.

61. Ibid. نوع لا ديني

62. Quran, 50:45.

63. Al-Baidawi quoted in 'Imarah, *Ma'rikat Al-Islām wa Usūl al-Ḥukm*, 156.

64. Ibid., 157.

65. Ibid.

66. Ibid., 160.

67. Mu'tazila (Mutazilite) is the religious movement founded in Basra, Iraq, in the first half of the eighth century by Wasil ibn 'Ata (d. 748), eventually becoming one of the important theological schools of what was considered Islamic "liberal" thinking.

68. ‘Imarah, *Ma‘rikat Al-Islām wa Usūl al-Ḥukm*, 160.
69. Ibid., 161.
70. ‘Abd al-Raziq, *Al-Islām wa Usūl al-Ḥukm* (1925), 22.

من الملاحظ البيّن في تاريخ الحركة العلمية عند المسلمين أن حظ العلوم السياسية فيهم كان بالنسبة لغيرها من العلوم الأخرى أسوأ حظ، وأن وجودها بينهم كان أضعف وجود، فلسنا نعرف لهم مؤلفاً في السياسة ولا مترجماً. ولا نعرف لهم بحثاً في شئ من أنظمة الحكم ولا أصول السياسة، اللهم إلا قليلاً لا يقام له وزن إزاء حركتهم العلمية في غير السياسة من الفنون.

71. See Muhammad al-Khidr Husayn’s book, *NaqD Kitāb Al-Islām wa Usūl al-Ḥukm* (1926), 42–44, where he names some twenty-six books, including books written on politics by early Muslim philosophers such as Abu Nasr al-Farabi and Abu Yusuf al-Kindi.

72. Ibid. Also see the version of Husayn’s book in ‘Imarah, *Ma‘rikat Al-Islām wa Usūl al-Ḥukm*, 254.

لم يكن حظ المسلمين من علم السياسة سيئاً، ولا وجودها بينهم أضعف وجود وعرفنا لهم في السياسة مؤلفات شتى: .... ألّف الكندي في السياسة إثني عشر تأليفاً منها رسالته الكبرى في السياسة ورسالة العامة.... وألّف أبو نصر الفارابي ثمانية مؤلفات في السياسة، منها السياسة المدنية...

73. al-Talbi, *‘Iyāl Allah*, 94.
74. Ibid.

نرى أن الحركات السياسية التي تتحدث عن الإسلام باعتباره ديناً ودولة قد تصدّى لها أناس عديدون في طليعتهم المفكر المصري علي عبدالرازق الذي حاول أن يثور على فكرة الإسلام دين ودولة، معتبراً أنّ الدين دين، والدولة دولة، ولا رابط بينهما، لكنه لم ينجح في ثورته تلك، رغم أنه ترك أتباعاً ينشرون أفكاره إلى يوم الناس هذا، ورغم أن فكره أصبح معمولاً به ضمنياً داخل العالم الأسلامي وبحكم الواقع.

75. Ibid.

8

The Implications of 'Abd al-Raziq's Study for the Debate over Islam and Politics

*T*HE ESSENTIAL ARGUMENT of *Al-Islām wa Usūl al-Ḥukm* remains at the center of a deep divide about the intended role of Islam, that is, whether Islam is fully realized as dīn (religion) alone, or is meant to encompass the role of both dīn and dawlah (religion and state). This work has presented the historical context of the disagreement, as well as the major lines of reasoning, as they developed, and asserts that 'Abd al-Raziq's book remains a groundbreaking and critical branch of thought in the contemporary controversy between the advocates of "secularist" and Islamist governance. In 'Abd al-Raziq's time, the primary challenge of Muslim intellectuals and politicians was to break free from occupying forces and, in the postcolonial period, to throw off models of governance that continued to advance colonial structures of hegemony. Because free exchange of ideas remains limited due to the strictures inherent in many of these regimes, the democratic paradigms that would foster necessary dialogue and experimentation have not been allowed to develop and thrive in an open manner. Advocates for separation of state and religion continue to be tarred with the brush of Westernization, a charge which unfairly attaches a stigma to the argument before it can be fairly engaged and understood. The concept of modernization has become so inextricably linked with the West that the political development of the Muslim world has been essentially hobbled by the association. Instead of being viewed as a process that each culture and tradition must claim and authorize, the process of modernization has been trademarked as particularly Western, corrupt in and of itself, but this understanding operates against the Muslim intellectual tradition, which encourages ongoing engagement with the texts in concert with, not in opposition to, human development, including the realms of social and political growth. To this end, the work of 'Abd al-Raziq offers an invaluable contribution to contemporary liberal discourse, honoring yet breathing fresh life into the intellectual and spiritual legacy of Egyptian scholar and reformer Muhammad 'Abduh.

More than eighty years have elapsed since the publication of *Al-Islām wa Usūl al-Ḥukm* in 1925. This study has examined the impact that the book had in its time and the controversy it ignited. The debate between the different contending parties of secularist and Islamist participants is still fierce today, and the central issue in the debate—whether Islam is only dīn (religion) or both dīn and dawlah (religion and state)—is likely to remain at the forefront of Muslim intellectual life for some time to come. During the days of 'Abd al-Raziq, the first task that faced Muslim, and especially Arab, intellectuals, as well as the political elite under colonial rule, was to bring an end to foreign occupation. Later, in the aftermath of colonialism, they found themselves struggling against another kind of "colonialism" and hegemony, namely, the dictatorships of their own rulers that had been presiding over their destinies since the early days of "independence." Despite the fact that this debate on the nature of the state and the place of Islam in politics began during those days, it has not found a fertile ground in which to develop fully in the post-colonial state, given the lack of freedom of expression in almost every single Arab country. Although most of the regimes in these countries, after "independence," have become secular in one way or another, they have severely lacked democratic settings, institutions, and forums that would have allowed such a debate to transform into an effective tool toward helping these nations to progress and develop favorably in order to improve the lives of their citizens and society, as other nations have. Within the context of examining the implications of 'Abd al-Raziq's work for the current debates over Islam and politics, this concluding chapter also deals with democratization issues in the contemporary Middle East.

In characterizing the essence of the difference between the definition of "politics" in Islamic civilization versus its meaning in Western civilization, some conservative scholars, such as Muhammad 'Imarah,[1] draw a clear line between the two. With regard to the first arguing that while there has never been any dispute in either premodern (classical or medieval) or modern Muslim thought over defining Islam as submission to God (in accordance with what was revealed to the Prophet Muhammad in the way of laws and normative principles), the meaning of politics within Islam is more of a moot topic. Before the encounter between Islamic civilization and Western civilization, which came through the Western colonial invasion of and encroachment on Muslim land, Arab-Islamic definitions of concepts were the only prevalent and popular ones in Arab dictionaries and encyclopedias; there was no disagreement in defining the word politics.[2] To present what he perceives as the

Islamic concept of politics, Muhammad 'Imarah borrows the definition made by Abu al-Baqā in his book *Al-Kulliyyāt* (*The Universals*), in which he defined politics (*siyāsah*) as:

> [the enterprise of] improving human beings by guiding them along the path of salvation in this world and the next . . . [through] deeds which bring people closer to goodness and keep them far from corruption and which [help them] organize [their] living in accordance with the norms of justice and Islamic righteousness.[3]

Such a definition of politics prevailed until the time of the encounter between Islamic civilization and Western civilization. This marked the beginning of the inflow of specific Western definitions of politics into Arab dictionaries. In 'Imarah's analysis, this caused a confusion and double-standard in concept and content that has become a problem facing Muslim intellectuals in whose minds Islamic and Western definitions were often confused.[4] The meaning of politics in the classical vocabulary of Islam does not stop at improving human beings in the current world only, "because the image of the human being is that of the Caliph (of God) who lives in this world as a crossing point to the Hereafter, which is better and everlasting."[5]

On the other hand, 'Imarah explains, politics in Western civilization "is confined to the organization of people's lives in this world only," in which case the human being becomes the master of this world. This exclusively worldly concept led to the secular ideology of separating religion not only from the "state" as an executive authority but also from all its structural, epistemological, social, educational, economic, moral, and philosophical aspects. In such a secular milieu, it becomes quite understandable why politics would be secular as well.[6]

While the semantic difference in defining politics is important to consider, reducing the debate on Islam and politics to merely semantic rhetoric is quite problematic. Secular and Islamist groups, reflecting different currents of religious and political thought, have been struggling in the Arab and Muslim worlds over Islam's place and role in politics. Within the rhetoric of the Islamists, the introduction of modernization to Arab and Muslim lands by colonial powers was meant to supersede and "override Arab-Islamic civilization with the intention to disfigure its national personality, to deform and distort its identity that characterized our *umma* and civilization throughout our long history."[7] 'Imarah argues that an important point to be emphasized here is that the core and essence of this debate has not been over Islam as belief or creed, nor over its morals and pillars; rather, the two contending groups are both comprised of virtuous Muslims and the struggle has been strictly focused on Islam's role in politics. However, one group has been looking only to the civil aspect of Islam (ahkām al-Shari'a) through a historical paradigm, whereas the other group sees Islam fused with politics and government, Islam being for them both a set of beliefs and a Shari'a. Thus, from the second group's perspective, if exiting the belief is an exit from the territory of the religion, then abandoning its Shari'a constitutes denial and ingratitude; it is unbelief and ignorance, a lapse from true Islam caused by weaknesses and shortcomings.[8] But even those in the second category do not agree on every aspect of Islam as politics, for they have their own divisions. One subgroup within the second category adopts a maximalist view of the Shari'a, taking into consideration the full range of texts, Quran and Sunna, in addition to the fiqh literature and the dicta of the great exponents of independent judgment (mujtahidūn), some giving pride of place to the early generations of Muslims (salaf). Another subgroup of the second category confines the Shari'a to the realm of goals, ideals, and objectives, thus treating the Shari'a as a dynamic process. This subgroup does not look at the Quranic verses and the prophetic traditions enshrining the penal code (ḥudūd) and the other legal provisions (ahkām) as comprising the essence of Shari'a or its totality, but rather as divine examples of the legal provisions and their implementation. Thus, the Shari'a is not identified with past manifestations but is more future oriented.

'Imarah draws further distinction, though with some exaggeration, between such groups that can broadly be described as "secularists" and "Islamists." On the one hand, the secularists refuse turāth (heritage) without being knowledgeable about it or even attempting to decipher its roots and what good it can offer for the present and the future of the whole community. Conversely, those who believe in turāth do not care about questions that secularists have and the sources of anxiety they experience in association with the idea of Islamizing life and politics.[9]

Although his claim that secularists refuse turāth altogether reflects some kind of an exaggeration, 'Imarah cautions that observing these contending parties debating insinuates that they appear to be engaged in "the dialogue of the deaf."[10] When the situation reaches such a point, the problem is that these groups are wasting the intellectual energies and faculties of thinking that could be used to help the umma wake up from its long sleep in order to face challenges and to progress as nations have progressed in other parts of the world, east and west.[11]

Briefly put, 'Imarah argues, these are the contending parties over this debate on Islam and politics and the position of religion in society:

> Those who take from Islam only the beliefs, the pillars, and the morals adopt the Western secular approach in looking at the religion of Islam and they have their own logic behind that. On the other side of the spectrum are those who take Islam in its totality, as a whole, and are committed to it completely. They refuse secularism and they call for implementing Islam as a *Shari'a*, a belief. Their disagreements are rooted in "the ground of Islam" and its camp, and within the framework of measures of independent judgment (*ijtihād*). Whereas disagreement between secularists, whether liberals or totalitarian, "is grounded in the West" as they embark from the thought of Western civilization and take their inspiration from its schools of thought.[12]

Arab-Muslim intellectual life has been experiencing this disparity since the beginning of modern colonialism which brought along with it the idea of "Westernization," thus creating this duality of secularists and Islamists. In other words, it has been a struggle between the "westernized" and the "fundamentalists" or Islamists. Each group has been trying to win over the other by repeating the exact same arguments and justifications without exerting real effort in understanding the justifications or arguments of the other group. In order for the dialogue to be effective, it is necessary for these groups to try to understand each other's perspective. Only when this dialogue becomes enlightened will it lead to a civilized plan to wake up the umma. Only then will the contending parties transform their disagreements into helping their nation(s) to progress as a unique umma with a distinguished civilization, using the experiences of such fierce battles against the many challenges it faces.[13]

Whether within the above characterization or in its diverse actuality, as long as there is an intellectual debate and dialogue on state and politics, state and religion, and the position of religion in society, *Al-Islām wa Usūl al-Ḥukm* will continue to occupy a place at the heart of such a dialogue. Although the arguments presented by 'Abd al-Raziq might not represent the most effective mode of argumentation, his book nonetheless constitutes a challenge to the Islamists' advocacy of an Islamic state, which has proven to be a major failure in every modern example, as will be briefly illustrated in this chapter. For the most part, religion has been exploited in an effort to oppress and control others, and to benefit the ruling elite of Islamists. Although 'Abd al-Raziq envisioned what would happen when religion is fused with politics, and when it becomes the tool used by an elite group with a specific agenda to determine the fate of a whole nation or region, his call for separation of religion and state has been bitterly criticized.

↝   *Muhammad 'Abduh Revisited*

MUHAMMAD 'ABDUH did not go as far as 'Abd al-Raziq on the issue of separating religion and state, though he tended to blame the prevailing corrupt conditions of authoritarian governments in Muslim countries on the ignorance of jurists and rulers. He faulted the jurists for not understanding politics and for depending on the rulers, thus failing to hold them (the rulers) accountable for their policies in government.[14] On the other hand, the rulers were responsible for corrupting the jurists and using them to promote their own benefits and agenda by making them produce *fatwas* (religious pronunciations) to vindicate the policies of their corrupt governments.[15] The absence of political unity and justice was, in 'Abduh's opinion, the result of the rulers' negligence, which has led to all of the evils that have befallen the Muslim community. An affinity with 'Abd al-Raziq's thought is clear in 'Abduh's argument that Muslim rulers seek exalted titles of princes, sultans, and the like, live opulently and ostentatiously, and further seek the protection of foreign nations to support them against their own people. Not only that, but they also usurp public funds for personal pleasure and fail to govern with justice.[16] It is to avoid this that 'Abduh repeats and insists that in Islam there is no final authority apart from the authority of God and the Prophet. Thus, he maintains, it is the duty of Muslims in the community to render advice to the ruler based on the Islamic concept of Shūrā or consultation. Therefore, when they call for the end of despotism and tyranny toward the welfare of their society, they are following the teachings of the Shari'a, not emulating foreigners.[17]

The influence of Muhammad 'Abduh's thought on 'Abd al-Raziq is reflected most clearly on the latter's repudiation of the caliphate system. 'Abduh's work insists that there is no final authority in Islam apart from that of God and the Prophet Muhammad. Islam, he maintains, never had a figure such as the pope, in whom both religious and civil offices are combined.[18] This is quite consistent with 'Abduh's view on religious authority; in other words, he has consistently argued that Islam is enjoined to overthrow religious authority because the only true relationship in Islam is the one between the individual and God. Elimination of the power of religious authority sets the human being free from any kind of supervision.[19] In this regard Abduh departs from the general classic interpretation of the word *khalīfa* (caliph), in that while most classical works had emphasized the Quranic verse that refers to man as khalīfat Allah (caliph of God) as a reference to the designation of the Prophet Muhammad and those who succeeded him for such a role, 'Abduh offers an interpretation in which each Muslim individual is responsible and accountable for the building of this civilization.[20] This explains well Abduh's known negative perception of the idea of the caliphate as a cause of corruption that deviated from the ideal Muslim society experienced during the time of the prophet. This is not dissimilar to an argument made by 'Abd al-Raziq discussed in chapter five of this study, when he affirms that "the caliphate was a disaster to Islam and Muslims, a source of evil and corruption that the religion of Islam and our world are rich enough and better off without it."[21] However as Charles C. Adams explains, 'Abduh, with all his emphasis on the spiritual character of religious exercises, defended the union of the civil and religious authority in Islam and favored retention of the essential system of canon law, although with far-reaching reforms.[22] Adams further elucidates:

> If any relation exists between the thought of Shaykh 'Ali and the doctrines of Muhammad 'Abduh, it is to be sought for in a certain spiritual and intellectual affinity, rather than in individual ideas. His historical approach to his subject, though a study of Islamic beginnings, which is not dissimilar in method to that of 'Abduh in the historical introduction to his *Risālat al-Tawhīd*; his conception of Islam as a spiritual religion, although he disassociates it from all political connections, 'Abduh did not do; his admission of the reasonable possibility of a universal religion, which embraces all men in a religious unity apart, however, from political unity; his general tendency to differ in thought and attitude from "those who know religion only as a hard and fast form"; above all the independence of his thought and the breadth of his view; these and other points of resemblance seem to indicate that he has been definitely influenced by 'Abduh and has imbibed much of his spirit.[23]

However, Adams is quick to point out the other side of 'Abd al-Raziq and the areas in which he surpassed the ideas of his mentor, 'Abduh, advocating a more liberal and revolutionary approach. The clear distinction is that while 'Abduh's main effort was "to infuse the Islamic heritage with modern ideas,"[24] 'Abd al-Raziq was a proponent of total separation between religion and politics, epitomized by his call for a "secular" state. Ultimately, this is what sets 'Abd al-Raziq on the opposite side of the spectrum, given the fact that his revolutionary conception of the state stands as a modern antithesis of the classical Sunni theory of the caliphate discussed earlier.

As alluded to earlier, and as Yvonne Haddad has put it, 'Abduh's efforts to infuse the Islamic heritage with modern ideas eventually led to a division among his disciples. Some of his followers, such as Rashid Rida, saw his vision of a revitalized Islam as the only answer for the salvation of the society.[25] Others, like Ali 'Abd al-Raziq, advocated a separation between religion and state as well as encouraging the secularization of society.[26] Neither of the two groups succeeded in their mission, however. As mentioned in previous chapters, Albert Hourani made the same observation when he argued that 'Abduh's thought, with regard to Islam and modern civilization, has been manifest in various degrees in the works of his followers, which developed into a "conservative" versus a "liberal" approach. Ironically, as Albert Hourani explains, although 'Abduh's purpose was to prove that the two—Islam and modern civilization—are compatible, one group of his disciples, represented by Muhammad Rashid Rida, carried his insistence on the unchanging nature and absolute claims of the essential Islam toward a strict Hanbali fundamentalism. Although the other group of 'Abduh's disciples leaned more toward his views on modernity and civilization, it tried to dissolve the relationship 'Abduh created between Islam and modern civilization and replace it with "a de facto division of spheres of influence,"[27] such as with Ali 'Abd al-Raziq, who "has been influenced, to a certain extent, by 'Abduh's ideas, [but] has advanced beyond them in many essential respects."[28]

⮩   *Khalid Muhammad Khalid*

KHALID MUHAMMAD KHALID makes clear his choice of democracy (before he abandoned that position in 1981 as I explained in the first chapter).[29] In his earlier book *al-Dīmuqrātiyyah Abadan*[30] (*Democracy Forever*), he discusses the problem of politics in the Middle East by drawing a distinction between dictatorship, which characterizes most of the regimes in the region, and the democracy that the region lacks. He maintains that a democratic system is based on legislative, juristic, and executive authorities, and that it distributes responsibility between these three powers. Given the fact that the democratic system derives its existence and legitimacy from the people, it is important for the people to participate, through their representatives, in proposing the improvements they desire. Such progress should be discussed in a democratic atmosphere in order to be consistent with the interests of the whole society, which might have conflicting interests sometimes.[31] In such a democratic system, the function of the parliament is not only to legislate, but also to observe and check as well. Thus, a democratic government is careful in executing and implementing laws because it is required by the distribution of responsibilities and the system of checks and balances. Such a democratic system represents the sovereignty and security of the people because the laws are not emanating from the will of an absolute dictator; instead, they reflect the will of the people and the necessary guarantees toward the government. Though a totalitarian regime might be able to implement improvements in the system quickly, it is done at a high expense, whereas a democratic system following the will of the people usually guarantees that the laws are implemented by the choice of the people toward their political progress. Thus is the difference between dictatorship and democracy: the first is a system that seeks quick fixes, the other helps in establishing a renaissance. Renaissance is a progress upward to the better, a progress in the human, political, economic, literary, and intellectual existence of a nation reflecting a continuous process of freedom in all its aspects.[32] In other words, Khalid argues that dictatorship might bring quick improvements but it does not establish a renaissance, which makes the difference between the two quite clear.

Most importantly, Khalid explains, in the absence of democracy and within a totalitarian setting, healthy debates and dialogues are curtailed, thus disrupting any intellectual progress in people's thought and freedom of expression. In the Middle East, both secular regimes—in their colonial and postcolonial representations—and religious totalitarian regimes have been equally oppressive and intolerant of free speech.

What happened to Ali 'Abd al-Raziq in the immediate aftermath of the publication of his book is quite representative of this. As mentioned earlier, al-Azhar Supreme Council not only condemned and denounced 'Abd al-Raziq's book, but also expelled the writer from the circle of 'ulama and terminated his membership in its council. It is interesting to note that even for those conservative scholars, such as Muhammad 'Imarah, who thought 'Abd al-Raziq had the right to express his opinion, the action of al-Azhar was perceived as a partisan and political decision carried out under the pretext of religion. As 'Imarah argued, what was at issue was "the statement included in *al-Azhar* Supreme Council's decision when it stated that 'the religious government' is an inseparable part of the Islamic *Shari'a*,"[33] reflecting severe intolerance of free speech. On the other hand, the reality is that, more than three decades after the declaration of his advocacy of separation of religion and state in Islam, Khalid Muhammad Khalid retracted his commitment to democracy and renounced his belief in political secularism in what Leonard Binder understandably described as "fear and confusion."[34]

~&   *Muhammad al-Talbi*

CONVERSELY, OTHER MUSLIM thinkers, such as Muhammad al-Talbi, have provided a unique analysis that favors the implementation of Western democracy without undermining Islamic tenets. Al-Talbi, however, does caution against taking "democracy" for granted, arguing that although Western democracy has been the most effective political system, it is not one model of democracy but a collection of democracies, some of which might become "the ugliest cover for tyranny and despotism, such as the democracy of the Proletariat."[35] Al-Talbi further maintains that "we then need to take away the holy or divine aura from democracy because it might be a façade, a camouflage for democracy, yet it is by no means the most effective cure for all times."[36] Al-Talbi then delves into discussing the Quranic concept of Shūrā, maintaining:

> The Quran clearly and undisputedly calls for al-tashāwur[37] (consultation) in the umma affairs, thus refusing arrogance and, consequently, tyrannical rule. However, the Quran is not a constitution, because if it were a constitution it would have been outdated and time would have surpassed it as many constitutions and ruling systems have been outdated, and as, no doubt, [other] systems would when time has surpassed them. The Quran, then, provides the freedom for and responsibility of regulating the consultation [system] to the umma in the organizations it chooses.[38]

The Quran, al-Talbi further argues, calls for true Shūrā in conformity, both in form and practice, with the events of time and place; but this should be done without any fanaticism or bigotry. Such a system of Shūrā would provide justice, harmony, and prosperity for every individual. Al-Talbi maintains that "thanks to the maturity of our people in this current stage and on account of our confrontation with all kinds of falsifications and distortions, it will be most desirable if we can realize [our] goal by means of democracy."[39] Another important point al-Talbi draws attention to is that if democracy in its modern sense did not exist in periods of early Islamic history, it was also absent from Western history in which political systems were derived from concepts of monarchy by divine right. Most importantly, history set aside, the essential thing is that neither the Quran nor the Sunna includes anything that contradicts democracy. On the contrary, both the Quran and the Sunna call for and justify democracy, a point that many reformist leaders have been trying to illuminate and confirm in their theoretical attempts.[40] In reference to such reformists, al-Talbi mentions the Moroccan thinker and politician 'Allal al-Fasi (1910–1974) and the Tunisian writer Khair-Eddin al-Tunisi, maintaining that "it is perhaps no coincidence that the first modern constitution throughout the Arab and Islamic world is the Tunisian constitution issued in 1861, during the days of Khair-Eddin."[41]

↦   *Examples of Incompatibility: Sudan and Afghanistan*

THE ISLAMISTS CONTINUED to experience their own internal divisions. In addition to the early divisions noted by 'Imarah, political Islam has manifested in recent years in many radical groups fighting fiercely for changing secular governments in some Muslim countries into regimes with an "Islamic" agenda. The most notable feature of some of these agendas is the incoherence they display as far as their advocacy of a system that rules by each of these group's perception and articulation of the Shari'a.

Recently, with the introduction of such alternative media outlets as satellite channels and the Internet, things have changed dramatically despite the fact that the nature of the regimes in the Middle East has hardly changed. Not only that, but when religion and politics are fused together, as will be seen in extreme cases like the Taliban and the Islamist regime in Sudan, no self-identified "Islamic" system or regime has yet to produce and translate the religion's sacred ideals as a social reality. The examples below from Sudan and Afghanistan reveal that those who claim to rule by an "Islamic state" turn, immediately after assuming power, into a tool for different kinds of oppression in the society.

THE SUDANESE SCENE: HASAN AL-TURABI

The influential voices of various Islamist movements have emerged to renew the call initially made by Hasan al-Banna in 1928—in the wake of 'Abd al-Raziq's book—for an Islamic state. Some of these movements have succeeded in assuming power through military force, such as the case with the former Sudanese National Islamic Front (NIF) led by Hasan al-Turabi[42] and the totalitarian regime they have enforced in the Sudan since June 30, 1989.[43] Currently the NIF is split into two movements: the National Congress (NC) led by the current military leader of Sudan, Umar al-Basir; and the Popular Congress (PC) led by al-Turabi. Al-Turabi is a leading theoretician of Islamism in North Africa and the Middle East as well as the leading ideologist of the former National Islamic Front in the Sudan and the acclaimed power behind the Sudanese Islamist dictatorial regime, led by Umar al-Bashir, which has exercised all forms of oppression against Sudanese citizens. Al-Turabi believes that the difference between Islamic fundamentalist states and Western democracies is that the former are striving to achieve democracy through a unified belief in God and the latter have put their faith in the government of man. Democracy in the West has the effect of splintering societies along religious lines and puts the material concerns of man above the pursuit of God. Islamic fundamentalist states will achieve democracy after a divine unity is attained.[44] However, after almost twenty years in power, the experience of the Islamists in the Sudan has been a total failure. Al-Turabi's "means of pursuing his goals have often violated the selfsame ideals, and the failure of even these radical methods to achieve the stable Islamic state he desires condemns him."[45] His dream of an Islamic state has been obscured by the reality in Sudan. Likewise his hope for an Islamic renaissance has been shattered by Sudan's strife. Al-Turabi's critics have charged that he is "a complex figure of high ideals and low tactics who may have prevented Sudan from developing into a successful secular state and who as yet to realize an Islamic one."[46] 'Abd al-Raziq's ideas still represent a counterargument as well as a challenge to the views of such Islamists as Hasan al-Turabi.

In juxtaposition, it is interesting to mention here Abdelwahab El Affandi, author of *Turabi's Revolution*[47] (1991) and a product of Sudanese Islamism, who argued in his book *Who Needs an Islamic State* that the concept of the Islamic state should be abandoned in favor of a concept of the "state for the Muslims." Such a state, in El Affandi's perspective, should necessarily be "democratic" not authoritarian.[48]

THE AFGHANI SCENE: THE TALIBAN

Along with the Sudanese experience discussed above, the example of the Taliban's[49] Islamist regime in Afghanistan serves as one of the recent manifestations of abusing religion to oppress citizens. Although both regimes can safely be characterized as representing radical and oppressive Islamism, the Taliban displayed severe extremism on many issues, including the deprivation of women's rights. After taking over Kābul in 1996, the Taliban leaders began to institute an uncompromising regime seeking to enforce a "puritanical" way of life based on their Wahhābī-inspired interpretation of Islam.[50] They immediately created the "Ministry for Ordering What Is Right and Forbidding What Is Wrong" to impose and enforce rules of proper conduct. Their leader, Mullah Muhammad 'Umar, led the Taliban as *Amīr al-Mu'minīn* (Commander of the Faithful). He was the supreme leader in a strictly hierarchical system of rule. Members of special Shūrā councils, composed of high-ranking Taliban leaders, advised him on various matters. Ultimately, 'Umar was the only individual who could issue an official edict. Many of the Taliban edicts had little to do with traditional Islam or the teachings of the Quran and were based, at least in part, on ancient tribal Afghani-Pashtun laws and customs. Much of Taliban legislation also reflected disenchantment and estrangement from modern life.[51] The Taliban continually issued new rules, using Radio Kābul and trucks equipped with loudspeakers to announce them. The rules of conduct eventually covered almost every aspect of social behavior, even forbidding things such as clapping.[52] Not only that, but the Taliban banned music and dancing, shut down movie theaters and television stations, destroyed public works of art and statues that depicted living beings, and forbade the consumption of alcoholic beverages. Men were ordered to grow full, untrimmed beards (in accordance with what they believed to be orthodox Islam) and were rounded up and beaten with sticks in an effort to force prayer in the mosques. All these actions are in sharp contrast with the teachings of the Quran reflected in such verses as, "Let there be no compulsion in religion."[53] The Taliban further strongly enforced the traditional custom of *purdah*, the veiling and seclusion of women from men. Women were ordered to cover themselves from head to toe in *burqas* (long, tent-like veils). The most striking action in their claim to rule by Islam is the fact that girls' schools were closed down and women were forbidden to work outside their homes. As a result, hospitals and orphanages lost almost all their staffs, which had been primarily female, and children in orphanages were left without caretakers. In a country where hundreds of thousands of men had been killed in warfare, widows found themselves unable to work to provide basic necessities for their families.[54]

Despite the fact that very few of the actions taken by the Taliban under the pretext of religion are defensibly Islamic, the point of depriving women of education, in particular, deserves some attention. A close look at both the Quran and the Hadith reveals a clear emphasis on encouraging education and the pursuit of knowledge regardless of gender. The very first Quranic verses revealed even appear to invalidate the Taliban's agenda, stating: "Read, in the name of your Lord who created—created *al-Insān* [the human being] from clots of blood. Read, your Lord is most Bountiful one, who by the pen taught *al-Insān* what he/she did not know. Indeed *al-Insān* transgresses in thinking himself his own lord, for to your Lord all things return."[55] Hadith reports also provide indications that the Prophet Muhammad encouraged education among his Muslim umma irrespective of gender. For instance, we read in one such Hadith, among reports that have been classified as sound (*sahīh*), that the prophet is reported to have said: "Seek knowledge from the cradle to the grave"; while in another sound Hadith we read, in reference to the prophet's wife, 'Ā'isha: "Learn half of your religion from that woman." According to this saying, 'Ā'isha not only taught women, but both men and women at such an early point in history as the seventh century.

'Abd al-Raziq's call for separating religion and state becomes indispensably significant as we see factions such as the Taliban abusing religion to further their own authoritarian interpretations of Islam and to sanction and enforce the oppression of women. This paradox poses some legitimate questions, such as why should women renounce their religion in favor of even political secularism if it clearly provides them with such important rights? The answer to this question is empirical, which is the fact that when religion, which carries the weight of centuries of tradition, has been separated from politics and remains a private matter, women have enjoyed considerable rights. On the other hand, as previously noted, when religion and politics are integrated together, it has thus far proven to be to women's detriment. 'Abd al-Raziq's theme, reflected in *Al-Islām wa Usūl al-Hukm*, guards against such abuse by a group of Islamist elites erroneously claiming to be ulū al-amr (those in authority).

↩   *The Egyptian Scene After 'Abd al-Raziq*

THE BATTLE BETWEEN Islamist and secular intellectuals has continued since the first decade of the twentieth century. The history of modern Egyptian culture is interposed by such battles fought between these two forces. In the analysis of Sabry Hafez,[56] in 1925 the traditionalist Islamists won the battle over Ali 'Abd al-Raziq's book, which had called for separating religion from politics, and succeeded in dismissing the author from his position at al-Azhar. Yet, Hafez maintains, in 1926 the Islamists' campaign failed to convict Taha Husayn—the leading Egyptian intellectual of the time—of blasphemy for advocating a Cartesian approach to the study of Arabic culture in his book *Fī al-Shi'r al-Jāhilī* (*On Pre-Islamic Poetry*). Consequently, in 1927, "the Muslim Brothers Association was formed, to press home the counterattack on the modernists."[57] However, the 1930s through to the 1940s witnessed a period of frustration for the traditionalists when they failed to make any gains over the following two decades.[58] Only in 1959 were they able again to secure a significant victory, "when al-Azhar proscribed Naguib Mahfouz's novel, *Awlād Hāratnā*" (*The Children of Our Quarter/Neighborhood*—largely translated as *The Children of Gebalawi*). In later years other plays, including *Al-Hussain: The Revolutionary*, and *Al-Hussain: The Martyr*, both by 'Abd al-Rahman al-Sharqawi, were also banned.[59]

Another noteworthy shift against the Islamists occurred during the regime of Jamal 'Abd al-Nasser (1952–1970) when he launched a major crackdown on the Egyptian Muslim Brothers and their affiliates, forcing many of them into exile.[60] Yet, before modernists could enjoy such a break under Nasser, the defeat of Egypt by Israel in 1967 came as a "gift" for the Islamists, which they used to blame the whole modernist project for this national failure. This marked "the beginning of a determined counter-offensive to re-legitimize discredited forms of religious-political discourse."[61] The argument against books such as Ali 'Abd al-Raziq's *Al-Islām wa Usūl al-Hukm* was thus renewed. Unfortunately, both Arab and Muslim modernists in their different generations and schools—just like their Islamists counterparts—have failed to present a viable theory of the state. Such modernists as 'Abd al-Raziq were perceived as deviating away from an accepted historical view of Islam and its relation to the state; 'Abd al-Raziq's theory was classified as drawn more from non-Muslim ideas on Islam and the caliphate as those articulated by Sir Thomas Arnold, as explained earlier.[62] Thus, the same argument emphasized earlier that was made by Muhammad Rashid Rida in 1925 against 'Abd al-Raziq's book stating that "it was the latest attempt by the enemies of Islam to weaken and divide it from within"[63] found resonance in 1967 with Egypt's defeat by Israel.

The factions involved in these debates have been blaming one another for the failures that have plagued the Middle East, as well as other parts of the Islamic world, for almost a century. And despite the continued debates between these diverse political groups, the situation has hardly changed or improved. Perhaps the urgent question that needs to be addressed is: is there a possibility for the creation of a defensibly Islamic environment in which different groups can debate issues of state and religion, and state and politics, and conduct dialogue openly and democratically toward improving the troubled situation? One of the major forces that has hampered the creation of such an environment is the dictatorial regimes that have been ruling over Arab countries for extended periods of times. This problem is further compounded by the strong support most of these regimes have enjoyed from the West, particularly from the United States of America, a fact that has made getting rid of these regimes almost an impossibility. An important question being discussed by political scientists and Muslim thinkers is the role the United States can play in fostering democracy in the region as opposed to supporting dictatorship to safeguard its own interests.

This lengthy reflection on 'Abd al-Raziq's important work, while aiming at providing a new perspective on a work that has been at the center of debate for a considerable period of time, has gone beyond that and moved toward scrutinizing the condition of Islam in general and the state of Islam's complex representations, cultural discourses, and historical developments as these bear upon the age-old issue of the relationship of Islam and the state. The fact that 'Abd al-Raziq's book continues to be debated is proof of its continuing relevance today. Throughout, different epochs have produced different models and intellectual discourses about these issues. The intervention of the West created new conditions, putting the question of Islam's relationship to modernity at the forefront of intellectual life. Increasingly, it becomes clear that an atmosphere of openness and tolerance is requisite for this debate to take place freely and openly. Ultimately, as long as 'Abd al-Raziq's argument challenges existing ideas, his book will remain an important and pivotal factor in contemporary Muslim discourses.

NOTES

1. I use Muhammad 'Imarah as an example of these views.
2. 'Imarah, *Al-Islam wal Siyāsah*, 9.
3. Abu al-Baqā quoted in 'Imarah, *Al-Islam wal Siyāsah*, 13.

استصلاح الخلق بإرشادهم إلى الطريق المنجي في العاجل والآجل... والأفعال التي يكون فيها الناس معها أقرب إلى الصلاح وأبعد عن الفساد . وتدبير المعاش على سنن العدل والاستقامة الإسلامية.

4. 'Imarah, *Al-Islam wal Siyāsah*, 13.
5. Ibid., 13–14.
6. Ibid., 14.
7. 'Imarah, *Ma'rikat Al-Islām wa Usūl al-Ḥukm*, 5.
8 Ibid., 6.
9. Ibid., 7.

10. Ibid.

11. Ibid., 7–8.

12. Ibid., 6–7.

فالذين يأخذون من الإسلام، فقط، العقائد والشعائر والعبادات والأخلاقيات يتبنون الموقف العلماني الغربي في النظر إلى الدين الإسلامي ولهم في ذلك منطق، ولديهم من الدعوة إلى إسلامية الدولة والمجتمع قلق يسوقون الحجج على أنه مشروع. والذين يأخذون الإسلام جميعًا، ويلتزمون به كاملًا، يرفضون العلمانية ويدعون إلى تحكيم الإسلام في الشريعة تحكيمه في العقيدة. أما خلافاتهم فإنها قائمة على أرض الإسلام وفي معسكره، وفي إطار الإجتهاد المحتكم إليه والمحكوم بمعاييره، كما أن خلاف العلمانيين — الليبراليين والشموليين قائم على أرض التغريب. ينطلقون من فكرية الحضارة الغربية، ويستلهمون مذاهبها.

13. Ibid., 8.

14. Muhammad 'Abduh, *Al-A'māl al-Kāmila*, ed. Muhammad 'Imarah (Beirut: al-Mu'ssassa al-'Arabiyya li al-Dirāsāt wa-al-Nashr, 1972), 3:530–531 (Haddad's translation, 53).

15. Ibid.

16. Muhammad 'Abduh, *Al-Muslimūn wa al-Islam*, ed. Tahir Tanahi (Cairo: Dār al-Islam, 1963), 36–45 (Haddad translation, 53).

17. 'Abduh, *Al-A'māl al-Kāmila* 1:354 (Haddad translation, 54).

18. 'Abduh, *Al-A'māl al-Kāmila* 3:185–186, 288 (Haddad translation, 53).

19. Ibid., 284 (Haddad, 41).

20. 'Abduh, *Al-A'māl al-Kāmila* 4:135 (Haddad, 46).

21. 'Abd al-Raziq, *Al-Islām wa Usūl al-Hukm* (1925), 36.

22. Adams, *Islam and Modernism in Egypt*, 267.

23. Ibid., 267–268.

24. Haddad, "Muhammad 'Abduh," 59.

25. Ibid.

26. Ibid.

27. Hourani, *Arabic Thought in the Liberal Age*, 169.

28. Adams, *Islam and Modernism in Egypt*, 259.

29. As mentioned in Chapter 1, although Khalid reverted to the conventional Islamist terminology in 1981, he continued to advocate tajdīd (renewal) and still believed that Shūrā (consultation) is mandatory in Islam and is exactly equivalent to the concept of "democracy" in its current usage, as Nazih Ayoub noted.

30. Khalid Muhammad Khalid, *Dīmuqrātiyyah Abadan* (*Democracy Forever*) (Beirut: Dar al-Kitab al-'Arabi, 1944), 54.

31. Ibid., 55.

32. Ibid., 56.

33. 'Imarah, *Ma'rikat Al-Islām wa-Usūl al-Hukm*, 8.

34. Binder, *Islamic Liberalism*, 158.

35. al-Talbi, *'Iyāl Allah*, 91.

36. Ibid., 92.

37. *Tashāwur* is another Arabic Quranic noun, such as Shūrā, meaning consultation.

38. al-Talbi, *'Iyāl Allah*, 91.

القرآن يدعو بصفة واضحة وبدون منازع إلى التشاوُر في شؤون الأمة، فهو إذن يرفض الاستبداد
بالرأي وبالتالي الحكم المستبد، لكن القرآن ليس بدستور، ولو كان دستورا ليلي وتجاوزه الزمن
كما بليت دساتير ونظم حكم عديدة، وكما ستبلى لا محالة نظم عندما يتجاوزها الزمن بدورها.
فالقرآن يترك، إذن، للأمة حرية ومسؤولية تنظيم التشاور في المؤسسات التي تختارها.... القرآن
يدعو إلى الشورى الصادقة التي تتكيّف في شكلها بما يتفق مع إحداثيات الزمان والمكان في دون
تشنّج وتصلب، وتوفّر العدل والإنسجام والإزدهار لكل إنسان. فإن كنّا اليوم، بحكم نضج شعوبنا
في مرحلتنا هذه، وبفضل التصدّي إلى كل أنواع التزييف والمغالطة، نستطيع أن نحقق الهدف عن
طريق الديمقراطية، فياحبذا.

39. Ibid., 90.

40. Ibid.

41. Ibid.

42. Hasan Abdullah Dafa'allah al-Turabi was born in 1932 into a religiously conservative Islamic family in eastern Sudan. He received strong Islamic schooling, earned a Master's degree in Law from the University of London and later a Ph.D. from the Sorbonne in France. He joined the faculty of Khartoum University as professor of law and later dean of the College of Law. He became a leader in the Sudanese Muslim Brotherhood movement, a group pressuring the government to adopt an Islamic constitution and implement Shari'a laws. After spending time as a political prisoner after a coup in 1969, he reorganized the Brotherhood as a political party and reconciled with the dictator, Numeiri. In 1983 Numeiri adopted Shari'ah laws for political—not ideological—motives; this adoption was bitterly opposed by insurgent forces in the south and by Sudan's Western allies. Numeiri was overthrown while visiting the United States and free, multiparty elections were held. The Brotherhood, now a broader-based Islamist party called the National Islamic Front, was the third-largest party in parliament. This government was under pressure from the rebels, Western nations, and its own army, and was not able to resolve the critical problems Sudan was facing. As the leader of an important party since the mid–1970s, al-Turabi was appointed to a variety of high government positions though he failed to be elected to a parliament seat. See Abd al-Salam Sidahmed, *Politics and Islam in Contemporary Sudan* (New York: St. Martin's Press, 1996), 105.

43. For recent political developments in Sudan, see Abdullahi A. Gallab, *The First Islamist Republic: Development and Disintegration of Islamism in the Sudan* (Aldershot, Hampshire: Ashgate, 2008).

44. Ahmad S. Moussalli, "Hasan al-Turabi's Islamist discourse on democracy and shura," High Beam Research, http://www.highbeam.com/library/doco.asp?docid=1G1 :15031995&refid=ink_d5&skeyword=&teaser= (accessed January 2009).

45. Gregory Sanders, "Dr. Hasan al-Turabi: His Political Philosophy in Context of Religion and Progress," http://titan.zort.net/~gsanders/text/alturabi.html (accessed January 2009).

46. Ibid.

47. For more on al-Turabi, see Abdelwahab El-Affendi's *Al-Turabi's Revolution: Islam and Power in Sudan* (London: Grey Seal Books, 1991).

48. Abdelwahab El Affendi, *Who Needs an Islamic State?* (London: Malaysia Think

Tank [MTT], 2008; first edition published in 1991). Available on the Internet at http://www.iseas.edu.sg/iframes/16apro8.htm, accessed January 2009.

49. This refers to the Taliban radical Islamist movement in Afghanistan that controlled most of the country from September 1996 to November 2001. The Taliban movement was created in 1994 by a warlord, Muhammad 'Umar (a.k.a. Mullah 'Umar), in the southern Afghanistan city of Kandahar. The name Taliban, meaning "student," refers to the movement's origins in Islamic religious schools, or madrasas, although most members knew war all their lives and attended the madrasas only for rudimentary religious training. During the 1980s, Afghanistan was occupied by the Union of Soviet Socialist Republics (USSR) and ruled by a Soviet-backed government. The Taliban movement emerged out of the chaos and uncertainty of the Afghan-Soviet War (1979–1989) and subsequent civil war in Afghanistan. Afghanistan's long war with the USSR was largely fought by *mujahidīn* (Islamic guerrilla) factions with assistance from the United States; Pakistan also provided places of refuge, military training, and other support. After the Soviets completed their withdrawal in 1989, civil war broke out between the mujahidīn factions and the central government. Afghanistan's central government had long been dominated by the country's majority ethnic group, the Pashtuns, but after the Soviet withdrawal a coalition government that included Tajiks, Uzbeks, Hazaras, and other minority groups came to power. The Taliban emerged as a faction of mujahidīn soldiers who identified themselves as madrasa students. The Taliban consisted mostly of Pashtuns intent on once again dominating the central government in Kābul. (from "Taliban," Encarta Encyclopedia 2004: http://encarta.msn.com). For a detailed study on the Taliban, see Ahmed Rashid, *Taliban* (New Haven: Yale University Press, 2001).

50. Encarta Encyclopedia 2004: http://encarta.msn.com
51. Ibid.
52. Ibid.
53. Quran, 2:256.
54. Ibid.
55. Quran, 96:1–8.

إقرأ باسم ربّك الذي خلق. خلق الإنسان من علق. إقرأ وربّك الأكرم. الذي علّم بالقلم. علّم الإنسان ما لم يعلم. كلا إن الإنسان ليطغى. أن رآه إستغنى. إن إلى ربّك الرجعى.

56. Sabry Hafez, "The Novel, Politics and Islam: Haydar Haydar's *Banques for Seaweed*," *New Left Review*, vol. 5 (September 2000): 117–141.
57. Ibid.
58. Ibid.
59. Ibid.
60. Ibid.
61. Ibid.
62. In reference to Sir Thomas W. Arnold's book *The Caliphate*, which 'Abd al-Raziq mentioned on page 15 of the original edition of *Al-Islām wa Usūl al-Ḥukm* (1925).
63. Hourani, *Arabic Thought in the Liberal Age*, 240–241.

GLOSSARY

aḥkām: Rules or ordinances.

aḥkām al-Sharīʿa: provisions of Sharīʿa.

al-Afdal/al-afDal: the best.

ʿAlid Imamah/Imāmah: The Imamate or leadership of Ali's descendents in Shiʿa Islam.

ʿālim: a scholar; the singular form of ʿulamā.

ahl al-shawka: the people of power and influence.

ahl al-ahwa: the people of desires and indulgence.

ahl al-ḥal waʾlʿaqd: the people of consultation who can enter into a contract or dissolve it.

al-amr bil maʿrūf wa-al-nahi ʿan al-munkar: commanding what is right and forbidding what is wrong.

al-Ḥākimiyya li Allah: sovereignty belongs to God, a concept invoked by many Islamists, such as Sayyid Qutb and Abu al-Aʿla al-Mawdudi.

al-taqwah: piety; fear or consciousness of God.

al-Wahy: God's revelation.

al-wuqūʿ fī hamʾat al-iḥlād: falling into atheism.

arkān al-ḥukūmah: ordinances of government.

asāla: rootedness.

ʿasabiyya: solidarity based on blood ties. Plural: ʿasabiyāt.

asās al-ḥukm: the basis of government.

ʿatāyā: donations.

al-Azhar: the most prestigious educational center and Sunni Islam foremost seat of learning, located in Cairo, Egypt.

Bayʿah: oath of allegiance.

Bayt al-Māl: the state treasury.

bid'ah: innovation.

dalālah: error/blasphemy.

dastūr: constitution.

dawlah: state; temporal power.

dīn: religion or way; Islam.

dunyā: the physical world; material existence.

farD: obligatory, mandatory.

farD kifāya: a communal obligation that can be carried out by some members of the Muslim community on behalf of the rest.

fatwa: legal ruling or opinion.

fay: taxes.

fiqh: Islamic jurisprudence.

fitna (plural, fitan): discord; a period of trial or calamity for the Muslim community.

fitra: natural disposition.

hadātha: modernity.

Hadith: a collection of volumes of the Prophet's tradition; a report or narrative of something the Prophet said or did.

Hanafi: one of the four Sunni schools of Islamic jurisprudence; attributed to Abu Hanifah of Kufa (d. 767 C.E.). Considered least conservative among the four.

Hanbali: The most conservative of the four Sunni schools of Islamic law; attributed to Ahmed ibn Hanbal (d. 855 C.E.).

harām: forbidden.

hudūd: limits; the punishments stipulated in the Quran for certain crimes.

hujja: clear-cut evidence; proof.

hukumāt al-amr al-waqi': governments of reality.

hukm shar'ī: rule by Islamic law.

Hurūb al-riddah: the Wars of Apostasy during the Caliphate of Abu Bakr.

Ijmā': consensus of 'ulama, especially in matters of law.

ijtihād: independent inquiry or reasoning, especially in jurisprudence; exertion.

i'lām (from 'ilm): informing.

imān/emān: faith or belief.

imam: top leader in the hierarchy of the Shi'a clergy system; also, leader of a prayer congregation in both Sunni and Shi'ī Islam. The word Imam is also used by some scholars interchangeably as Caliph.

imāmah: leadership; the male descendents of Ali and Fatima in Shi'a Islam. Also used sometimes to denote "caliphate."

imārah: emirate.

insijām: compatibility or harmony.

irshād: guidance.

irtidād: apostasy (renouncing Islam).

I'tiqād: belief.

jāhiliyya: ignorance; the age of pre-Islamic paganism.

jihād: struggle, striving, exertion; a just war or in self-defense. Largely misinterpreted as "war against non-Muslims."

jizia: the poll tax paid by non-Muslims under classical Muslim rule.

kara'im amwālihim: their precious possessions.

khalīfa: caliph.

khilāfah: caliphate.

khilāfatist: an advocate of the caliphate.

kufr: unbelief, ungrateful, rejection of God's religion.

li-khilāfat al-nubuwwa: vicegerent of the prophet.

Maliki: one of the four Sunni schools of Islamic law; attributed to Malik ibn Anas (d. 795 C.E.); dominant in North Africa and Muslim Spain.

maḥārim: sacred prohibitions.

Manarist: a follower of Rashid Rida's Manar School.

maqāsid wa usūl: goals and principles or roots.

muballigh: conveyor, transmitter, missionary.

mubāya'a: contract, act of allegiance.

mughālata: fallacious argument.

mujtahid: one engaged in ijtihād; a scholar who formulates Islamic law.

mujtahidūn: plural form of mujtahid.

mulk: monarchy.

murtaddīn/murtaddūn: apostates.

nikāḥ: marriage.

nubwwa: prophethood.

nukūs: withdrawal, retreat.

quwwah qudusiyyah: holy power.

Qiyās: reasoning by way of analogy, especially in Islamic law.

'aqlī: reason-based.

Quran: considered by Muslims to be the Word of Allah (God) revealed to the Prophet Muhammad in Arabic between 610 and 632 C.E.

ra'yy: personal opinion or reasoning, especially in law.

risālah: message.

Saḥāba: the prophet's companions.

saḥīḥ: sound/authentic or correct; the canonical Hadith collections of Bukhari and Muslim.

salaf: the early generations of Muslims.

salaf al-umma: the early Muslim community.

Salafī: conservative Sunni reformists that advocate returning to the Quran, Hadith, and the example of the earliest community.

Saqīfa: The day when the Ansar (supporters of the prophet) and the Muhajirīn (those who migrated with him from Mecca to Medina) met to elect a leader in the aftermath of the prophet's death.

Shafi'ī: one of the four Sunni schools of Islamic law; attributed to Muhammad ibn Idris al-Shafi'i (d. 820 C.E.).

Shahādah: the testimony of faith; the first pillar of Islam, that there is no God but God and that Muhammad is the messenger of God.

sharʿ: provision of Shari'a.

sharʿī: Shari'a law-based.

Shari'a: "the path"; divine law; system of law and life based on the Quran and Sunna of the prophet.

sharʿī tablīghī wa tatbīqī: sharʿī (law-based), tablīghī (message-based), and tatbīqī (practice-based).

shubhah: ambiguity.

Shūrā: consultation.

sultan: power, authority; a Muslim ruler.

Sunna: the exemplary behavior of the prophet.

taʿassobāt: social cohesions based on blood ties or tribalism.

taʿassub: fanaticism.

ta'dīb: discipline, correction.

tafsīr: interpretation and commentary on the meaning of the Quran.

tajdīd: reform or renewal.

tandhimāt al-dawlah: government systems.

Tanzimat: Turkish for Reorganization.

tashannuj: rage/spasm (in discussion).

turāth: heritage.

'ulamā (ulama, 'Ulamā): scholars with expertise in Islamic law sciences (Quran and Hadith, especially Islamic Law).

ulū al-amr: those in authority.

umma: nation; the worldwide Muslim community; a group/family/community of Muslim nations; community of believers.

usūl: foundations, roots.

usūl al-fiqh: the science or roots of Islamic jurisprudence; namely the Quran, the Sunna, Ijmāʾ, and Qiyās.

wafd: delegation.

wājib: obligation or duty.

wakīl: agent.

walī al-amr: guardian; also, a person in authority (singular of ulū al-amr).

wujūb al-Imāmah: obligations of leadership.

wujūb al-khilāfah: obligations of the caliphate.

yaḥkum: to govern or rule.

yumaththil: represents.

zaʿāmah: leadership.

zaʿāmah mulūkiyyah: monarchical leadership.

SELECT BIBLIOGRAPHY

'Abd al-Mawla, Mahmoud. *Tanzhimāt al-Mujtama' wa al-Dawlah fī al-Islam (Organization of Society and State in Islam)*. Tunis: Al-Sharkia al-Tūnisiyyah lil Tawzī', 1973.

'Abd al-Raziq, Ali. *Al-Islām wa Usūl al-Ḥukm: Baḥth fī al-Khilāfah wa-al-Ḥukūmah fī al-Islām (Islam and the Foundations of Rule: Research on the Caliphate and Government in Islam)*. First Edition. Cairo: Matba'at Misr, 1925.

———. *Al-Islām wa Usūl al-Ḥukm: Baḥth fī al-Khilāfah wa-al-Ḥukūmah fī al-Islām*. Includes comments and criticism by Mamdouh Haqqi. Beirut: Dār Maktabat al-Hayāt, 1966.

———. *Al-Islām wa Usūl al-Ḥukm: Baḥth fī al-Khilāfah wa-al-Ḥukūmah fī al-Islām*. Sousa, Tunis: Al-Marif House for Print and Publications, 2001.

'Abdel Kader, Soha. *Egyptian Women in a Changing Society: 1899–1987*. Boulder, Colo.: Lynne Reinner Publishers, 1987.

'Abduh, Muhammad. *Al-A'māl al-Kāmila (The Complete Works)*. Ed. Muhammad 'Imarah. Beirut: al-Mu'ssassa al-'Arabiya li al-Dirāsāt wa-al-Nashr, 1972.

———. *"Al-Tasawwuf wal Sūfiyyah" (To Be a Sufi and Sufism)*. In *Al-A'māl al-Kāmila*. Vol. 3. Ed. Muhammad 'Imarah. Beirut: al-Mu'ssassa al-'Arabiya li al-Dirāsāt wa-al-Nashr, 1972.

———. *Risālat al-Tawhīd (The Theology of Unity)*. Ed. Muhammad Muhy al-Dīn 'Abd al-Hamdi. Cairo: Matba'at Muhammad Sabih and Sons, 1966.

———. *The Theology of Unity*. Trans. Ishaq Musa 'ad and Kenneth Cragg. London: Allen and Unwin, 1966.

———. *Al-Muslimūn wa al-Islam (Muslims and Islam)*. Ed. Tahir Tanahi. Cairo: Dār al-Islam, 1963.

'Aboud, 'Abd al-Ghani. *Al-Dawlah al-Islāmiyyah wa-al-Dawlah al-Mu'āsirah (The Islamic State and the Contemporary State)*. 1st edition. Cairo: Dār al-Fikr al-'Arabī, 1981.

Abu Zayd, Nasr Hamid. "Enlightenment in Islamic Thought." Online version, 2004. http://www.kath.de/akademie/rahner/vortag/enlight.html, 1–10.

Adams, Charles C. *Islam and Modernism in Egypt: A Study of the Modern Reform Movement Inaugurated by Muhammad 'Abduh*. New York: Russell and Russell, 1968.

Affendi, Abdelwahab El. *Al-Turabi's Revolution: Islam and Power in Sudan*. London: Grey Seal Books, 1991.

———. *Who Needs an Islamic State?* London: Malaysia Think Tank (MTT), 2008.

Afghani, Jamal al-Din al-. *Al-A'māl al-Kāmilah li Jamal al-Din al-Afghani (The Complete Works of Jamal al-Din al-Afghani)*. Ed. Muhammad 'Imarah. Cairo: Egyptian Public Association for Publication, 1966.

Amin, Ahmed. *Duhā al-Islam (The Forenoon of Islam)*. Cairo: n.p., 1936.

'Aqqad, 'Abbas Mahmoud al-. *Muhammad 'Abduh*. Cairo: Dār al-Kitāb al-'Arabī, 1969.

Arnold, Sir Thomas W. *The Caliphate*. Oxford: Clarendon Press, 1924. Reissued with an additional chapter, New York: Barnes and Noble, 1966.

'Awwa, Muhammad Salim al-. *Fī al-Nizhām al-Siyāsī li al-Dawla al-Islamiyya (On the Political System of the Islamic State)*. 6th edition. Cairo: al-Maktab -Misri al-Hadith, 1983.

Ayalon, Ami. "Egypt's Quest for Cultural Orientation." The Moshe Dayan Center for Middle Eastern and African Studies, Tel Aviv University. Online version, 2004. http://www.dayan.org/D&A-Egypt-ami.htm, 1–34.

Ayoub, Nazih. *Political Islam: Religion and Politics in the Arab World*. London: Routledge, 1991.

Balādī, Sādiq al-. "75 'Āman 'Alā Sudūr *Al-Islām wa Usūl al-Hukm*," ("75 Years After the Publication of *Islam and the Foundations of Rule*"). http://www.althakaf aaljadeda.com/296/sadik.htm. Accessed 2007.

Balawi, Mutlaq al-. *Al-'Uthmāniyyūn fī Shamāl al-Jazīra al-'Arabiyya: 1908–1923 (The Ottomans North of the Arabian Peninsula: 1908–1923)*. Beirut: Arab Encyclopedia House, 2007.

Banna, Hasan al-. *Five Tracts of Hasan al-Banna*. Trans. Charles Wendell. Berkeley: University of California Press, 1975.

———. *Majmū'at Rasā'il al-Imām al-Shahīd Hasan al-Banna (Collected Tracts of the Martyred Imām Hasan al-Banna)*. Beirut: Dār al-Andalus, 1965.

———. *Memoirs of Hasan al-Banna Shaheed*. Karachi: International Islamic Publishers, 1981.

Baqillani, Abu Bakr al-. *Al-Tamhīd*. Ed. Mahmoud Muhammad al-Khudayri and Muhammad 'Abd al-Hadi Abu Rida. Cairo, 1947.

Bates, Daniel, and Amal Rassam. *Peoples and Cultures of the Middle East*. Englewood Cliffs, N.J.: Prentice-Hall, 1983.

Bellah, Robert N. *Beyond Belief: Essays on Religion in a Post-Traditional World*. Berkeley: University of California Press, 1991.

Berque, Jacque. *Egypt: Imperialism and Revolution*. Trans. Jean Stewart. London: Faber and Faber, 1972.

Binder, Leonard. *Islamic Liberalism: A Critique of Development Ideologies*. Chicago: University of Chicago Press, 1988.

Black, Antony. *The History of Islamic Political Thought: From the Prophet to the Present*. Edinburgh: Edinburgh University Press, 2001.

Cleveland, William L. *The Making of an Arab Nationalist: Ottomanism and Arabism in the Life and Thought of Sati al-Husri.* Princeton: Princeton University Press, 1971.

Cooper, John, Mohamed Mahmoud, and Ronald Nettler, eds. *Islam and Modernity: Muslim Intellectuals Respond.* London: I. B. Tauris Publishers, 1998.

Cragg, Kenneth. "Muslim Encounters with the West." *The Encyclopedia of Politics and Religion.* Ed. Robert Wuthnow. 2 vols. Washington, D.C.: Congressional Quarterly, 1998.

Deeb, Nashawi al-. "Muhakamat Sheikh Azharī Asbaha Wazīran lil-Awqāf," (A Trial of an Azharite Scholar Who Became a Minister of Endowment), *al-'Arabī* 11, no. 884 (November 9, 2003).

Farhad, Kazemi. "Perspectives on Islam and Civil Society." In *Islamic Political Ethics: Civil Society, Pluralism, and Conflict,* 38–55. Ed. Sohail H. Hashmi. Princeton: Princeton University Press, 2002.

Fouad, 'Abd al-Fattah Ahmed. *Ibn Taymiyya and His Position from Islamic Philosophical Thought.* Alexandria: Egypt Book Public Corporation, 1980.

Gallab, Abdullahi A. *The First Islamist Republic: Development and Disintegration of Islamism in the Sudan.* Aldershot, Hamshire: Ashgate, 2008.

Gellner, Ernest. *Nations and Nationalism.* Oxford: Blackwell, 1983.

Ghannam, Suleiman al-. *Political, Regional, and International Environment in the Arabian Peninsula during the Emergence of King Abdul Aziz to Establish the Modern Saudi State.* Riaydh: Maktabat al-Ebaikan, 1999. Published in Arabic; given the long title, I have only included the English translation.

Ghazali, Abu-Hamid al-. *Al-Iqtisād fī al-I'tiqād (The Golden Mean in Belief).* Includes commentary by Insaf Ramadan. Damascus: Qutayba Printing, Publishing and Distribution Press, 2003.

Gibb, Hamilton A. R. *Studies on the Civilization of Islam.* Ed. Stanford J. Shaw and William R. Polk. Boston: Beacon Press, 1962.

Haddad, Yvonne. *Contemporary Islam and the Challenge of History.* Albany, N.Y.: SUNY Press, 1982.

———. "Muhammad Abduh: Pioneer of Islamic Reform." In *Pioneers of Islamic Revival,* 30–63. Ed. Rahema Ali. London: Zed Books, 1994.

Hafez, Sabry. "The Novel, Politics and Islam: Haydar Haydar's *Banques for Seaweed.*" *New Left Review* 5 (September 2000):117–141.

Hamza, Fuad. *Qalb al-Jazīra al-'Arabiyya (The Heart of the Arabian Peninsula).* 2nd ed. Riyadh: al-Nasr Modern Library, 1968.

Haqqi, Mamdouh. *Naqd wa Ta'līq (Comments and Criticism),* in 'Abd al-Raziq, *Al-Islām wa Usūl alHukm,* 1966.

Haykal, Hasanayn. *Mudhakkirāt fī al-Siyāsah al-Misrīyyah.* Cairo, 1951.

Haykal, Muhammad Husayn. *Waladī (My Son).* Cairo: n.p., 1931.

Hijazi, Yasir. "*Al-Islām wa Usūl al-Hukm*: Ma'rkiat al-Dīn wa-al-Siyāsa," (*Islam and the Foundations of Rule*: The Battle of Religion and Politics) http://www.the newlibya.com/october25/Asalaamhkm.htm accessed 2007.

Holy Bible: King James Version. Michigan: Zondervan Publishing House [n.d.].

Holy Quran: English Translation of the Meanings and Commentary. Medina: King Fahd Holy Quran Printing Complex, 1990.

Hourani, Albert. *Arabic Thought in the Liberal Age, 1798–1939.* Oxford: Oxford University Press, 1962.

Husayn, Sheikh Muhammad al-Khidr. *NaqD Kitāb Al-Islām wa-Usūl al-Ḥukm.* In ʿImārah, *Maʿrikat Al-Islām wa-Usūl al-Ḥukm,* 1989.

Husayn, Taha. *Mustaqbal al-Thaqāfah fī Misr (The Future of Culture in Egypt).* Trans. S. Glazer. Washington, D.C.: American Council on Learned Societies, 1954.

Huwaidi, Fahmi. *Al-Islam wa-al-Dīmuqrātiyyah (Islam and Democracy).* Cairo: Markaz al-Ahrām lil-Tarjamah wa-al-Nashr, 1993.

Ibn Jamaʿa. *Taḥrīr al-Aḥkām fī Tadbīr Ahl al-Islam (Summary of the Rules for the Governance of the People of Islam).* Ed. Khair Eddin al-Tunisi. Beirut: Dar al-Kutub al-ʿIlmiyya, 2003.

Ibn Khaldun. *The Muqaddimah: An Introduction to History.* Trans. Franz Rosenthal. Ed. and abridged by N. J. Dawood. Princeton: Princeton University Press, 1989.

Ibn Tamiyya. *Al-Siyāsa al-Sharʿiyya.* Online original Arabic Text. http://arabic.is lamicweb.com/Books/Taimiya.asp?book=8 (accessed July 2007).

Ibrahim, Zakeria. *Ibn Hazm al-Andalusī.* Cairo: Egypt Publication House, 1966.

ʿImarah, Muhammad. *Al-Islam wa-al-Siyāsah: Al-Radd ʿalā Shubuhāt al-ʿIlmāniyyīn (Islam and Politics: Responding to the False Arguments of Secularists).* Cairo: Dār al-Tawzīʿ wa-al-Nashr al-Islāmiyyah, 1993.

———. *Al-Islam wal Sulta al-Dīniyyah (Islam and Religious Authority).* Cairo: Dar al-Thaqāfa al-Jadīda, 1979.

———. *Al-Islām wa Usūl al-Ḥukm: Dirāsa wa-Wathāʾiq (Islam and the Foundations of Rule: A Study and Documentations).* Beirut: Arabic Association of Printing and Publishing, 1972.

———. *Al-Saḥwah al-Islāmiyyah wa-al-Taḥaddi al-Ḥadārī (Islamic Revival and Civilizational Challenge).* Cairo: Dār al-Mustaqbal al-ʿArabī, 1985.

———. *Maʿrikat Al-Islām wa-Usūl al-Ḥukm (The Battle of Islam and the Foundations of Rule).* Cairo: Dār al-Shurūq, 1989.

Ismaʿil, Sayf al-Dīn ʿAbd al-Fattāh. *Al-Tajdīd al-Siyāsī wa-al-Wāqiʿ al-ʿArabī al-Muʿāsir: Ruʾyah Islāmīyyah (Political Renewal and Contemporary Arab Reality: An Islamic Vision).* Cairo: Maktabat al-Nahda al-Misriyyah, 1989.

Kaylani, Shams-Eddin al-. *Al-Imam Muhammad ʿAbduh: 1849–1905.* Damascus: al-Ahālī Lil-Nashr wa-al-Tawzīʿ. First Edition, 2001.

Kamguian, Azam, and Mona Basaruddin, eds. Bulletin of "Committee to Defend Women's Rights in the Middle East" 15 (August 2003). *Institute for the Secularization of Islamic Society.* http://www.isisforum.com/women/bulletin15. htm#Iran

Katib, Ahmed al-. "Ibn Tamiyya Supports the Theory of Tyranny and Oppression." http://www.iraqcenter.net/vb/archive/index.php/t-3276.html. Accessed 2007.

Kelsay, John. "Civil Society and Government in Islam." In *Islamic Political Ethics: Civil Society, Pluralism, and Conflict*, 3–37. Ed. Sohail H. Hashmi. Princeton: Princeton University Press, 2002.

Kerr, Malcolm H. *Islamic Reform: The Traditional and Legal Theories of Muhammad 'Abduh and Rashid Rida*. Berkeley: University of California Press, 1966.

Khalid, Khalid Muhammad. *Al-Dīmuqrātiyyah Abadan* (*Democracy Forever*). Beirut: Dār al-Kitāb al-'Arabī, 1974.

———. *Min Hunā Nabda'* (*From Here We Start*). Cairo, 1950.

Khan, Qamar-ud-din. *Al-Mawardi's Theory of the State*. Lahore, Bazm-i-Iqbal, [n.d.].

Kurdi, Abdulrahman Abdulkadir. *The Islamic State: A Study Based on the Islamic Holy Constitution*. London: Mansell Publishing, 1984.

Lambton, Ann K. S. *State and Government in Medieval Islam*. Oxford: Oxford University Press, 1981.

Lapidus, Ira M. *A History of Islamic Societies*. Cambridge: Cambridge University Press, 1988.

———. "The Separation of State and Religion in Early Islamic Society." *International Journal of Middle Eastern Studies* 6, no. 4 (October 1975).

———. "State and Religion in Islamic Societies." *Past and Present*, no. 151 (May 1996).

Lawrence, Bruce. *Defenders of God: The Fundamentalism Revolt Against the Modern Age*. New York: Harper and Row, 1989.

Madelung, Wilfred. "The Shiite and Kharijite Contribution to Pre-Ash'arite *Kalam*." In *Islamic Philosophical Theology*. Ed. Parviz Morewedge. New York: SUNY Press, 1979.

Mawardi, Abu al-Hasan 'Ali al-. *Al-Ahkām al-Sultāniyya wa-al Wilāyāt al-Dīniyya* (*The Ordinances of Government and the States of Religion*). Ed. Ahmed Mubarak al-Baghdadi. Kuwait City: Dar ibn Qutayba Publications, 1989.

Mitchell, Richard P. *The Society of the Muslim Brothers*. London: Oxford University Press, 1969.

Moussalli, Ahmad S. "Hasan al-Turabi's Islamist discourse on Democracy and shura." High Beam Research: http://www.highbeam.com/library/doco.asp?docid=1G1:15031995&refid=ink_d5&skeyword=&teaser (accessed 2009).

Munson, Henry Jr. *Islam and Revolution in the Middle East*. New Haven: Yale University Press, 1989.

Muti'i, Sheikh Muhammad Bakhit al- (a.k.a. Bakhit). *Haqīqat Al-Islām wa Usūl al-Hukm* (*The Truth about Islam and the Foundations of Rule*). Cairo: The Salafiyya Publication, 1926.

Nasr, Seyyed Hossein, and Oliver Leaman, eds. *The History of Islamic Philosophy*. Routledge History of World Philosophies. Vol. 1. London: Routledge, 1996.

'Owf, Ahmed Muhammad. "Al-'Arab fī Jāhiliyya" (Arabs in the Jāhiliyya). On-line version of *Minbar al-Islam* magazine. http://www.islammemo.cc/article1. aspx?id=26493, accessed 2007.

Parvez, Manzoor. "Islamic Liberalism and Beyond." Book Review. *American Journal of Islamic Social Sciences* 7, 1:1–9. Online version http://www.algonet. se/~pmanzoor/Binder.htm (2009).

Rahnema, Ali, ed. *Pioneers of Islamic Revival*. London: Zed Books, 1994.

Raihani, Amin al-. *The Modern History of Najd and the Biography of Abdul Aziz bin Abd al-Rahman al-Faisal al Saud, King of Hijaz and Najd and Their Supplements*. Published in Arabic. Beirut: Arabic Studies and Printing Publishing Foundation, 1980.

———. *Arab Kings*. 2nd ed. Beirut: Arabic Studies and Printing Publishing Foundation, 1986. Also quoted in al-Balawi.

Rayyis, Muhammad Diyā' al-Dīn al-. *Al-Islām wa-al-Khilāfa fī al-'Asr al-Hadīth: Naqd Kitāb al-Islām wa-Usūl al-Ḥukm*. Beirut: Al-'Asr al-Hadīth lil-Nashr, 1973.

Reid, Donald M. "Arabic Thought in the Liberal Age: Twenty Years After." *International Journal of Middle Eastern Studies* 14, 4 (November 1982).

Rosenthal, Erwin. *Political Thought in Medieval Islam: An Introductory Outline*. Cambridge: Cambridge University Press, 1958.

Safran, Nadav. *Egypt in Search of Political Community: An Analysis of the Intellectual and Political Revolution of Egypt, 1804–1952*. Cambridge, Mass.: Harvard University Press, 1961.

Sa'īd, Rif'at al-. *Al-Irhāb al-Muta'aslam: Limādha wa Matā wa ilā Ayn? (Islamized Terrorism: Why, When, and to Where?)* Cairo: Amal Publishing, 2004.

Salvatore, Armando. *Islam and the Political Discourse of Modernity*. Reading, U.K.: Ithaca Press, 1997.

Sanders, Gregory. "Dr. Hasan Al-Turabi: His Political Philosophy in Context of Religion and Progress." http://titan.zort.net/~gsanders/text/alturabi.html (accessed 2009).

Sayed, Youssef (Yusuf) al-. *Rashid Rida wa-al-'Awda ila Manhaj al-Salaf (Rashid Rida and the Return to the Salaf Manhaj)*. Cairo: Mirette, 2000.

Sayyid Marsot, Afaf Lufti al-. *A Short History of Modern Egypt*. Cambridge: Cambridge University Press, 1994.

Shaw, Stanford J., and Ezel Kural Shaw. *History of the Ottoman Empire and Modern Turkey*. Vol. 2. Cambridge: Cambridge University Press, 1988.

Sherwani, Haroon Khan. *Studies in Muslim Political Thought and Administration*. Fourth edition. Lahore: Ashraf Press, 1963.

Sidahmed, Abd al-Salam. *Politics and Islam in Contemporary Sudan*. New York: St. Martin's Press, 1996.

Sidahmed, Abd al-Salam, and Anoushiravan Ehteshami, eds. *Islamic Fundamentalism*. Boulder: Westview Press, 1996.

Sirrs, Julie. "The Taliban's International Ambitions." *Middle East Quarterly* 8, no. 3 (2001). Online version: http://www.meforum.org/article/486 (accessed 2009).

Smith, Charles D. *Islam and the Search for Social Order in Modern Egypt: A Biography of Muhammad Husayn Haykal.* Albany: State University of New York Press, 1983.

Smith, Wilfred Cantwell. *Islam in Modern History.* Princeton: Princeton University Press, 1957.

Tabarī, Muhammad ibn Jarīr al-. *Tafsīr al-Tabarī.* Cairo: Dār al-Maʿārif, 1961.

Talbi, Muhammad al-. *ʿIyāl Allah: Afkār Jadidah fī ʿAlāqat al-Muslim bi Nafsihi wa bil Ākharīn (Children of God: New Ideas on the Muslim's Relationship with Himself and Others).* Tunis: Sras Publishers, 1992.

The Columbia Encyclopedia, Sixth Edition. New York: Columbia University Press, 2001. Online Version: http://www.bartleby.com/65/ca/caliphat.html

Thornton, Ted. "Sati al-Husri (1880–1968)." *History of the Middle East Database.* http://www.nmhscool.org/tthornton/mehistorydatabase/sati_alhusri.php (accessed 2009).

Tibi, Bassam. *The Challenge of Fundamentalism: Political Islam and the New World.* Los Angeles: University of California Press, 2002.

———. *The Crisis of Modern Islam: A Preindustrial Culture in the Scientific-Technological Age.* Salt Lake City: University of Utah Press, 1988.

———. "The Idea of an Islamic State and the Call for the Implementation of the Shariʿa/Divine Law." Middle East Information Center. Online article. http://meddleeastinfo.org/article4480.html (accessed 2009).

Tripp, Charles. "Sayyid Qutb: The Political Vision." In *Pioneers of Islamic Revival,* 154–183. Ed. Ali Rahnema. London: Zed Books, 1994.

Voll, John O. *Islam: Continuity and Change in the Modern World.* Boulder: Westview Press, 1982.

Wahba, Hafiz. *The Arabian Peninsula in the 20th Century.* 3rd ed. Cairo: Afaq Arabic Publishing. http://www.edwardtrimnell.com/middleeast-worldwari.htm, accessed 2007.

Watt, W. Montgomery. *Islamic Philosophy and Theology.* Edinburgh: Edinburgh University Press, 1985.

———. *The Formative Period of Islamic Thought.* Oxford: One World Publications, 1998.

Wazzani, Muhammad Hassan al-. *Al-Islam wa-al-Dawala (Islam and the State).* Fez, Morocco: Alwazzani Association, 1987.

Weiss, Bernard G. *The Spirit of Islamic Law.* Athens: University of Georgia Press, 1998.

Wuthnow, Robert, ed. *The Encyclopedia of Politics and Religion.* 2 vols. Washington, D.C.: Congressional Quarterly, 1998.

INDEX

Abbasid dynasty (750–1258), 20

'Abd al-Hamid II, 5–6

Abdalla bin Hussain, Emir (Jordan), 46

Abd al-Rhaman I, 20

'Abd al-Raziq, Ali: controversy following publication of *Al-Islām wa Usūl al-Ḥukm*, 61–67; critiques of, 8–9, 103–18; and disagreement among Muslim scholars on roles of revelation and reason in character of caliphate, 22; Egyptian context and intellectual setting of, 7, 55–67; and Ibn Khaldun, 34; and opposition to re-establishment of caliphate in Egypt, 49–51; overview of works on relationship of state and religion, 1–5; scholarship on writings of, 9–16; and theory of the caliphate, 7–8, 35, 40, 70–86, 128–29; thinking of about government as institution distinct from religion, 8, 90–100; works of as case study of relationship between Islam and the state, 9, 123–38

'Abd al-Raziq, Bayt Āl (father of 'Abd al-Raziq), 60

'Abd al-Raziq Pasha, Mustafa (brother of 'Abd al-Raziq), 60

'Abdel Hadi Pasha, Ibrahim, 61

'Abduh, Muhammad, 7, 49, 55, 57, 58–59, 105, 128–30

Abdul Aziz al Saud, King (Saudi Arabia), 45, 46–47

Abdul Hamid II (1876–1909), 40–43

Abu Bakr (632–634), 19, 20, 26, 74, 79–83, 107, 109

Abu Dā'ūd, 91

Abu 'Isa Muhammad al-Tirmidhi (d. 892), 91

Abu Jafar Muhammad ibn Jarir al-Tabari (838–923), 97, 102n26

Abu Musa al-Ash'ari, 91

Abu Zayd, Nasr Hamid, 11–12

Adams, Charles C., 9, 10, 15–16, 105, 129–30

Afghani, Jamal al-Din al- (1838–1897), 43, 57–58

Afghanistan, and Taliban, 110, 134–36, 141n49

ahl alḥal wal-'aqd (people of authority who loosen and bind communities, or those who bring issues to a solution), 26

'Ā'isha (wife of Prophet Muhammad), 136

Al-Aḥkām al-Sulṭāniyya wa al-Wilāyāt al-Diniyya (The Ordinances of Government and the States of Religion) (al-Mawardi 1989), 23–24

al-Azhar Supreme Council (Egypt), 4, 49, 60, 61–62, 88n32, 131–32

Al-Dīmugrātiyyah Abadan (Democracy Forever) (Khalid 1974), 130

theory of, 24; critiques of 'Abd al-Raziq's position on religion and, 103–18; influence of 'Abd al-Raziq's ideas on debate over Islam and politics, 15; Muslim debate on relationship between religion and, 2, 15, 55–56; overview of 'Abd al-Raziq's works on relationship between religion and, 1–5; works of 'Abd al-Raziq as case study of interaction between Islam and, 9, 123–38. See also caliphate; government; political science

Sudan, Islam and contemporary government of, 110, 133–34, 140n42

Sufism, and Wahhabi doctrine, 59

sultan: 'Abd al-Raziq's use of term, 50–51; role of in Ottoman Empire, 41

Sunnan al-Tirmidhi (Abu 'Isa Muhammad al-Tirmidhi), 91

Sunni, and development of theory of caliphate, 5, 19–35

Tahtawi, Rifa'a Rafi', al- (1801–1873), 95–96, 98

tajdīd (reform or renewal), 3, 119n9, 139n29

Talbi, Muhammad al-, 10, 15, 104, 118, 132–33

Taliban (Afghanistan), 110, 134–36, 141n49

Thornton, Ted, 13

Tibi, Bassam, 11

tradition, and Muslim debate on relationship between state and religion, 2–3. See also modernity and modernization; turāth

tribalism, Arabs and concept of, 94

Tunis, and constitution of 1861, 133

Tunisi, Khair-Eddin al-, 133

Turabi, Hasan Abdullah Dafa'allah al-, 133–34, 140n42

turāth (heritage), 126

Turkey: Kemalist government of and abolishment of caliphate, 6, 20, 41; and young Turk Revolution, 42–43. See also Ottoman Empire

'ulama (scholars with expertise in Islamic law sciences), 3

'Umar, Muhammad, 135, 141n49

'Umar ibn al-Khattab (634–644), 20, 75, 81–82, 91

Umayyad dynasty (661–750), 20, 21

umma/umam (nation or community of nations), 3, 32, 125

usūl al-fiqh (study of sources of Islamic jurisprudence), 7

'Uthman ibn 'Affan (644–656), 20, 21

wafd (delegation), 48

Wahba, Hafiz, 47

Wahhābi movement (Arabia), 59

Waladī (My Son) (Haykal), 104

Wasil ibn 'Ata (d. 748), 121n67

Watt, Montgomery, 17n11

Westernization: and colonialism, 127; and concept of separation of state and religion, 123

Who Needs an Islamic State ? (El Affandi), 134

Wilson, Woodrow, 47

Wingate, Reginald, 48

women's rights, and Taliban in Afghanistan, 135–36

World War I, and Ottoman Empire, 47

Young Turk Revolution, 42–43

Zaghlul, Saad, 48

Zawahri, Ayman al, 4